CULTURAL GIVING

Successful donor development for arts and heritage organisations

Theresa Lloyd

Arts & Business *working together*

Institute of Fundraising

The Monument Trust

Other titles by Theresa Lloyd

Why Rich People Give

A Guide to Giving

Arts & Business, the Institute of Fundraising, and The Monument Trust have supported this book. The facts presented and views expressed, however, are those of the author and not necessarily these organisations.

Published by Directory of Social Change
24 Stephenson Way
London NW1 2DP
Tel: 08450 77 77 07
Fax: 020 7391 4804
E-mail: publications@dsc.org.uk
The Directory of Social Change is a Registered Charity no. 800517

Editing, design and production Laura McCaffrey

Printed and bound by Russell Press

A catalogue record for this book is available from the British Library.

Whilst all reasonable care has been taken to ensure the accuracy of this publication, the author nor the publisher cannot accept responsibility for any errors or omissions.

ISBN-10   1 903991 80 3
ISBN-13   978 1 903991 80 0

To A Wealthy Man Who Promised A Second Subscription To The Dublin Municipal Gallery If It Were Proved The People Wanted Pictures

William Butler Yeats

You gave, but will not give again
Until enough of paudeen's pence
By Biddy's halfpennies have lain
To be 'some sort of evidence',
Before you'll put your guineas down,
That things it were a pride to give
Are what the blind and ignorant town
Imagines best to make it thrive.
What cared Duke Ercole, that bid
His mummers to the market-place,
What th' onion-sellers thought or did
So that his plautus set the pace
For the Italian comedies?
And Guidobaldo, when he made
That grammar school of courtesies
Where wit and beauty learned their trade
Upon Urbino's windy hill,
Had sent no runners to and fro
That he might learn the shepherds' will
And when they drove out Cosimo,
Indifferent how the rancour ran,
He gave the hours they had set free
To Michelozzo's latest plan
For the San Marco Library,
Whence turbulent Italy should draw
Delight in Art whose end is peace,
In logic and in natural law
By sucking at the dugs of Greece.
Your open hand but shows our loss,
For he knew better how to live.
Let paudeens play at pitch and toss,
Look up in the sun's eye and give
What the exultant heart calls good
That some new day may breed the best
Because you gave, not what they would,
But the right twigs for an eagle's nest!

Acknowledgements

This book could not have been written without significant generosity from a number of people.

First are the funders, whose support has enabled me to engage leading professional contributors, cover the editorial and production costs, and allocate a budget for marketing and promotion. The early support and endorsement of The Monument Trust was extremely encouraging. Arts & Business has not only contributed financially, but provided access to its research data and will be helping significantly with the promotion of the book. The Institute of Fundraising also provided financial support and acted as the conduit for the charitable donations; this involved setting up and monitoring a bank account and administering the invoices from contributors and suppliers. I am also very grateful to two anonymous trusts whose support ensured that the project would go ahead.

Key to the concept of this guide is that it draws on the experience of donors, arts and heritage organisations and expert advisers. I owe a special debt to Trevor and Lyn Shears who have been willing to be quoted extensively about their giving to the arts and heritage. Their journey is both inspiring and informative. Other donors have spoken off the record; their knowledge and participation has been enormously helpful.

A number of arts and heritage organisations from around the country and across a wide spectrum of sectors have been generous with frank descriptions of their donor schemes and ideas about volunteer leadership, what it takes to make them work, and what they have learned. Very busy people spent time describing their approach, checking versions of the text, providing data and photographs. No-one whose participation was requested declined to help. They are listed in Contacts.

In addition to these case studies a number of leading authorities provided advice on their areas of expertise. These cover a number of specialist topics including communications, data protection, endowments, events, legacies, naming, recruitment, research, US fundraising and wealth screening.

The culture sector owes a huge amount to these contributors, who have freely shared their experience and knowledge, as well as to several consultants and other practitioners who gave encouragement, particularly as the ideas for this book were being developed.

One person in particular should be mentioned: Graham Elliott of haysmacintyre contributed the entire chapter on the complex and frustrating area of relevant tax-related issues, particularly Gift Aid and VAT.

I am also indebted to Bill Conner for reassuring me that my occasional plagiarism of my own work, *Why Rich People Give*, is in the best traditions of many of the greatest composers, including Handel, the restoration and support of whose house and the activities inside it is the subject of one of the case studies.

Its chair, Christopher Purvis, has also been very supportive of this project, as have John Botts CBE, Dame Vivien Duffield CBE and Sir Nicholas Goodison, all of whom were generous with their time, experience and ideas. And I am delighted that Vernon Ellis not only shared his ideas about what matters to donors but agreed to write the foreword.

As well as the large group of people who helped pro bono, I have been supported by a group of professional colleagues. David Dixon and Janet Reeve have suggested, researched and written case studies. In addition David has not only written Chapter Six, on audience development, but contributed significantly to the thinking on how to manage individual giving, in Chapter Seven. Janet has reviewed and made very helpful suggestions on several of the special topics in Chapter Eight, and agreed to make time to read the final text in the week before moving house. I am delighted that Susan Mackenzie, who helped with some of the analysis for *Why Rich People Give*, was also involved with this book, providing critical support on data analysis and input on the bigger picture. As much as for their professional input, I am hugely grateful to these colleagues for their enthusiasm, commitment and constant encouragement during what seemed like a very tight timetable. All of these people agreed to undertake these tasks at well below their normal fees.

This also applies to Laura McCaffrey, who managed the editorial, design and production processes gently but firmly, encouraged me (not always successfully) to remove superfluous text, and whose calm professionalism struck exactly the right note towards the end of the project. In this she was helped by my assistant Lindsey Clarke, who joined me in June and whose competence and reliability has transformed my work generally and contributed to this project in particular.

Finally, I have very much appreciated the support of John Martin, publishing manager at the Directory of Social Change.

If, in spite of this broad-based interest and freely-given advice, there are errors, omissions or a lack of clarity, that is entirely my own responsibility.

Essentially, this guide is a collaboration. Those involved have contributed because they believe passionately, as I do, that the arts and cultural heritage in the UK should thrive, because they underpin our values, spiritual recreation, idea of beauty and a sense of identity and community. Whether the focus is gardening or grand opera, poetry or pottery, they inspire and may unite in shared pleasure. The alliance of enthusiastic commitment, money and competence which developed this guide should be mirrored in the successful partnerships – based on shared passions, values, understanding and mutual respect – between trustees, senior managers, artistic leaders, artists, experts, visitors, audience members and individual donors. This collaboration will help the arts and heritage to flourish.

However we all recognise that encouraging individual giving is not of itself enough to enable the arts to thrive. There needs to be an integrated approach to leadership, governance, strategy, financial planning and learning from others. This book is intended to be a contribution to that learning process, and the entire culture sector owes a debt of gratitude to all who have supported it so generously.

We are most grateful to all the photographers who have waived their reproduction fees for this book.

Contents

Foreword

By Vernon Ellis

Most arts and cultural organisations find it hard to make ends meet. I am chairman of two opera companies so I have some experience! Traditionally, most are dependent on public funding and, when times have got very tight, have relied on public funding to bail them out.

But times are changing. I think that there is now a general realisation that, right or wrong, bail-outs can no longer be relied upon. Moreover, right or wrong, the level of public funding of the arts is unlikely to increase materially. Even more seriously, there is every chance that funding levels will decline in the face of a general squeeze on government budgets and the pressure of the Olympics.

On top of this, the future for corporate support is uncertain. There is scope for corporate sponsorship certainly and some companies are interested in wider support that combines elements of employee engagement and corporate responsibility. But the longer-term trends are unclear.

There are two elements of a response to this. More must be done by arts and cultural organisations themselves to become more resilient, more open to new business models, more creative – administratively as well as artistically – whilst keeping to their core mission. Mission, Models, Money (which I chair) is a collaborative initiative amongst cultural organisations and funders to find enduring responses to these challenges.

The other response is to increase the level of private funding, particularly from individuals. We often tend in this area to look to the US where they have stronger traditions of individual philanthropy and certainly cultural organisations are much more reliant on private giving. But the culture, and the tax regime, is different there. Not all ideas transfer, though some will.

We might also look at the emerging good ideas and approaches coming out of the new trends in social investment, where money can be invested in new ways, other than straight capital or revenue grants. But the examples are still rare in the arts and cultural sector.

So, what we still need most is a quantum leap in the ability of organisations to tap into the potential offered by the new wealth structure in the UK. There is a broad base of enthusiastic support for most cultural organisations. Moreover, I believe that there is a cadre of people who support the arts and heritage not because it's a "good deal", but because they care passionately about them and want them to flourish. That is certainly true of my own support of the arts. But arts and cultural organisations are often just not efficient enough at translating more of this personal passion into higher level financial support.

There are, of course, many success stories, but also some horror stories. There are some very good development organisations and some less good ones.

What we need is a distillation of real-world experience into best practice and practical advice. This is what this book offers. And advice not just for the development office but for trustees, senior and executive management. I strongly believe that "development" is not just something to be done by the development office but should be something built into the culture of the entire organisation.

This work has been conceived, written and co-ordinated by Theresa Lloyd, who has extensive experience of advising cultural organisations about strategic planning, governance and fundraising, and has also been able to draw on her detailed knowledge of major donors, based on the research undertaken as director for *Philanthropy*UK, described in her book *Why Rich People Give*.

There are many lessons in the book for all of us who care about the way forward for cultural organisations and want to secure the future for the artistic endeavours we love, whether as artists, managers, trustees or supporters.

Vernon Ellis is chairman of English National Opera and The Classical Opera Company, trustee of the Royal College of Music and several other musical organisations, chairman of Mission, Models and Money and international chairman of Accenture. He is also a supporter of many arts organisations through the Vernon Ellis Foundation.

Introduction

This book is about encouraging individual giving to culture – to the arts, to heritage, to those activities through which we recreate our spiritual lives, affirm our values and interests, and share enjoyment as observers, participants and practitioners. These interests can take a myriad of forms – going to the theatre, visiting a great house, walking in a protected woodland, singing in a choir or developing a garden – from window box to rolling acres. The support sought may be for venues such as concert halls or art galleries, projects such as exhibitions or festivals or opera productions, the conservation and cataloguing of treasures of the past, investment in contemporary art, or the training of young talent.

And as throughout history, the motivations of those who become involved in such support are varied and mixed. At the same time, people may wish to enhance their city, support a talented individual, put something back into an art form which has given them pleasure, have opportunities to share that pleasure with like-minded donors, and be recognised for discerning generosity.

Over the centuries, the arts have been predominantly funded by private patronage. The history of art is as much about the sometimes turbulent relationships between artist, composer or writer and their patron as it is about wider trends. Indeed, although there have been exceptions, it is only relatively recently that artists (in whatever field) have embarked on a creative endeavour without a prior commission, whether from church, king, city, guild or individual benefactor. For their part, the patrons would, as now, see their support as part of their place in society and in history.

For many, the support and embellishment of their community was an expression of communal pride, and the artistic investment was not confined to churches and palaces. Builders of medieval hospices throughout Europe commissioned great artists to ornament the rooms for the sick. Examples include the hospital of Santa Maria della Scala in Siena, which only recently ceased to serve the city as a hospital after some 800 years. Its vast pilgrim hall was built in the 1430s, with a huge cycle of paintings commissioned in the 1440s from a number of leading artists. In the same century, the Hospices de Beaune were established in Burgundy in the wake of the devastation of the Hundred Years War. The mission specified by the founder, Nicolas Rolin, was primarily to support the poor and the ill:

[Every morning] *"white bread must be given to the poor asking for alms before the doors of the hospital."* [Everything must be done so the poor] *"be received there, fed and cared for, at the expense of the hospital, until they regain their health or are convalescent."*

As in Siena, the founder also had a vision of the power of art, both to transform the experience of the beneficiaries and, perhaps, to glorify his reputation. An inventory of 1501 lists a large number of objects including furniture and tapestries, and the outstanding polyptych by Rogier van der Weyden of the Last Judgment.

The interaction between art and social welfare, and the idea that the poor would benefit from great art, and not only in churches, was not confined to mainland Europe. St Bartholomew's Hospital, founded in 1123 and granted by Henry VIII to the City of London in 1546, always attracted significant philanthropy. In the 1730s the artist William Hogarth decorated the Grand Staircase with two magnificent paintings depicting the biblical stories of The Good Samaritan and Christ at the Pool of Bethesda which illustrate the spirit of the hospital's work. The Great Hall, built to the designs of architect James Gibbs in the 18th century, is covered inside with large wallboards listing individual donors, including members of the royal family, and the amount they contributed. Around the same time, successful ship-builder and sailor Captain Thomas Coram established The Foundling Hospital to provide care for homeless children he found living and dying on the streets of London. He was assisted by his friend, the artist William Hogarth, who like Coram was childless. In 1739, George II granted a Royal Charter for the establishment of a Foundling Hospital and Hogarth personally contributed paintings to decorate the walls of the new building. His example inspired many other contemporary British artists to donate works to this pioneering and philanthropic institution, creating the first British art gallery. The rich and influential were encouraged to come to view the pictures as well as the children, in the hope that they might commission works from one of the exhibiting artists and contribute to the work of the Hospital.

Handel was also a supporter and presented an organ to the Foundling Hospital Chapel which he christened with a special performance of Messiah (the "Foundling Hospital version"). In his will, Handel bequeathed to the hospital a fair copy of Messiah and so created a musical tradition which continues to the present day through the Coram Family's Handel Concert held each February to celebrate his birthday.

There is no doubt that the Christian traditions of Europe underpinned this commitment to the poor, even among those not noticeably pious. And it was not

The Benefactor's Panel at Barts.

only the wealthy who contributed. Ordinary citizens helped those in need and also participated in commissioning important works, including paintings, churches, cathedrals, monasteries, public works and civic buildings, by means of relatively small subscriptions. A pattern of support emerged that has been common ever since, whereby a mass of small gifts is bolstered by major donations from one or more rich individuals.

Victorian charity was also largely religious in its motivation, with Quakers a particularly prominent force. Henry Wellcome, who founded one of the world's richest foundations, declared he wished to be rich in order to fund medical research for the glory of God and the good of mankind. Andrew Carnegie, in contrast, remarked in his Gospel of Wealth in 1889 that: *"the man who dies rich dies disgraced"*, thereby suggesting that philanthropy was a social rather than a religious obligation. He, like so many others, included funding of cultural activities – in his case libraries and church organs – in his philanthropic portfolio, seeing it as an integral part of improving the lives of the poor.

The town halls of Victorian Britain, like those of medieval Italy, are monuments to civic pride and to patronage by successful local business people supported by local subscription. Concert halls, art galleries and museums were being funded and opened around the country. They ranged from the major and broad-based to the small and specialist. Before the Tate Gallery opened in 1897, with a collection of 65 works donated by Henry Tate to the nation, a trust was formed in 1890 by the Reverend Stopford Brooke. He bought Dove Cottage, home of the poet Wordsworth, and opened it to the public a year later.

Explaining the aims and ideals of the first board of trustees, Brooke wrote: *"There is no place... which has so many thoughts and memories as this belonging to our poetry; none at least in which they are so closely bound up with the poet and the poems... In every part of this little place [Wordsworth] has walked with his sister and wife or talked with Coleridge. And it is almost untouched. Why should we not try and secure it... for the eternal possession of those who love English poetry all over the world."*

Meanwhile, in 1895 the National Trust was founded by three Victorian philanthropists – Octavia Hill, Sir Robert Hunter and Canon Hardwicke Rawnsley. Concerned about the impact of uncontrolled development and industrialisation, they set up the National Trust to act as a guardian for the nation in the acquisition and protection of threatened coastline, countryside and buildings. Essential to the vision is the concept of access, and in 2004 an estimated 50 million people visited the National Trust's open-air properties, and the pay-for-entry sites were visited by more than 12 million people. The Trust now has 3.5 million members.

However, notwithstanding the huge growth of organisations such as the National Trust, together with charities in the social welfare sector funded by individual donors, there is no question but that two world wars and the advent of the welfare state changed attitudes profoundly. While the philosophy of individual giving in the 20th century was inevitably influenced by the philanthropic principles of the wealthy businessmen of the 19th century, the establishment of the Arts Council, conceived of by J M Keynes and formed by the Attlee Government in 1945, marked an enormous change in attitudes to support for the arts. Launching the Arts Council in a broadcast, Keynes remarked with confidence: *"We look forward to the time when the theatre and the concert hall and the gallery will be a living element in everyone's upbringing, and regular attendance at the theatre and at concerts a part of organised education."* The original objective was not only to provide public funding for artists and arts organisations, but also to ensure universal access.

A key component of the vision was the integration of access and organised education. At the same time, however, the establishment of the welfare state in the wake of World War II gave rise to a new and significant change in conceptions of altruism in the UK, the role of the state and responsibility for the provision of public goods. It marked the beginning of what became an increasingly common tendency to marginalise charities and to belittle individual giving. Indeed, for some 20th-century collectivists the word "charity", which had once brought to mind working-class traditions of giving, began to take on objectionable connotations of hierarchical values and unfashionable pieties.

Today, however, charities have become essential organs of civic society: the "third sector" offering important alternatives to the state and sustaining independent values against centralising pressures of conformity. Although some 40% of charity income is from public sources, not only has private giving survived the challenge of a changing social context, but some of the biggest gifts from wealthy people over the last 50 years have gone to universities, museums, galleries and cultural organisations.

However, we have not returned to pre-welfare state attitudes. The positioning of art and heritage as the preserve of the rich or the pursuit of an elite is a phenomenon of populist journalism, reinforced by most politicians. This is despite the numbers: 50 million visits to the National Trust a year, six million visitors to the Tate galleries, over five million to the British Museum. In a recent Arts Council survey, 25% of the sample (over 6,000 people) had been to a play or drama in the previous 12 months, and 40% had listened to classical music in the last four weeks. (By contrast 12.8 million attend Premier league football matches each year.) And, of course, this is just the tip of the national iceberg of interest and participation in the arts and heritage. The philanthropic idea, manifest for centuries, that access to the arts for all, or as many as possible, is part of being in a civilised and caring society, and should be an integral part of "organised education", needs to flourish again. But, as we shall explore in Chapter One, attitudes to the role of the state are changing. And as well as the impetus of vision and philanthropy, economic forces are also at work as people realise that culture is good for business. In Liverpool and Manchester, research by the Institute for Public Policy Research (IPPR) has clearly shown how a vibrant cultural life is helping to bring skilled people back to city centres. (This is and discussed further in Chapter Two.) Creativity and culture is increasingly viewed as an essential part of the regeneration package, and a characteristic of great cities.

In a sense we have come full circle. But over the same period as we have seen the essential role of the individual philanthropist decline and begin to be recognised again, we have also seen two other significant developments. The first is an inevitable result of processes such as the reduction of cultural studies in formal education – that the value of the arts is not obvious to those who wish to contribute to social welfare. The arts have to learn to attract those who are not as yet frequent visitors or audience members. The IPPR report gives strong ammunition for those who wish to make the case for the role of culture in contributing to community life and active citizenship.

More importantly, few organisations are as effective as they could be at engaging the support of those with real potential to be committed and major donors – the people who already know about them, love the art form and attend regularly.

The other key development over the past two decades is that there is increasing professional expertise and experience in the field of fundraising and development in the UK. The purpose of this guide is to share that experience and inspire the reader to creative plagiarism. There is something for everyone in the range of ideas and practical examples featured.

Before giving these in detail, the first chapter considers the context within which potential donors and cultural organisations seeking support are operating.

Chapter One

The attitudes to the role of the state in the UK and the US

This book is a practical guide to encouraging individual giving to cultural organisations. It could be argued that, particularly in the arts, all that matters is the personal passion for the artfom and the link between individual and institution. However, as in the fields of education, health and social welfare, for organisations to be effective at soliciting significant gifts, it is important that their leaders understand the context within which major donors operate, the beliefs and influences that inform their approach to giving, and their view of whose job it is to fund the provision of culture.

While each individual carries a very personal range of feelings, there are broad research-based indications which can provide an insight.

In thinking about giving, especially to the arts and heritage, many look wistfully across the Atlantic, either in the hope that US donors will fund them when UK donors have not, or that somehow US levels of funding can be obtained in the UK without the commensurate investment in developing relationships and in the context of a very different culture of asking and giving.

In Chapter Eight we explore what is needed to fundraise in the US. And while the main focus of this guide is the UK, and what has been and can be achieved here, this chapter will also refer briefly to other countries, particularly the US, and why experience there is so dissimilar[1].

The role of the state and the development of philanthropy

The motivations and attitudes of private donors in any country are inextricably bound up with perceptions of the role of the state: in which sectors should it intervene, for what aspects of their lives should people take personal responsibility, and what is the function of private philanthropy.

---

[1] *Some organisations have been effective at soliciting support from US donors, see Chapter Eight.*

The US

In the US, there has been extensive research and commentary on attitudes to the job of government – a role seen as profoundly different from that in the countries of origin of many of its citizens. As Claire Gaudiani has pointed out[2], citizen generosity has *"created a social environment where capitalism could flourish without destroying democracy"*. More than that, such giving – seen as investment – has contributed to economic development alongside the spur of capital investment. It is argued that the values – drawn from the Judeo-Christian tradition – which underpin generosity in the US are essentially about enlightened self-interest; the purpose or impetus is to establish a social structure of mutual support and upward mobility so that people may become "responsible citizens"[3]. The act of the Good Samaritan restored the man on the road to Jericho to productive life[4]. It is suggested that the same values of fairness and honesty underpin investor confidence and hence capitalism.

However, as we shall see, influences are complex and motivations mixed. Philanthropy is also a pragmatic response to the risks to social cohesion arising from unfettered capitalism. It softens some of the more negative impacts of competition and wealth concentration – the Darwinian world of the survival of the fittest which we currently see in some emerging economies. In this way, philanthropy helps to distribute wealth and, most important, opportunity and upward mobility, which are seen as good for society and democracy. American philanthropy is considered by most commentators as entrepreneurial, creative and individualistic.

Furthermore, the lack of any relationship with or knowledge of the recipient that is inherent in the provisions of services by the state also minimises the sense of reciprocal responsibility and commitment that was also the hallmark of pre-welfare state philanthropy in the UK. For many, not only in the US, this awareness of mutual obligation and interdependency is essential for a sense of being part of a community.

But in recognising the overall benefits to society and accepting that the imperfections of democratic capitalism, tempered by responsible citizenship, nevertheless provide one workable social model, we should also acknowledge that the motivations of individuals are likely to be mixed. This is borne out by research in the US and the UK, and, increasingly, elsewhere.

---

2. The Greater Good – How Philanthropy Drives the American Economy and Can Save Capitalism *2003*.
3. Benjamin Franklin, quoted by Claire Gaudiani.
4. See the eighth and highest stage of generosity described by Maimonides, the Jewish philosopher and teacher, which is to help the person in need to become productive and independent – helping people to help themselves.

Many of these themes identified in the UK studies are echoed in research from other countries, such as Germany, Australia and, of course, the US. But while there are common motivations and concerns about society, there are also very significant differences. These are integrally linked with attitudes to the role of the state; the most documented comparisons are between the US and the UK, with recent research in Australia[5] indicating attitudes closer to those prevalent in the UK than in the US.

It is worth spending some time exploring these ideas, since so often politicians berate the wealthy for not apparently giving as much as their US counterparts, without appearing to understand the very different culture and tax regime (for the wealthy) which pertains across the Atlantic.

Values, attitudes to the state and control – does the US think differently?[6]

A major part of US giving is linked to community. People with wealth feel they have a responsibility to embellish their community and indeed that a range of high-quality local amenities, particularly cultural and medical, reflects well on their own success in business or enterprise. So wealthy people who do not contribute risk being perceived as not "doing their share" while benefiting from other people's support.

In the Francie Ostrower research in the US, almost everyone (over 90%) rejected the idea of reducing or even eliminating the tax incentive for giving and having the government/state use the increased revenue to support the types of welfare and cultural activities which benefit from philanthropy. Comments on the alternatives included *"that's socialism"* and *"if I wanted to live that way I'd move to Sweden"*.

Part of the reason for giving, and for giving the maximum for which they receive a tax reduction, is a marked antagonism to the idea of any extension of government expenditure, and the proposition that their taxes would otherwise be contributing to the growth and maintenance of a welfare state. Creating a foundation is seen as a way of *"not giving all your money to the government in taxes"*.

There was also scepticism about the ability of the government to provide an effective substitute for private philanthropy. (Scepticism about government competence is reflected in the UK and German research.) But beyond the perceived

---

5. Encouraging wealthy Australians to be more philanthropic. *Denis Tracey 2005.*
6. *For this analysis the main US sources have been* Why the Wealthy Give, *by Francie Ostrower, published in 1995, and* The Mind of the Millionaire, *which presents findings from a national survey on* Wealth with Responsibility, *published by Paul Schervish and John Havens in January 2002.*

impracticality of the idea is a stronger view that a vital aspect of philanthropy is that it allows individuals to support the causes they value. Linked to that is the question of influence, or even control. *"If government took over, then unless I become a legislator, how can I have a say?"* And there was a fear about an "official line". *"This country is about freedom of choice."*

As this demonstrates, donors argue that it is desirable that philanthropy places a significant level of the funding of welfare and other activities in private hands and outside the government domain. They value the individualism in terms of choice, initiative and impact which they believe the current system represents. For these reasons, philanthropy represents more to donors than a mechanism for channelling money to worthy causes. It is seen as representing some of the most valuable and even defining elements of American society. For one woman in the Ostrower research, philanthropy is *"the idea of giving and citizen participation – and I think that's what America's all about"*. One man talked about *"the whole difference between our system* [that is, the American approach] *and the European system, where the government fills the gap and the people don't do anything"*.

Philanthropy not only sustains a set of organisations; it sustains a set of values.

Giving as a norm

As important as maintaining "control", in the US philanthropy is an integral and defining element of elite culture. This is crucially linked to the nature and functioning of upper-class culture in American society. Characteristic of the people who formed the basis of the US research was that they live in an environment in which giving is a norm, and regard philanthropy as an obligation that is part of their privileged position. It is seen as a responsibility that goes with success.

The US may lack the aristocratic and sharply defined class distinctions and social traditions that still linger in the UK, but the analysis of philanthropy in the US shows that American elites do fashion a separate cultural world for themselves by drawing on and refining elements and values from the broader society.

Philanthropy becomes a mark of class status that contributes to defining and maintaining the culture and organisational boundaries of elite life. As donors put it, philanthropy becomes a *"way of being part of society"*, and *"one of the avenues by which society makes its connections"*.

We know that this is not the case in the UK. Hard though it may be to define the social elite, we understand that the extent to which elite philanthropy opens doors to the highest levels of British society is limited[7], and that there are many people who are perceived to be members of the upper levels of the social hierarchy in the UK who are not major donors, particularly to cultural activities.

Furthermore, those who are perceived to aspire to elite status are sometimes despised for apparently displaying their wealth through giving, and such sentiments can be a disincentive.

Indeed, there is an apparent paradox that "outsiders" (whether new rich, members of ethnic minorities, or immigrants) may see charitable giving as a way to become an "insider", although in the UK, unlike in the US, giving is not seen as an attribute of the social elite[8].

What about tax incentives?

As discussed, philanthropy in the US is a social institution that takes on meaning in the context of a cultural emphasis on individualism and private initiative, and a mistrust of government power and large-scale bureaucracy. (These themes are not confined to the elite, but are found more generally in American society.) These underlying values provide a framework in terms of which philanthropy as a social institution makes sense. The existence of such a framework is important, as it is not obvious nor necessary that philanthropy would be valued by elites, or anyone else.

It appears that the introduction of tax incentives for giving in other countries, including the UK, has not automatically – or not yet – resulted in fostering comparable levels of philanthropy. At the very least, this implies that for a culture of giving to flourish, tax incentives are not enough; there must be clear expectations of the role of individuals and a belief that the wealthy must take responsibility for certain aspects of society, associated with an ethos of respect for the values of individualism and enterprise which underpin wealth creation.

However, the absence of tax incentives can be a major constraint, particularly among those who have had the opportunity to compare the situation in the US and the UK, let alone in countries in mainland Europe.

---

7. One American fundraiser based in the UK told me that it had taken her some time to realise that the royal patron of the arts organisation for which she worked would certainly not ask an individual for money, and that even a very major gift would not produce a private invitation to the home of the patron.
8. An issue highlighted with the revelations about donations and loans to the Labour Party associated with recommendations for honours in Spring 2006.

Comparing the tax structures

There are increasing demands to change the systems and tax regimes of countries ranging from the UK to India, from Russia to Australia. Every analysis points out that while the tax regime is not a motivator to give, the absence of an encouraging regulatory framework can be a significant deterrent to major giving.

As we have seen, people are viewing the use of the tax system in their charitable giving as a form of hypothecation – earmarking taxes for a specific purpose – "telling the government what to do with my money". As pointed out in *The Millionaire Givers*[9], the belief in the US among many donors interviewed that "a free market system fosters a giving environment" coexists rather curiously with the way in which high tax rates function as an incentive to give. The highest number of foundations of all sizes was created during the period of highest tax rates in the US. No-one is suggesting that tax mechanisms alone create a culture of giving. Nevertheless, they underpin major philanthropy, just as they encourage donations from the less well-off.

In the research, several people made a link between the US culture of giving and the question of tax incentives. In the US, cuts in direct taxation in the late 80s acted as a disincentive to the act of giving itself[10]: *"If it were not for the savings in taxes – the notion that the government really is participating in a gift – I think there would be an awful lot less giving".*

Similar ideas were expressed in research in Australia[11], although there was a broader range of views and for many it was not a "deal-breaker", but they might give less. As Dame Elisabeth Murdoch[12] says: *"Much of what I do would not be possible if I didn't get a tax deduction. Occasionally, I do help causes which don't have tax-deductibility (sometimes you just have to), but my main distribution of funds is tax-deductible. If that was not so, I would not be able to give as much."*

A fundamental difference between the tax regimes in the US and the UK is that in the US it is possible to make an irrevocable gift of a capital sum, obtain tax relief at the time of making the gift, and still enjoy the benefit of the income (which can be assigned, for example, to children) from the capital until a specific date, sometimes the death of the donor. This way, the donor enjoys the benefit of the tax relief

9. The Millionaire Givers: Wealth and Philanthropy in Britain. *Howard Hurd and Mark Lattimer Directory of Social Change 1994.*

10. *See an article in* Trust Monitor *in 1990 by Mark Lattimer, based on research by Dr. Teresa Odendahl conducted with 135 very wealthy US donors in 1987.*

11. Giving it Away, *based on interviews with 60 individuals and families in Australia, by Denis Tracey 2003.*

12. *Former wife of media magnate Rupert Murdoch and an entrepreneur and philanthropist in her own right.*

at the time of making the gift decision. This is what is meant by most "planned giving" in the US, and it accounts for a significant proportion of major gifts received, particularly for endowments for cultural, education and medical institutions.

At the time of writing, tax benefits available in the UK are still not equivalent to those in the US for major gifts of capital in the lifetime of the donor, although there is an active coalition of organisations campaigning under the umbrella of the Charity Tax Reform Group for "Lifetime Legacies". The proposals are described in the Additional Information.

Works of art and other gifts in kind

As well as donations of money, in the US, arts organisations are soliciting whole or fractional gifts of works of art – an increasingly popular approach as the value of art is ever-rising. In January 2004, the Goodison Review[13] recommended (among other proposals) tax reforms in the UK for gifts of works of art similar to those available in the US, although the tax relief would be based on the valuation at the time of the initial commitment.

Another feature of the US system is that tax relief is available on other gifts in kind, not only works of art. This has a major impact on the apparent level of charitable giving in the US. Gifts of old clothes, obsolete computers, redundant toys and a whole range of second-hand goods qualify for tax relief. Recipient and donor have a vested interest in assessing the worth of the donated article at its highest probable value. The recipient adds the value of gifts received to the total annual income, and the donor obtains a receipt which can be used in the year-end tax process to claim tax relief. This process reminds the taxpayer of the benefits of tax relief, and reinforces the benefits of giving from an early age. It is one of the practices which underpins a culture of giving.

In the UK such giving, which sustains charity shops and welfare charities, is not "counted" by the donors, nor does it feature in individual giving statistics, although the shop income, for example, will appear in the accounts of the recipient charity. In recent years, gifts in kind, including property, jewellery, shares, works of art, cars and food (from the food industry) have accounted for about 25% of US reported giving[14]. Statistics comparing US and UK giving as a percentage of gross domestic product are not comparing like with like.

13. Goodison Review – Securing the Best for our Museums: Private Giving and Government Support. *January 2004.*
14. *As reported by Mike Hudson in* Managing at the Leading Edge, *published in March 2004. He points out that there has been a significant increase in non-cash donations in the US; from 1988 to 1997 they grew from 12% to 28% of all gifts. His source is* The New Profit Almanac and Desk Reference, *Murray Weitzman et al, Independent Sector, 2002.*

Other differentials

There are many other ways in which the attitudes to wealth and the approach to philanthropy differ between the US and UK. Probably the most significant is in the realm of volunteer activities, particularly board membership. This is explored in Chapter Eight.

The UK – a mixed funding economy

The UK research[15] revealed a range of views about the proper extent of the role of the state, but virtually universal agreement that the state should pay for "basics", including health and education, that the public sector cannot do everything, but that private philanthropy should lever rather than substitute for government funding. At the same time, charities were seen as more effective and more likely to be able to be pioneering – creating models of best practice not always taken up by the public sector. For some the potential of change on a macro scale justified, and indeed required, advocacy and lobbying to multiply the impact of a successful initiative or to address root causes.

In recognising that the state will never be able to provide for all demands, it is suggested that attitudes to this issue in the UK are changing, and perhaps becoming more like those in the US. The start of the change was dated to the Thatcher era. However, there are still many who feel that the state is not funding its core responsibilities, and that the private donor, via charities, is picking up what should be state-funded activities.

Delivering core education was seen as the role of the state but providing extra investment – for talented or disadvantaged children, for example – was considered a proper, or inevitable, role of private individuals. There was a range of views, including among arts funders, about the extent to which the state should continue to support the arts. Although those giving substantial sums to the arts were by no means the majority, they were among the most vocal about the need for government either to do more, or at least to be more honest and direct about what it is up to. Several made the point that if government wishes to support free entry as a matter of state policy, or promote "accessibility", the museums and galleries and theatre and opera houses to which this applies should be fully funded to provide this service.

---

15. This is drawn from Why Rich People Give, by Theresa Lloyd, based on interviews with 100 wealthy people, published in 2004.

There is a tension between the understanding that the state cannot provide for all needs and the reluctance of people to give if they feel the impact will immediately be diminished by an equivalent reduction in government or other public sector support. Long-term government commitment to a consistent minimum would help to address this concern[16].

Another reason cited for a mixed funding approach was the lack of ownership and the risk of detachment from a sense of corporate or community responsibility that can arise if the state is too prescriptive. Many criticised what they saw as the increasingly controlling nature of government, and the adverse impact on self-help, volunteering and local community spirit. In these contexts, it was observed that private giving is a manifestation of commitment and involvement by and within a wider community, sharing responsibility and demonstrating mutual support – an essential feature in the US, and manifest in the UK to some extent in areas away from London.

But as well as changing attitudes to the role of the state and whose job it is to pay for the arts and heritage, there are changing patterns in the ways that donors engage with the organisations they support. We look at these in the next chapter.

16. In the Arts Council survey mentioned in the Introduction, nearly 80% of people thought that arts and cultural projects should receive public funding.

Chapter Two

Beyond current philanthropy

As well as changing attitudes to the role of the state and whose job it is to pay for social benefits, particularly the culture sector, there are broader developments in the ways that philanthropists engage with the non-profit sector.

Giving trends in the UK[1]

Based on recent trends in both demographics and philanthropy, the UK appears to be on the brink of a sea-change in charitable giving – one that will result in sustained, higher levels of giving by a greater number of individuals.

First, we are in the midst of a significant global, inter-generational transfer of wealth. From 1998 until 2052, "baby boomers" and the Second World War generation will pass on their estates to their heirs and to charity. In the US alone, this wealth transfer is conservatively estimated to be worth $41 trillion, with $6 trillion being bequeathed to charity[2]. Moreover, the wealthier the individual, the more generous they are likely to be: estates of $20 million or more typically leave an average 49% of their value to charity and only 21% to heirs[3]. These patterns are likely to be similar in the UK. Furthermore, the proportion going to charity is more likely to increase than decrease, as fewer baby boomer couples are having children: it is predicted that 21% of women born during the 1960s will remain childless, compared with 14% of women born in 1931[4].

Meanwhile, a new type of donor is emerging – young, self-made and socially conscious – who is giving rise to new ways of giving. Of those interviewed for *Why*

---

1. This section is excerpted and adapted from A Guide to Giving, 2nd edition, edited by Susan Mackenzie, Association of Charitable Foundations 2005. First edition written by Theresa Lloyd, 2003.
2. J Havens and P Schervish (1999) Millionaires and the Millennium: New Estimates of the Forthcoming Wealth Transfer and the Prospects for a Golden Age of Philanthropy, Boston College Social Welfare Research Institute, Boston.
3. "Doing well and doing good", The Economist, July 29 2004, London.
4. The SAGE Research Group, London School of Economics, citing M Evandrou and J Falkingham.

Rich People Give, 70% were self-made, half of whom were entrepreneurs and half were professionals, largely in finance.

These statistics are supported by the *Sunday Times Rich List*, whose editor, Philip Beresford, has observed that, in 1989, 75% of the List had inherited their wealth and 25% were self-made. By 2005, this ratio had been reversed. Beresford also notes that, with this shift *"has come much more willingness to talk about wealth, not to be ashamed of it, to be proud of what they have achieved* [5]. Citing the increasing levels of liquid wealth resulting from company sales, he predicts that *"within the next five years the number [of entrepreneurs] who have sold their business for £50 million or more will make up around 30% of the* Rich List, *compared to 15% today"*.

As described in *Why Rich People Give*, these new philanthropists are using their wealth and business experience to create private foundations, start up or support emerging models in philanthropy, test innovative approaches to social issues, and volunteer their time and expertise. They are engaged and pioneering, have ambitious goals, seek impact and demand accountability. Moreover, as traditional foundations and government have begun to adopt aspects of these new approaches, the key distinction in philanthropy is no longer the conventional structure of giving (individual, family, foundation), but rather the aspiration of the giver.

Examples of emerging approaches in philanthropy include:

● **New types of financing for charities**

Social investors are utilising risk-based capital and quasi-equity to finance charities and social enterprises, filling a gap in the funding market. Organisations offering loans to charities include Venturesome and Charity Bank, both incubated by the Charities Aid Foundation. The Esmée Fairbairn Foundation, a significant funder of the cultural sector, has also invested in this field[6].

● **More strategic and more engaged donors**

Many new philanthropists – especially business entrepreneurs and City professionals – want to do more than write a cheque; they also want to use their experience and expertise to support the charity more closely. They are

---

5. *Conference speech, 14 April 2005.*
6. *One example of a new approach is the development of syndicates to purchase outstanding string instruments for virtuoso players; a scheme conceived and promoted by Nigel Brown. Further information can be obtained from www.nwbrown.co.uk/articles/article03_02.asp .*

willing to invest a significant amount of capital – including funding core costs – and take significant risks to test innovative ideas. An example is Impetus Trust, the UK's first general venture philanthropy organisation **(www.impetus. org.uk)**. Two recent government initiatives – the Adventure Capital Fund and Futurebuilders – also offer a mix of financial and non-financial support.

This interest is not confined to the UK. The European Venture Philanthropy Association has 30 members from nine countries.

● **Targeting gaps in current services**

New donors are challenging the traditional ideas reviewed earlier, that government should provide for all social care, education and health services, and that any private funding in these areas would "let government off the hook". Recognising that government resources are finite, they are defining new roles for private donations – which are more able than government to accept risk – within public services. New Philanthropy Capital (NPC), a charity that advises donors and funders on how to give more effectively, has highlighted various ways private donations can augment public service delivery. These include testing and promoting new, innovative approaches (e.g. palliative care centres for cancer patients), serving people who do not receive government funding (e.g. counselling support for families of disabled children), and subsidising a higher level of care than the government provides (e.g. in-home care for the terminally ill).

● **The rise of the social investor**

Social investors aim to harness the power of market forces to achieve sustainable economic growth in disadvantaged communities. By seeking a financial return, in addition to a social return, they are able to attract significant private investment that otherwise would not be available. Examples of new models include Community Development Finance Institutions (CDFI) and Community Development Venture Capital (CDVC). Community Investment Tax Relief (CITR), introduced by the UK Government in 2002, has further spurred community investment, as shown by the success of CITR accounts offered by Charity Bank.

● **Focus on impact, accountability and transparency**

As they become more strategic in their giving, donors increasingly want to see the impact of their support. This goes beyond outputs, such as the number of people served, to address the longer-term outcomes and impacts on beneficiaries, such as improved health or self-esteem. New ways to assess these impacts are being developed. For example, in the 1990s, American venture philanthropy fund REDF pioneered a new measurement tool – social return on investment (SROI) – which measures social returns (such as increased income from new employment) as well as financial returns. In the UK, the New Economics Foundation has developed a portfolio of tools to help understand and measure social returns. Furthermore, donors, drawing on their business experience, are demanding increased accountability and transparency from charities. They want to be confident that their money is being used both effectively and efficiently.

● **Improved information flows**

Publicly-available information on charities generally has been wanting. However, this is beginning to change, as several new initiatives aim to improve the quantity and quality of information flows in the sector. These include online resources, such as the Charity Commission's Register of Charities, and the online charity directory, GuideStar UK, as well as research into different areas of charitable activity and tailored advisory services for donors from organisations such as New Philanthropy Capital, independent advisers and via private wealth managers.

What does this mean for culture?

It may be thought that little of this is relevant to the small museum in the North-East, or the regional touring opera company, or indeed a national art gallery. But the crucial factor is that the potential donors to these organisations have many choices, and not only in respect of other arts organisations or traditional charities; their friends may be encouraging them to become more involved in social investment; they may not see the arts and heritage as an essential part of their lives, or as an appropriate focus for charitable giving. This guide is not about addressing these macro issues, but it is essential that those within cultural organisations with responsibility for their future financial security understand the broader context within which philanthropists and their advisers are operating.

The rise of the "donor-investor", understanding their expectations and treating them appropriately is a recurring theme of this guide.

Measuring the impact of culture

Of the many developments cited, there are two which should concern us. The first is the focus on the measurement of "impact". The concerns of policy-makers and public funders of the arts are, it might be thought, some way removed from those of the individual ticket-buyer and supporter. People may be sceptical about the idea that the impact of the "transformative powers of the arts" on people's lives and on the development of a "creative business" sector is measurable. However, it is important to be aware of the very lively debate around these matters since the ideas have had such an effect on public funding, and therefore on the positioning and case made by those who solicit such funds. In Spring 2006, two publications explored these issues. They are *Culture Vultures*, edited by Munira Mirza and published by Policy Exchange, and *From Access to Participation*, by Emily Keaney, published by the Institute of Public Policy Research. The comments that follow are drawn from these analyses.

Some say that those seeking public funds have been very successful. Since the National Lottery was set up in 1994, it has awarded £2 billion for the arts in Britain. In the new millennium, Labour announced the single biggest increase in support for the arts: £100 million over three years on top of a £237 million base. In 2003, it topped this with an extra £75 million to Arts Council England. Furthermore, one of this government's most popular and effective policies was free admission to the national galleries and museums. "Creativity" has been a vital facet of New Labour policy-making.

But alongside this growing interest in the arts has been a change in the way they are perceived or presented. The Arts Council and DCMS (Department for Culture, Media and Sport) tell us that the arts are (now) not only good in themselves, but are valued for their contribution to the economy, urban regeneration and social inclusion.

Urban regeneration experts and planners argue that major new cultural buildings like the Lowry Centre in Salford or the Sage in Gateshead are key to reviving former industrial towns. Up and down the country, arts organisations – large and small – are being asked to think about how their work can support government targets for health, social inclusion, crime, education and community cohesion. Galleries, museums and theatres are busy measuring their impacts on different policy areas to prove they are worth their subsidy. When the government decided to curb its spending on the arts in 2005 by £30 million, many people within the arts sector felt much of their socially-oriented work had been overlooked. As Sir Nicholas Serota of the Tate put it: *"I've obviously failed to persuade government that [Tate Modern] matters as much as a new hospital or school."*

The problem is that there is surprisingly little evidence for these claims, and as Sara Selwood points out, the failure to "prove" the social value of the arts has led to an even more desperate (and wasteful) search for evidence, resulting in a heavy burden on arts organisations to collect data.

Some may also claim that the result is an arts policy that is more about therapy and "well-being" than artistic quality. Andrew Brighton of Tate Modern, writing from the perspective of a curator and arts professional, sees the rhetoric of social inclusion as a deeply anti-democratic strain in the arts. Current arts policy, he argues, misunderstands the universal power of art and leads to a tick-box culture of political bureaucracy which all artists should be wary of. However, it may be that, as in areas such as social welfare, new-style philanthropists will be influenced to look for other outcomes than artistic excellence. As one policy think-tank put it: *"Broader social and economic arguments for the arts are essential in today's political, business and economic environment. Both public and private funders are increasingly likely to demand practical outcomes and robust evaluation*[7]*"*. If that is to be the case, the responsibility of aesthetic excellence is simply not enough. Artists and cultural organisations are under greater pressure to prove that they can transform society.

It is in this area that the overlap between professional and amateur, and between passive observation and participation becomes blurred. Robert D. Putnam's book charting the decline of associational activity in America may have been entitled *Bowling Alone*[8], but he draws as many of his examples from cultural activity as he does from sporting activity. He suggests that just as, at its height, social capital was manifest in the membership of choirs, town bands, amateur acting groups or simply "gathering round the piano", so its decline is manifest in the increasing tendency of people to consume culture either in their own homes (watching television or listening to recorded music) or as members of a large and fairly anonymous audience (going to the cinema or concerts).

Britain, too, has a long history of "amateur" or civic participation in culture – including among those who are less well-off. There was a proliferation towards the end of the 19th century of organisations such as working-men's schools and reading rooms which provided their members with access to the work of writers, philosophers and poets, and were greeted eagerly as sources of educational enrichment.

Despite the development of new technologies, these traditions have continued to the modern day. Indeed, the post-war years saw the emergence of a range of new opportunities for collective cultural endeavour, with people joining camera and film clubs, drawing and pottery classes, rambling groups and conservation societies, to take just a few examples. For anyone with musical ability – including Tony Blair and

---

7. *J. Cowling (ed) 2004* For Arts Sake? *Institute for Public Policy Research.*
8. Bowling Alone: The Collapse and Revival of American Community *by Robert D. Putnam. New York: Simon & Schuster, 2000.*

Chapter Two

Ed Grundy in *The Archers*[9], to name but two – playing in a band became almost a rite of passage.

Today, this sort of activity remains widespread – though new technologies and new trends give it an ever-changing face. Examples include family history groups, book clubs, salsa classes, creative writing courses, holidays catering to amateur archaeologists and painters, or web groups devoted to discussing new films.

At the same time, during the post-war years, the development of modern electronic technologies and the rise of mass-entertainment industries put pressure on this sort of cultural participation. As the NHS took charge of people's health and town planners re-engineered cities, the Arts Council, the BBC and other national cultural organisations came to see their job as to support professional artists and mediate between them and the public. Cultural bodies were – and, to some extent, have remained – slow to support new forms of popular cultural participation, such as pop music and filmmaking[10].

The report from the IPPR on which this analysis is based is not deriding passive enjoyment, nor arguing that all cultural policy should be directed at promoting active engagement in artistic and heritage activity. It acknowledges that the enjoyment of, say, listening to classical music, watching a film, visiting a historic landmark or attending a lecture on architecture, can be just as valuable in itself, and just as beneficial in other respects, as more active forms of engagement. Indeed, the two tend to feed off each other. Hearing great performances can inspire people to make music themselves, a visit to a stately home can stimulate interest in an individual's own family history, or the history of their own locality, and so on.

However, these two reports, published within weeks of each other, highlight a debate which provides the context for the development of private support of the cultural organisations, particularly by individuals. If the leaders of such organisations want to influence the focus of the agenda, for example, by emphasising the importance of artistic excellence, risk, innovation and investment in new talent, they must speak out.

There will be opportunities to do so. In June 2006, The Arts Council of England responded to government demands that it adopt a "democratic vision for culture" with its corporate plan for 2006 to 2008. The emphasis is on "participation in all that

9. The Archers *is a popular BBC radio series, based on a fictional family and village, that has been running for several decades.*
10. Mulgan 1997 Saturday Night and Sunday Morning*; Stroud: Comedia.*

we do" and the six stated priorities are: taking part in the arts, children and young people, the creative economy, vibrant communities, internationalism, and celebrating diversity. There will also be a new 10-year strategy for the visual arts. The previous plan focused on the artist as the "life-source" of the Council's work. This plan includes a commitment to launch a "public value" enquiry, and promises a review in 2007 of the portfolio of regularly-funded organisations "to ensure it reflects the cultural and artistic aspirations of the country".

The formal arts funding system appears to have gone along with the prevailing focus on social exclusion and the idea that material deprivation is not its only cause. In this context, the argument for excellence ("elitist") may be more complex than a reference to what is on the walls or on the stage of an institution. As we note from research and from stories such as that of donors Trevor and Lyn Shears (see page 38), there is great interest in education, in increasing access and in embellishing the local community. But there is no current evidence that individual donors are looking to measure effectiveness in the culture sector in the same way that they might evaluate investment in social welfare, although of course there is the potential for analogous assessment in the related fields of education, encouraging access and outreach. On the contrary, those who may be demanding in terms of the assessment of the impact of their support in social welfare fields, may trust their own judgment of the arts and heritage which they support because of a passion based on knowledge, shared enjoyment and appreciation of musicians, artists or curators.

But people do not operate in silos; those involved with public funding may interact with major and influential grant-making trusts, and they in turn have trustees who may also make personal decisions about support of the arts and heritage. That is why it is important that those directing cultural organisations should be aware of and perhaps participate in the debate, to ensure that their view of what matters, whatever they think that may be, is heard in the appropriate places.

Provision of information

Along with the measurement of impact we have noted the focus on accountability and transparency. Even if the newer individual donor does not adopt the same rigorous analytical approach as they may with their investment in social welfare charities[11], it is likely that cultural organisations may be increasingly expected to distribute to donors an accessible annual report and accounts, as do their colleagues in the service delivery sector. Some already do: Glyndebourne (very dependent on

---

11. NPC produces detailed reports identifying the effectiveness of different types of intervention in various types of social welfare organisations. These are downloadable for free at www.philanthropycapital.org .

support from individual donors) publishes an annual report (Life and Times). This not only includes descriptions and photographs of the works performed, statements from the chairman and general director and the story of the seven year gestation period for each production, but also a central double-page spread showing a breakdown of the costs of the Festival and the sources of funds. Furthermore, there is a two-page financial review and, of course, a list of all the major donors. See Chapter Four for further discussion of annual reports.

The purpose of this book is to be a practical guide to engaging individuals; as part of that process organisations should have the vision, courage and competence to outline the facts of organisational financial life to their donors and prospects, explain the business model, and invite them to share as genuine partners in the long-term development of the organisation. For the newer philanthropists and donor investors who are now part of the potential marketplace, as we have seen earlier in this chapter, the principles of this approach will not be strange, although they may not have heard it from cultural institutions. This book is not directly about engaging in the broader debate about governance and leadership in the culture sector, but successful individual donor development depends on addressing those issues. The practical overlap between that debate and this book arises where, as for all cultural organisations, the concern is about covering core costs and building reserves and endowment. (Endowments are discussed in Chapter Eight.)

The current situation and the outlook for the next few years

There are a number of people considering future funding models for the arts. Prominent among these has been Adrian Ellis of Adrian Ellis Associates. There are several useful reports generously available on the website (www.aeaconsulting. com). The company's *Review of Charitable Giving Vehicles and their use in the US and Canada*, commissioned by the Maecenas Institute of Arts & Business (see Additional Information for contacts) contains an introduction which also concludes that public funding for culture is unlikely to increase.

There are also several presentations developed for the Clore Leadership Programme (see page 305) that look at the very changing demographics and expectations of donors and users, and among other guidance identify the relationship between mission, capital and capacity which is at the heart of the challenges faced by many cultural organisations. Examples of the impact of distorting this triangular relationship are given in the section on Gifts in kind and restricted gifts in Chapter Eight.

Adrian Ellis analyses the over-extended and under-capitalised arts sector, pointing out that the current funding model, and, indeed, the way funding is sought, leads to further strain on resources rather than strengthening core competencies and capacities.

Another organisation looking at these and related issues is Mission, Models, Money (**www.missionmodelsmoney.org.uk**). It is driven by a concern to "catalyse debate about issues of organisational and financial sustainability, leading to changes in mind-set, approach and working practices in arts and culture organisations, and the infrastructure that supports them". This initiative too is part of a dynamic process based on a recognition that the traditional approaches to crises in arts management – essentially to seek more public funding – will be as unsustainable as they have proved to be in the past. Like this book, the Mission, Models, Money approach is to learn from best practice, and is supported by Fellows from the Clore Leadership Programme (see Additional Information for more details).

So there is general agreement that it is more important than ever to focus on the development of sustained support from individual givers. This holds true despite recent very positive moves in public funding and sponsorship of the arts. As we noted earlier, the Labour Government has overseen a massive increase in Lottery and Arts Council funding. The Government certainly argues that it has made an unequalled commitment to the arts, and this was endorsed in 2004 by Sir Christopher Frayling, who said that it was "a golden age" for the arts[12]. Over the same period, business sponsorship of the arts has also increased dramatically, as we see in the report from Arts and Business in Additional Information.

In advocating increasing investment in developing individual donor support, we do not underestimate the importance of continuing corporate involvement. The case and methodology for doing so lies outside the scope of this guide and is well explained by Arts and Business. And strategic alliances with corporate sponsors may offer opportunities to reach their clients and their staff.

But all the indications are that the "golden age" is passing. There is increasing demand within the cultural sector (not least from Lottery-funded projects whose annual funding costs are significantly higher than before), a likely standstill in public arts funding, albeit at a higher level than hitherto, the possibility of ticket-buyer choice in the allocation of Lottery funds and the focus on the Olympics, with a knock-on effect not only in London.

At the same time, there has been significant investment in understanding the issues surrounding individual giving, not only in the arts and heritage sectors. In January

12. The Guardian, *4 November 2004.*

2004 the National Audit Office published its report on income generated by the museums and galleries[13]. In May that year the DfES (Department for Education and Science) published the report *Increasing voluntary giving to higher education*, covering many issues relevant to the culture sector, particularly the need for a culture of asking within institutions[14]. *Why Rich People Give* looked in depth at donor motivation and expectations, many of them explored in this guide. And although nothing has yet been done about the key recommendations, it was the Treasury which commissioned the Goodison Review[15], also published in January 2004, which has a major focus on encouraging gifts in kind to the arts by private individuals. Matters relating to individual donors are covered in the draft Charities Bill.

Some organisations are taking the findings and lessons of all this to heart. With this raised awareness has come increasing investment and professionalism – some of it in the culture sector, as featured in case studies in this guide. But there is a wide spectrum. In practice, most cultural organisations benefiting from philanthropy demonstrate a mixed funding portfolio. A summary snapshot of a number of the case study contributors[16] showed that total income was roughly equally divided among public funding, development income and earned income, which was largely through box office/visitor fees. Income from individuals accounted for roughly 35% of total development income, although this ratio ranged widely, from 6% to 90%. Half of the organisations had legacy income, although for the most part this was immaterial. Legacies are explored at length in Chapter Eight.

Investment in development has been encouraged by projects such as the Maecenas Initiative of Arts & Business and the Clore Leadership Programme (see Additional Information for further details). The City University has run an arts administration course for some time and is launching (in Autumn 2006) a Cultural Leadership Programme. In June 2006, the Anglia Ruskin University in Cambridge announced a restructuring of its Masters degree in arts management to cover "the essential core skills required to manage arts and cultural organisations in the 21st century". It will include marketing, business planning, strategy, finance, IT and fundraising. But despite these developments, some would claim that there has been insularity in the cultural sector; that there is relatively little skills and employment transfer with other

---

13. *Theresa Lloyd was a member of the Expert Panel for this review, which can be found on www.nao.gov.uk.*

14. *This can be downloaded from www.dfes.gov.uk/hegateway.*

15. *Securing the Best for our Museums: Private Giving and Government Support, available from www.hm-treasury. gov.uk/media/B9D/02/ACF10B6.pdf.*

16. *We emphasise that these figures should be viewed in the context of an inherent sample bias: most of the contributors of financial data are London-based performing arts organisations, and almost all have had significant capital income and expenditure in the last five years.*

non-profit sectors, and that very few cultural organisations engage staff who are members of the Institute of Fundraising.

Alongside the standstill or decrease in public and corporate funding, and increasing professionalism, there is also increasing competition from outside the sector. Even if we discount the arrival of "new philanthropists" and focus on more traditional donors and income sources, there is no room for complacency. Reference has been made to the higher education sector and there is no doubt that there is increasing investment and competence in raising money from alumni as well as major donors who may have had no connection with the university. A growing number of hospitals are setting up or re-energising separate trusts with an explicit focus on capital campaigning and the establishment of endowments. They are soliciting funds across the board, from small donations to major gifts. And, of course, there is no let-up in the needs of social welfare and international development organisations, not only for disaster relief.

So it can be argued that it is more important than ever that those cultural organisations that are not yet investing sufficiently in engaging and sustaining a relationship with their audiences, exhibition visitors, readers, and current donors are failing the very people that they exist to serve. This is particularly important for the organisations that do not have a place on the national stage. There could be a risk that there will be a similar pattern to that observed in the charity sector: larger and national organisations do well because of investment, reputation and branding; small (local) ones may also do well, with leadership and sufficient investment, because they don't want or need to grow too much and have a local monopoly (as in the case of hospices, for example). It may be the medium and smaller ones that lose out, unless they demonstrate an understanding of and investment in the elements that go to make success in individual giving.

Before we look at these, let us consider the attitudes of donors.

Chapter Three

Why people support the arts and heritage

This chapter is based on research about the motivations of the wealthier. But there is no reason to suppose that the attitudes of those with fewer resources, but who nevertheless make what to them is a significant commitment to a cultural organisation that they love, differ significantly.

Notwithstanding the changing perspectives of some newer and younger donors, there is still a significant pool of traditional and potential supporters for whom involvement in the arts is a matter of passion, relationships, shared creativity and fun. Furthermore, people who adopt a venture philanthropy approach to their investment in social welfare often recognise that measuring "impact" and "effectiveness" in the arts and heritage is about trusting their own judgment. They regularly visit houses and gardens and attend performances, exhibitions and other presentations in the institutions they love and support. They can see for themselves that the theatre is packed with a wide range of people, that the exhibition is of outstanding quality and interest, that the young dancers are rising to the challenge of their training, and that the curatorial and conservation work enjoys a world-class reputation. The assessment of peers, critics and respected fellow-donors reinforces or supplements that assessment.

This chapter is about motivations for serious giving, at whatever level. In the culture sector more than any other, there are opportunities for relationships that are about transactions rather than philanthropy. The difference is crucial, and is explored in the next chapter. Before looking further at cultural giving in particular, it might be helpful to consider motivations in general[1].

Influence and motivation – the wider perspective

Whatever the legal framework or attitudes to the role of the state, people in similar situations display very different approaches to philanthropy. There is a wide

1. *A detailed analysis of this topic can be found in* Why Rich People Give, *by this author, from which much of this chapter is drawn.*

spectrum of factors that influence their motivations. These range from the traditions and influences of faith, family and community, to the personal response to injustice, a perceived gap in social service provision, a passion for an art form. It is clear that core values and traditions embedded within the family, or central to people's upbringing, have an initial and powerful influence.

Faith and religious tradition

Research on both sides of the Atlantic shows that the influences of religion are, for many, central to the family values that form attitudes to giving. This is mentioned across all backgrounds. Not surprisingly, no distinction is made between community tradition, family and faith, since, in the experience of those for whom religion is important, these are interwoven.

The importance of a sense of duty or responsibility, to help the less fortunate or the disadvantaged, appears to transcend religious affiliation and the level of wealth in the household. There is a connection with the idea that giving is not just about money, but is a way of life; giving time is also linked to the concept of service to others. Many mention the importance of a sense of community, and the shared values and principles that underpin a cohesive society.

The immigrant experience

The immigrant experience – of either themselves or their parents – is central to most people from Jewish or Asian communities in the UK. There are deeply held cultural and religious values within such communities and it is difficult to disengage the factors surrounding immigration. Nevertheless, in the research some talked explicitly about the influence of their family coming to a new country and wanting to contribute to the society that had given refuge and opportunity. Strongly linked to this was parental encouragement to achieve and be successful from an early age.

Why people give

Whether donating time or money, most people have a range of motivations for giving. There is sometimes an inextricable overlap between general motivations and the reasons why people support specific causes. Criteria for selecting specific causes can be associated with these general factors, but also with personal and business experience, social networks, and where people live and work. Personal experience may include a specific trigger – for example a child's illness, being moved by a great artistic performance, or coming face-to-face with perceived injustice or waste of talent. The relationship with the cause may also have started in a number of other ways – through an introduction from a respected friend or business acquaintance, or attendance at an event, as we see in the Hallé example in Chapter Four.

It is also vital to distinguish between the passions and personal experiences that may lead an individual to become a giver in the first place, and the reinforcement donors get in seeing the impact of their support, knowing that they are making a difference, being properly thanked and meeting like-minded people.

Belief in the cause

Without doubt, the key impetus for the majority of people in research studies across the world is belief in the cause. For many, a passion for a specific cause is inseparable from motivation; the enthusiasm underpins and is reinforced by the affinity for and relationship with the individual organisations focused on the subjects of concern to the donor. Donors who care deeply about a generic cause – whether child poverty or opera – may well support more than one charity or institution focusing on those issues.

The UK research found it was common to see issues surrounding "putting something back" into society and a response to both emotional and intellectual engagement melded together. There was also a recurring combination of belief in the cause supported by confidence in the organisations supported. For some, the chosen cause was support of major institutions, particularly those with a cultural, educational or medical base. This was often linked to a sense of national as well as civic and personal pride. Birmingham, or London, or Manchester, or the North East, or the UK, were felt to benefit from and "deserve" outstanding hospitals, art galleries and so on.

"For fairly modest amounts one can make a real difference. I feel ashamed if we don't have a world-class opera house in London and if foreigners are expected to provide the money."

That person added that he *"wanted to make a difference in keeping London a great world city'.*

Being a catalyst for change

A related theme concerns people's desire to see *"something that otherwise wouldn't have happened"*. This was sometimes expressed as *"helping to create change"*, sometimes as *"having an impact"*, but always with the underlying wish to make a "real" difference. Another recurring theme in facilitating change was the wish to get "value for money" – effective and direct use of a financial contribution.

Several respondents expressed the desire to have an impact on individual lives – whether disadvantaged young people, talented artists, or people who lack opportunity more generally. Many linked their support of individuals to the benefits to society, partly to redress inequality but also to allow recipients to become more independent or to develop "intellectual capital". Others emphasised the satisfaction of observing the effects of their philanthropy – seeing the beneficiaries flourish. For some, these ideas come together in setting up a new organisation.

CASE STUDY

Southbank Sinfonia – the chairman's involvement: the importance of 'hands-on', enthusiastic and committed leadership

- **Training orchestra**
- **London**
- **Total income: £541,000**
- **Development income: £541,000**

By Janet Reeve

In 2002, Simon Over, now artistic director of Southbank Sinfonia, approached his friend Michael Berman to see if he could help with an idea for a new orchestral project. Simon is a talented conductor and accompanist and musical director of the Parliament Choir. For a long time he had harboured a dream to create a staging post for aspiring young musicians between music college and a professional career. He thought that if he could select 30 or so of the best music graduates and create a working orchestra with them for a year, they would be far better equipped to face the challenges of the real world of the working musician, and that it would be a stimulating ensemble to work with.

Michael Berman was himself an accomplished musician, but he made a living helping to develop early-stage technology businesses. He was captivated by Simon's idea and before long they were joined by Katharine Verney, a musician and educationalist with a background in human communication. She too became enthusiastic about the project. The small group of three began to develop a business plan. Raising funds was obviously a priority consideration.

At first, drawing on business experience, Michael assumed that the way to raise money for the arts was to employ a fundraiser on a commission basis i.e. retaining a cut of the money raised. He had conversations with various individuals who claimed they could do this, but he became more and more uneasy about them. Paying fundraisers on commission is greatly disliked by donors and for a number of reasons is strongly advised against. (See Chapter Eight for a more detailed discussion of this.) There are no shortcuts to successful fundraising. A leading businessman who had been involved in two major capital campaigns for cultural institutions advised Michael that the only way to raise money for a start-up project was to do it yourself.

Michael committed funds of his own and set about finding further seed-corn money to employ a general manager for the project. Together they mapped out a fundraising strategy and took advice from a fundraising consultant. The focus was on raising money from charitable trusts and individuals for basic costs, including bursaries for the players they intended to audition for the first year of Southbank Sinfonia – the name adopted for the project.

The team understood that, to be successful, it needed to harness the energy of influential contacts who could either donate money themselves or open doors to other sources of income. They also knew that there were important skills that only a development professional would have and they needed that expertise too. There was also the question of servicing donors. They decided to retain the consultant who was able to give concise, practical advice on specific approaches to donors. They were also fortunate to have secured the help of an experienced volunteer to help cultivate and service the donors. This included maintaining regular contact with donors, welcoming them to concerts, managing a number of cultivation events and starting up a membership scheme. The volunteer worked in the office more or less full-time.

With guidance from the consultant, the general manager made several successful applications to charitable trusts. Simon and Michael mapped out their networks and started to think about ways to cultivate their potential targets. Each recognised his responsibility for working hard at the fundraising. They worked closely with the consultant on how best to present their exciting idea to potential donors. They believed in their project and didn't shy away from asking for specific sums of money to support its different aspects. Individual donors were inspired by the unique nature of the Southbank Sinfonia programme and supporting players' bursaries appealed to them.They recognised the difficulties faced by talented young music graduates at the start of their careers and saw clearly the need for a professional "finishing school". Each individual musician would benefit by acquiring the essential knowledge and skills to survive and succeed as a professional musician.

Photo: David Costley-White

Southbank Sinfonia also planned to perform in venues throughout the UK, reaching hundreds of schoolchildren as well as a wider public audience.

Meanwhile, Simon and Michael had managed to find office space for the small team for a modest rent at St John's Church in Waterloo, London. The church also provided crucial rehearsal space for the orchestra. As part of the bargain, Southbank Sinfonia planned to give free "rush-hour" concerts at the church. These would give the young musicians valuable regular performance experience, as well as enhancing the life of the local community, and have proved to be tremendous opportunities for introducing people to the organisation, socialising and building relationships.

The partnership with St John's Waterloo has proved mutually beneficial. Four years on, Southbank Sinfonia is working closely with the church to redevelop the crypt. The orchestra has also been able to acquire more spacious offices to cater for its growing administrative team, as well as dressing rooms and extra rehearsal space for the players. There will also be room for other charitable organisations to share the space.

Southbank Sinfonia now has a staff of six, which includes a fundraising officer. It continues to invest in the services of the consultant for strategic advice and staff training, and has also used a freelance fundraiser to research and write applications to targeted trusts. It has twice tried to recruit a more senior fundraiser but has not yet found a candidate right for the organisation. Despite its impressive track record, some potential candidates view Southbank Sinfonia as a relatively unknown commodity. Meanwhile, it is doing well on existing resources.

Southbank Sinfonia has adopted an open, collaborative and positive approach that has paid dividends, both artistically and in fundraising terms. Players introduce concerts from the stage and chat to members of the audience after concerts. Supporters feel they are part of the event and are happy to be involved. The result is informal excellence.

The challenge for Southbank Sinfonia over the next few years is to move from start-up mode to sustainability. Fully aware of this, and with a secure base of donors established, it knows that it will need to invest further resources into the fundraising operation to retain and grow support.

Self-actualisation

A number of drivers can be categorised under the general heading of self-actualisation – the realisation of an individual's personality and development of some or all of its aspects. They involve issues surrounding integrity, personal engagement and commitment, as well as responses to intellectual and emotional sentiments. While for most people self-actualisation is not the initial motivator, the experience of the "psychic" benefits sustains their giving and is the basis for recurring commitment.

The motivating power of appreciation, whether for money or expertise, cannot be overstated. Most people emphasised the pleasure of being valued for their donations, and being respected by other donors, which in turn contributed to feelings of self-worth.

People used to leadership and decision-making gain an additional satisfaction by allocating money which would otherwise go to government. This is in part about keeping control and influence over the way their money is spent. It is also about competence, and the idea that giving money in a tax-efficient way is a better alternative to paying more taxes and having "Gordon Brown spending it".

Another significant potential emotional benefit is the dream of the philanthropic legacy. Although many major donors can celebrate major commercial and entrepreneurial achievements, and a few have made significant contributions in creative fields, there is a strong implication that the highest recognition of posterity lies in what benefactors are able to do for others. This is closely linked to the issue of the desire for recognition. We return to this in the next chapter.

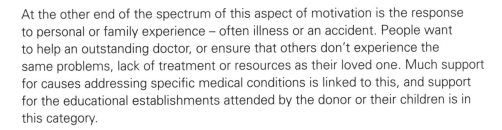

At the other end of the spectrum of this aspect of motivation is the response to personal or family experience – often illness or an accident. People want to help an outstanding doctor, or ensure that others don't experience the same problems, lack of treatment or resources as their loved one. Much support for causes addressing specific medical conditions is linked to this, and support for the educational establishments attended by the donor or their children is in this category.

The moral dimension

For many, one factor in their motivations is the satisfaction – to a greater or lesser extent – of their conscience. For most people, the basis of the values that prompt feelings of obligation are the influences explored earlier – of faith, family or community. Some link their sense of being privileged to both an obligation to those less fortunate and to wanting to help rebalance a sense of social injustice. The identification of others "less fortunate" varies. For many it covers a wide range, from family to community to wider society.

Financial support of those with much less, or going through hard times, is seen as part of the responsibility of wealth, and in some cases is a family tradition.

The theme of "putting something back" was mentioned by many, especially but not only by those who were immigrant in origin. And "putting something back" may also have a direct link with the arts: a lifetime of pleasure and stimulation at the opera, concert hall or museum or beautiful garden, (at least where it is known to be a non-profit organisation), is often given as a reason for a donation, even amongst people who no longer attend regularly, and this is certainly a theme for some legacies, for example, to the National Trust.

However, not everyone explains their philanthropy in those terms. A significant minority, including some who had made money and some who inherited, link their belief that they had been fortunate with the obligation to share. This sense of "deserving one's luck" was manifest across all backgrounds.

Relationships

It is not surprising that one of the major motivating factors reported by respondents across all categories is the fun, enjoyment and personal fulfilment of relationships with a range of people that charitable activity brings.

The pleasure in part derives from the broadening of perspective engendered by meeting people from a completely contrasting walk of life, often creative and dedicated to different goals. The sense of working in partnership with those who deliver the mission is very important for many donors, and retaining a place among a lively community of exemplary givers is a major motivator.

How giving is linked to social engagement and the desire or influence of joining networks is crucial to what constitutes or encourages a culture of giving. Culture in this sense is, amongst other things, about the attitudes, values, norms and "rules" that inform a society, while membership of a group within society (faith, family or community) which creates expectations of charitable giving is, as we have seen, a key determinant of philanthropy. In the absence of any such membership, joining and participating in a network or set of relationships in which giving is an essential and pleasurable component is a major step to normalising such behaviour.

In the absence of strong religious networks the cultural sector is ideally placed to create and sustain networks of people who share values, interests and community.

DONOR CASE STUDY

Trevor and Lyn Shears

By Theresa Lloyd

Background

Trevor and Lyn Shears are based in Newcastle. Trevor is Yorkshire born and bred. They established a charitable trust in 1996, after a successful management buy-out and public sale of his transport company. Having realised some £20 million, they soon afterwards, and with significant help from the local community foundation, placed £8 million into a charitable trust.

This endowment, with good investment, including in the shares of the transport company, now stands at £14 million, and they are distributing some £600,000 a year and expect this to increase.

The focus of the trust includes environmental issues, healthcare, transport-related activities (particularly old trams and trains), local causes and projects, and the arts, with a particular focus on singing, singers and opera. In many cases the latter two – local causes and music – overlap.

The focus on the arts was initially influenced by Lyn Shears. Her parents were not musical but she developed her passion for singing through the choir she joined aged 12. This helped hugely in later life when she was moving every two years; wherever she lived she joined the local choir, enjoyed the singing and met like-minded people.

Support of The Sage Gateshead

Photo: Mark Westerby

The Sage Gateshead.

"We learned about The Sage from George Hepburn, head of the Community Foundation serving Tyne & Wear and Northumberland." (For more about community foundations see Chapter Eight.)

"What fired us about the Sage was the education programme; everyone, especially young people, would be able to have an opportunity to engage in all kinds of music they might have thought was not for them. The Sage is about getting away from an 'elitist' image and getting people into enjoying all kinds of music. It's the biggest project we've ever done. We gave £300,000.

"Initially, we wanted to be anonymous. We were doing what we wanted because of our private passion for music. Then we had a huge change of heart; we wanted to encourage others and share that passion.

"The naming of a room in the Education Centre came much later. They came and offered us the opportunity to name the room. They have said that this will be in perpetuity.

"The nature of The Sage and its funding is unique; the building was funded by Gateshead Council and the Lottery. It is rented by the North Music Trust, and the business plan included commercial elements in the income mix.

"The Endowment Fund was to pay for the education programme. So we went into it on the same basis as Sage Group plc with its £6 million: the proposition that income from the endowment would support education for ever.

"It wasn't about the naming, but about supporting a locally-based international centre of excellence".

Examples of other support of the arts and heritage

Trevor and Lyn support several other arts and heritage organisations and projects, including:

a) The Samling Foundation

"We have supported this for three years and give £30,000 per annum which funds one of its masterclasses a year for six young singers. It invests in outstanding young people, bringing them together with world-leading artists to interact and produce new work, break down boundaries and establish innovative new networks. Through partnerships with The Sage Gateshead, local authorities and schools and the business community, it brings world-class projects, outreach programmes and performances thus fulfilling a unique role in the North East and Cumbria."

b) Tyneside Cinema

"We are giving £100,000 because it is an important building in the region and is into major new facilities for film and drama education, with links to local universities.

"Key for us is that organisations don't just exist in a vacuum; they must have tentacles reaching out into the community."

c) National Tramway Museum, Crich, Derbyshire

This is about a group of people preserving trams, and Trevor is very enthusiastic. But there is a lot more – including a woodland walk and sculpture trail and folk music events.

"We need to be able to educate and teach people about transport as part of their history. We got involved in the library, setting up electronic databases, creating a link to Sheffield University. It's about transport history and its importance in education. They act as consultants to TV producers, and generate income.

"We now contribute annually in perpetuity – £30,000 a year. It funds a post and they know it's ongoing."

d) Northern Stage

"We contributed an initial £10,000 towards refurbishment and are committed to £5,000 annually towards its educational programme.

"It is the largest professional producing theatre company in the North of England. With a permanently-employed group of actors, it is able to work closely with education and community groups across the North East."

e) Live theatre

"We are contributing £70,000 to the refurbishment fund and £10,000 a year to education and outreach. It's about live theatre on the quayside and working with local playwrights. It also has the largest free theatre and drama education and outreach programme in the city. It is committed to the vision that drama can be used constructively to empower participants and play a crucial role in their personal and social development."

f) Great North Museum

This is a Victorian Museum originally called The Hancock Museum, now linked with Newcastle University. Mr Hancock was a taxidermist. He collected and preserved specimens, and built up an amazing collection. It's a natural history museum – with live animals too.

This is closed for complete refurbishment until 2009. When re-opened it will:

● Be a gateway to North-East.
● Contain lots of artefacts with links to Hadrian's Wall.
● Be designed to link to the National Curriculum and have other education programmes, including outreach with local schools.
● Integrate three collections.

Trevor and Lyn have committed £100,000 capital and will support the education programme.

g) Them Wifees

"This is a drama group created by a group of women with major problems, including communication. They use plays as a form of acting therapy and teaching. We have provided £1,000 for core funding."

How they approach project or grant assessment

● See what the organisation does before they commit.
● Attend events.
● Make it clear they would like to attend education programmes.
● Request individual organisation reviews. They may not read them all the way through but always read the executive summary.
● Trust the people they are dealing with.

"For example, we have supported Seven Stories – the National Centre for the Children's Book. It's in Newcastle, on the quayside in an old warehouse. We take the grandchildren; we can tell if they like it."

In general

a) *"We see that many funders support a project for a maximum of three years or even just give on a one-off basis. Very few people are keen on core funding or making a long-term commitment. We are more inclined to long-term support."*

b) *"Also, we know that in some cases money we give is "allocated" to a specific project but in fact goes into general or core funding, since the project is in the budget and would happen anyway and we are happy with that. The organisation sets the budget and aims to raise the money to do it. An example is particular WWF projects."*

c) *"We are passionate about local excellence."*

d) *"We don't want the recipients to roll-out the red carpet so we tend to go to fewer things and we always pay for our tickets."*

e) *"We believe that education in the arts can inspire and uplift people, thus enabling them to better manage the problems of everyday life"*

Key points

● Most people are driven by more than one motive at the same time.

● Belief in the cause or mission is the main reason for giving substantial sums and recurring support.

● Knowing that you are making a real difference, to an overall mission or individual lives, is a powerful motivator.

● Civic pride, community support, and putting something back are also powerful drivers.

● Giving opportunities to others, whether young talent, or visitors and audiences who would not otherwise benefit, and sharing learning opportunities, matters to many.

● The rewards of relationships, with those who deliver the mission, with specialists, with beneficiaries and with other donors, cannot be overestimated.

As we see, belief in a cause is not the only reason for giving, and certainly not for continuing to give. The level and continuity of commitment is closely related to the degree to which the recipient is able to awaken and sustain a passion for the cause. The relationship between donor and recipient is crucial to the philanthropic experience. We look more closely at what donors expect in their relationships with the cultural organisations they support in the next chapter.

Chapter Four

What donors expect

T he main focus of this chapter is the expectations of donors, particularly those who have given what to them is a significant amount of money. These expectations may be unrelated to the absolute value of their gift, but are a reflection of the level of commitment they see themselves as having made. The more significant the gift for the donor, the more they are likely to expect the beneficiary to invest in the reciprocal relationship.

So while much of the focus of this review is about major gifts, for some donors and for some smaller organisations, relatively small donations – £1,000 or less – may lead to the same expectations.

Transaction or altruism

One of the most important factors to understand is the difference in the mind of a donor between a relationship based on a transaction and altruistic giving. Is the supporter driven by the benefits they might gain, or by the passion for the cause which may unlock significant investment? A benefit-driven approach to increasing support to a significant level carries the seeds of its own failure, if presented in terms of "value for money". And it is very important not to assume that all lower-level donors are transaction- or benefits-driven. Indeed, some people choose not to become Friends because they do not want the involvement offered with that status.

Many higher-level donors are not thinking primarily about "value for money", nor should they to be encouraged to do so. All the evidence is that the "rewards" are about knowing they are making a difference, and sharing their passions and interests with those who deliver the artistic mission, knowledgeable members of the professional team, and other like-minded donors.

They give because they want to see an organisation that they love thrive, to share in the improving standards and rising reputation, to support young and outstanding talent and to feel part of the creative team that enables great art to flourish.

One scheme which encapsulates many of these facets is the Chair Patrons programme at the Orchestra of the Age of Enlightenment.

CASE STUDY

**Orchestra of the Age of Enlightenment –
Chair Patrons Scheme**

- **Period instrument orchestra**
- **London and touring**
- **Total income: £2.6m**
- **Development income: £376,000**

By Janet Reeve

In 1993, the Orchestra of the Age of Enlightenment (OAE) decided to set up a scheme to raise annual donations from individuals based around an association with its orchestral "chairs". The idea came from a board member and donor who had seen a similar idea in action and thought it could be adapted to good effect at the OAE.

The OAE was founded in 1986 by a group of talented period instrument musicians who bucked the trend and decided to invite guest conductors to work with them rather than become a vehicle for a single conductor's artistic direction. This visionary spirit attracted a promising degree of support from like-minded entrepreneurial individuals who provided financial assistance and legal expertise, and opened doors to corporate sponsors. The board was made up of a proportion of musician members and committed volunteers with relevant expertise.

The non-playing board members and the musicians shared a passion for music and for the exciting adventure they had embarked on together in creating a new orchestra. The Chair Patrons scheme captured the essence of the relationship between volunteers and the lively group of musicians early on in the life of the organisation. All board members had given financial support already and those who were able immediately signed up as Chair Patrons. In the early days of the scheme, £2,000 brought an association with the principal player in one of the sections of the Orchestra, while the patron for the leader's chair donated £3,000. Board members who had signed up made further approaches to close friends who were enthusiastic about

Photo: Eric Richmond/Laing and Carroll

music. Soon eight or more couples had become Chair Patrons. This was a charitable donation. Patrons paid for their concert tickets and other events on top of their donations.

After each of the eight or so concerts each season at the South Bank Centre, Chair Patrons were invited to pay to dine afterwards with the musicians, forming what became known as the Dining Club. At first a working title, the name has stuck because it describes well the "clubby" gathering after concerts where friendships are made and much fun is had.

Twelve years on, the Chair Patrons scheme is still going strong. The donation has risen and a new higher-level of Benefactor has been introduced. In 2006 the OAE has 18 Chair Patrons and eight Benefactors and the scheme now generates nearly £150,000 a year before Gift Aid. This represents a substantial part of voluntary income and is impressive for an organisation with an annual turnover of £2.6 million.

The retention rate of donors at the OAE is significant. Taken over 10 years, the Chair Patrons Scheme (and the related Benefactors scheme) has generated in the region of £1 million with Gift Aid. The donors who have been contributing for a period in excess of 10 years are as valuable to OAE as one-off major donors, and arguably more so as they contribute vital unrestricted funds which enable it to plan ambitious concerts across the season. The organisation recognises the longevity of support and aspires to service the Chair Patrons and Benefactors as if they were major donors. It has recently invested in the recruitment of an experienced major donor manager to look after individual donors.

The long-standing relationships that have developed between musicians and donors are the life-blood of this orchestra. The warmth of the players and the intimacy they enjoy with their regular audience is noticeable. Supporters are often highly musical themselves and find enormous emotional and artistic fulfilment through close links with particular players and the "behind the scenes view" of orchestral life offered. Chair Patrons believe that the scheme is one of the best ways to support the Orchestra. The scheme enables OAE to work with some of the most talented orchestral musicians in the world, which in turn attracts top musical directors, soloists and conductors. The Chair Patron's donation is, therefore, the catalyst for a whole circle of events that enables the OAE to be regarded as one of the best orchestras in the world.

Donors themselves have been very effective in recruiting friends who in turn become donors. Close relationships also mean that it is not hard for the management to approach one of the Patrons for additional support when the need arises.

The OAE has a development team of three. One staff member is responsible for the management of individual giving, spending nearly three-quarters of her time managing the Chair Patron and Benefactor schemes. The dedicated team member is an excellent investment, but the responsibility for looking after the donors is shared and understood throughout the organisation. This is because excellent relationships have formed over the years, primarily at the Dining Club after concerts, but also, in many cases, through the shared experience of being on the Board. It is not often that artists are queuing up to have dinner with the sponsors, but at the OAE the musicians really do look forward to it.

Conclusion

The OAE has undoubtedly hit upon a successful formula and over time has built up a secure income base from its individual giving scheme, although it is, of course, subject to the usual rules on Gift Aid and VAT in relation to donations. While the OAE has maintained good relationships with its donors and some have been there from the start, some have fallen away and new ones have replaced them.

This is exactly as you would expect – people move away, some move on to support other things. What is clear from this case, however, is the crucial importance of developing relationships with donors and involving them in what you do. Donors feel more inclined to continue supporting when they can see exactly how their contribution makes a positive impact. The feeling of being part of a group or club is also a very important factor for success.

Donation as membership

Some are quite explicit about their expectations that giving at a certain level is about buying privileged access. At a low level it is simply seen as a "good deal" – membership of the National Trust or the Royal Academy was described as being in this category. It was noted that the tax treatment of such contributions was inconsistent, some being payable through Gift Aid or trusts and others not, and some organisations having to pay VAT in some cases. This is explored in detail in Chapter Nine.

Some people may start supporting the arts because it is seen as a "good deal", and may continue to contribute to certain organisations on that basis, but support others for which they have a real affinity in a quite different frame of mind. It is clear from the research for *Why Rich People Give* that supporters of cultural institutions make a clear distinction between those organisations which they support in order to obtain access to perceived real benefits – for example, priority booking or "free" entry to exhibitions – and those to which they make significant commitments, in order to make a real difference. Many are Friends, at various levels, of a number of heritage organisations, museums, galleries, opera houses and theatres. They are well-disposed to all, but passionate about a few. Within the same genre they may support several at relatively modest levels.

A typical opera-loving donor may support a number of opera companies at the level necessary to guarantee best seats for popular performances, and because they wish the companies well, but is likely to have a deep relationship (and go deeper into their pockets) for one or at the most two. This is not only because of belief in the excellence of the "product" and the team, but also because the involvement in the organisation which comes with and is a key part of the pleasure of major giving is time-consuming and emotionally engaging. Once people have two or three such organisations and relationships in their lives they may not have room for more, however exciting the new opportunity might be.

Before we explore the more complex areas of the nature of the relationship with the cultural beneficiary that reinforce a philanthropic partnership, we should focus on the benefits that even those driven by altruism may expect, even if it is not the primary or only reason for giving.

Special privileges

Because most arts and heritage organisations offer a range of special privileges, donors have come to expect it. The benefits are usually one form or another of special access – to a range of services and sometimes to key people.

"I don't expect it but I do appreciate it. I accept that there is privileged access for people who give money."

"They should definitely offer hooks for people who give time and money. Organisations are not very good at saying thank you. If you give money and can't get a ticket, it's a poor do. It's a way of saying thank you and can be a motivation to give more."

Many people took the view that benefits, while not being a determining factor, were important, and some recognised an ambivalence in their own position.

"I am more inclined to give money if they don't promise special access, but in practice having a special phone line for ticket booking is very nice."

For some major givers such arrangements are part of the overall package of recognition and involvement to be negotiated between donor and recipient.

"It's not a condition but I want things clarified beforehand – if my name will be on display, if there's special access and so on."

The forms of special access cited as desirable by interviewees included:

- Attendance at rehearsals.
- Visits to exhibitions outside public opening hours.
- Visiting projects under construction (for major capital gifts).
- The personal attention of the director.
- Seeing behind the scenes, such as building work-in-progress, conservation undertakings or other specialist activities.
- Avoiding the crowds, primarily attending exhibitions and other visual arts displays through, for example, private views (for high level supporters) or personal tours, escorted by curator or director (for major donors).
- Saving time and obtaining fast-track servicing. Examples included:
  - A hotline for tickets.
  - A special bar or bar area in the intervals.
  - A special area for collection of programmes and tickets.
  - A designated cloakroom (to save queuing at the end).
  - Free parking (not expected in London).

People expect to pay more for an allocation of scarce resources – usually tickets. It is not expected that the tickets will be free, just available. Some recognise that this is very much a mutually beneficial arrangement and should not be counted as charity in the same way as gifts to causes where there is no self-interest.

"I am a founder member of Glyndebourne. I don't consider that charity. I pay the premium to jump the queue. It's the same as being friends of ENO or ROH. If you get the benefit, it's not charity."

This question of when a cultural organisation is a "charity" is important. The interviewee just quoted seemed to be suggesting that it is in the eye of the beholder; for him and some others it relates to the nature of the relationship with the particular organisation, rather than anything to do with legal status.

Explaining that they are charitable organisations meriting philanthropic donations, just as in other sectors, is a crucial challenge for the cultural sector, particularly when planning legacy promotion, as we see in the contribution on legacies in Chapter Eight.

Others who say that they do not expect special access recognise that it may be necessary to offer it to ensure a committed donor base. Some make a distinction between those who do and do not receive public funds, citing the need for the latter to secure a recurring income basis on which to plan. Examples included the Royal Academy and Glyndebourne.

Four key points emerge from people's discussion of special access in the arts:

● Lower-level givers may see themselves as buying a service – a ticket hotline, a fast-track cloakroom – as much as being "charitable".

● Partly in response to promotion by arts and heritage organisations themselves, expectation of such services are now widespread, and most of those involved with fundraising strongly advocate their continuation.

● Some major donors see themselves as potential ambassadors, and argue that to perform that role well they need frequent (privileged) access.

● Some higher-level donors are very irritated by what they see as pettiness about charging for small things. They are not interested in the finer points of the rules related to tax issues (see Chapter Nine). Some expect to negotiate terms for access as part of the overall arrangements relating to the management of the relationship.

Sometimes those involved in the arts forget the excitement for those new to the sector of seeing "behind the scenes".

CASE STUDY

Hallé Concerts Society – Conductor's Circle Patrons

- Symphony orchestra
- Northwest
- Total income: £5.3m
- Development income: £734,000

By Fiona McLeod, development director

In February of 2006, a new sponsor to the Hallé held an event around a concert at The Bridgewater Hall in Manchester. As part of the day, the Hallé arranged a workshop for the sponsor's clients; this involved both writing and music creation along the theme of the concert – Romeo and Juliet.

Two of the guests noted a great interest in the Hallé and although not from Manchester, were very keen to become more involved. Over the next couple of months the Hallé kept in contact with them by letter and phone and in April invited them to a private dinner with the music director and other top-level donors. The guests had the opportunity to speak with like-minded people who already give philanthropically and to meet the music director, who invited them to attend one of his rehearsals in May. They accepted and, having no real understanding of the work involved in preparing for a concert, were thrilled to be given such an insight into the "back stage" work of the Hallé.

Following that rehearsal and concert, they decided to become more involved in both attending and giving and agreed to become part of the Hallé's individual patron programme at the highest level.

They have subsequently attended another concert where they met more of the patrons of the orchestra, which they much enjoyed. Now with their pledge of support, the Hallé has the opportunity to build this relationship and hopefully to encourage them to bring like-minded friends to concerts and events, or possibly to hold a dinner on behalf of the Hallé in their home.

Donation as philanthropy

It should be noted that it is not only major donors who may see their donation as entirely philanthropic. However, while some at every level may decline opportunities for involvement, for most the pleasure and psychic benefits come from enjoying the art form, seeing the organisation and the artists and other creative people associated with it flourish, and sharing this with others. The crucial role of the development office is to ensure that opportunities for these experiences are arranged and managed flawlessly.

Relationships with recipients

The way the recipient manages the relationship with the donor is an essential element in the successful development of a sustained commitment to that organisation. A key aspect is that the donors want to feel they are valued members of the team. They want to be appreciated for more than their money. They know that money is only one of the essential strands for a project. But donors also want recognition for the interest, concern and passion that motivates them, and that they assume they share with trustees and staff of the recipient organisation (and, in some sectors, with the ultimate beneficiaries), and for the expertise that is often the source of their wealth.

This aspect is all the more important if potential donors have the mind-set of the donor-investor, the rise of which was discussed in Chapter Two.

CASE STUDY

Birmingham Contemporary Music Group

- **Orchestra**
- **Midlands**
- **Development income: £197,000**
- **Total income: £650,000**

By Stephen Newbould, artistic director

Birmingham Contemporary Music Group (BCMG) has found a novel way of linking donors directly with their work. BCMG exists to commission and perform new works from living composers and, through its Sound Investment scheme, creates what it describes as a partnership between audiences and BCMG to support composers.

The budget for each new work (usually between £5,000 to £15,000) is divided into £100 Sound Units in which any audience member (or other supporter) may "invest". The donor can buy Sound Units in the works of their choice, or Floating Sound Units if they do not have a preference for a particular composer. Naturally, BCMG has other sources of funds and so commissions still go ahead even if the whole sum needed has not been raised in "investments". However, without the additional money generated from the Sound Investment scheme each year, the organisation's ability to commission would be curtailed.

As at 2005/06, there were generally between 30 and 55 Sound Investors per commission. BCMG usually premieres three to four Sound Investment commissions each season. So far the scheme has raised £150,000, which is very significant in the context of funds available for commissioning new classical music. Sound Investors live all over the UK, and many are London-based. BCMG says that Sound Investors often buy Sound Units as gifts or to celebrate a special occasion.

Payments can be made by credit card (including online via BCMG's website), by cheque or through a direct debit monthly instalment scheme, paying from £10 a month.

It is made abundantly clear that this is not an investment scheme within the meaning of the Financial Services Act since the "investors" are really making a donation, have no rights over the resulting composition and will not receive any return on their investment (donation). All donations are eligible for Gift Aid.

BCMG has premiered well over 50 new Sound Investment works, and in total has given over 200 performances of these new works. Many have been broadcast by the BBC and taken up by other ensembles around the world.

When a donor invests they are sent an Investment Certificate with further information about the composer and piece they are supporting. Regular updates are given to the donor as work on composition progresses, and donors are invited to rehearsals and to a special reception at the premiere.

At this reception, the composer presents the "investor" with either a free signed copy of the title page of the score, or the exclusive opportunity to buy the full score, also signed by the composer. The donors' names are listed in the score and concert programme, and investors have guaranteed tickets for the premiere performance. After this BCMG continues to send any press reviews, and pass on news of future performances.

Clearly, many people enjoy the experience, as there is an extremely high re-investment rate, with over two-thirds of investors continuing their support after their initial investment.

One donor quoted on BCMG's website says:

"... to be present at a rehearsal where an imaginative composer, a skilled story-teller and a handful of dedicated musicians turn a few deceptively simple phrases into a magical musical event; to hear for the very first time a new composition brilliantly inspired by the poignant imagery of a talented artist and to share the experience with fellow Sound Investors – what could be more exciting?"

Anne Fletcher, a Sound Investor in commissions by Judith Weir with Indian storyteller Vayu Naidu, and Howard Skempton. April 2005.

An interesting aspect is that the scheme has brought BCMG many new audience members, thus reversing the usual picture.

Many Sound Investors are general music lovers coming to contemporary music as a relatively new thing, attracted by the idea of the scheme. They then get hooked.

Essential features of the donor-beneficiary relationship

Good communications

The importance of effective communication was constantly stressed in discussions about the management of the relationship between donor and recipient. Key points that came out of interviews included:

"I want a personal letter of thanks, that's all."

"You can't thank people enough, charities shouldn't be afraid to write too often. Too many charities become production lines. You lose people if you don't really make it personal. They must keep in touch regularly, make people feel part of the team, keep people informed."

"I would give 10 out of 10 to an organisation which came back after a year and asked for 30 minutes of my time to explain what had happened to the money and project and what was achieved."

"I want to be appreciated and not taken for granted. I expect no say in how the money is spent. I back an organisation, project or person; it's for them to decide. I want a continuing relationship."

The preferred content of the communication and the forms it should take vary between individuals, but the need for ongoing connection was firmly emphasised. Interviewees repeatedly mentioned the importance of establishing good contact at the outset, of maintaining it throughout the relationship, and giving time and thought to the process. There was also recurrent reference to the need for personalised communication rather than "production lines".

Particularly in the cultural sector, donors assume that those they deal with share their passion about the art form, and an interest in the current programme of activities and in the members of the creative team who "make it happen". Those in the development office who manage the relationship must be able to empathise with the donor, and to communicate impeccably and appropriately. It is worth pointing out that even if the individual donor uses a charitable trust, this should not mean that they are dealt with by a "trust fundraiser" who they see as responsible for institutional foundations.

Information

In the interviews, there was a widespread call from donors for the provision of regular – and useful – information about the progress of the recipient organisation or cause.

People spoke with appreciation of the unexpected short personal note, phone call or email about a success or milestone for the organisation or project, and their regret at careless or mass-produced data bearing little relation to the focus of their support.

Appreciation and recognition

Most people interviewed wanted some form of appreciation or recognition for their philanthropic giving from the recipient. But there was a wide spectrum of views about the form this should take, ranging from a private expression of appreciation at one end to public and publicised recognition at the other.

In Chapter Six, David Dixon explores what might be called the mass-market end of the donation spectrum, pointing out that at lower giving levels it would simply not be cost-effective to deal with everyone on a completely individual basis. But people should feel that they matter to the organisation. One former very distinguished chair of several leading organisations in the cultural sector told me that he wrote personally to everyone who gave more than £1,000. For some organisations that figure should perhaps be £500.

"Manners Makyth Money"[1]

"The response from the people I help is 99.99% of what is needed. I like it when people thank me and say they could never have done it without me."

As we have seen, interviewees felt that there should be a clear – and personalised – thank you from beneficiaries for their contributions. Although this seems a fairly modest request, several donors interviewed spoke of inadequate expressions of gratitude for major gifts, including standard letters for six-figure sums. Those who were themselves givers and also had experience as fundraisers were particularly emphatic about the importance of looking after major donors.

"You must nurture people, not drop them when you have got the money. They must be included in the future even if they do not continue to give. It is not about one-off deal-making. You must make them feel special."

This relates to two other facets to this complex area – loyalty and legacies. Many of those who support organisations year after year report feeling undervalued compared with a one-off major donor. Few organisations in the cultural sector have a process or formal scheme for recognising loyalty. One is the National Trust.

1. *From a conversation with Sir Nicholas Goodison.*

CASE STUDY

The National Trust – Patrons at the National Trust – recognising loyalty

- **Heritage**
- **National**
- **Total income: £315m**
- **Development income: £68m, including £48m in legacies**

By Justine Webb, head of major gifts

Morte Point in North Devon.

The National Trust Patron scheme was launched in 1997 to recognise those who had made a single gift or cumulative gifts of £10,000 or more since its centenary year in 1995. It also launched a Benefactor programme for those giving £500 a year or more. The Patron scheme was offered to those who already "qualified" and to a number of "prospects" who it was thought might like to become Patrons. The launch was marked by a dinner with HRH The Prince of Wales. Since then it has not been proactively promoted, but Benefactors mingle freely with Patrons at National Trust events. The Trust knows, anecdotally, that some donors aim for this level of involvement.

Patrons are invited to the same events as Benefactors, but are given special Patron Life Membership. There are already over 100 Patrons and the Trust is planning to have an annual dinner exclusively for regularly-giving Patrons.

In addition, there are some 20 Grand Patrons who have given £100,000 or more, singly or cumulatively. Many of these live overseas and their relationship with the Trust is usually managed on an individual and bespoke basis, depending on their interests and when they are in the UK. The Trust believes that even if donors do not make a gift for a year or two, this programme gives a reason to keep in touch and keep cultivating its Patrons. *"Patrons enjoy being kept up to date with projects they support. They often make further, generous, unsolicited gifts when they can see a need."*

Trust research shows that existing Benefactors and Patrons say they did not join the scheme for the benefits, nor do they expect them. But they do appreciate them and say that it gives them a much deeper insight into the work of the National Trust – and, of course, means that they keep giving, usually larger amounts over time. This is borne out by the figures.

Awareness of recurring commitment is easier for performing arts organisations with box offices. This is explored more in Chapter Six.

However, it is possible for galleries with free entry for the main collection to capture information and develop schemes recognising long-term commitment, as we see in the cases of the National Portrait Gallery and the Hayward Gallery.

Growing individual supporters

CASE STUDIES – Tales of two galleries

National Portrait Gallery

- **Visual arts**
- **London**
- **Total income: £12m**
- **Development income: £3m**

By Janet Reeve

When Pim Baxter joined the National Portrait Gallery in 1997 to head up the communications and development department, the Gallery had 300 individuals on a mailing list. It had done well on capital fundraising and had established several important corporate sponsorships, but very little had been put in place to grow revenue support through membership schemes and regular individual giving.

Recognising the problem of capturing data when general entrance to the Gallery was free, Pim put a system in place to obtain as many names and addresses as possible through the ticket buying process for paid exhibitions. (See data protection guidance in Chapter Eight.) She created a membership scheme which initially cost £24 a year to join. The cost has since risen to between £25 and £45, depending on how people pay and joint membership deals. Though Members receive discounts at the shop and in the restaurant and a copy of the

Photo: Andrew Putler

The Regency in the Weldon Galleries.

Gallery's newsletter, the main draw for Members is free entry to exhibitions and priority booking for special events. The Gallery has secured 2,700 members so far and a further 30,000 have joined "Patron Mail" – an email information service and a great way to grow new Members.

At the other end of the scale, Pim set about growing a body of Life Patrons who donate £20,000 in one year or £5,000 a year over four years, and Patrons who give £1,000 per annum. Working with the finance department, benefit levels were approved by HM Revenue & Customs (HMRC). Life Patrons were asked to split their donation, paying £3,200 without any tax breaks to account for benefits and the remaining £16,800 as a donation. The Gallery now has 15 Life Patrons. The Gallery's £1,000 Patron level works on the same principle of a split between donation and paying for the benefit element (£880/£120). The Patron group has 82 members, and with focused attention from dedicated staff, is growing all the time.

In response to demand for a level between membership and Life Patrons, the Gallery has recently introduced Associates who pay £250 a year, again with a subscription/donation split. This has proved popular, with 42 members so far.

Pim has been well supported by the director of the Gallery as well as a sub-set of the Development Board which acts as a working group on individual giving. She also has three dedicated members of staff working on individual giving, having this year created the new post of major donor development manager, and sees the total revenue growing as a result. Research plays an essential part in identifying new individual prospects for the Gallery at all levels.

The success of the Gallery's Patrons scheme and others like it is based on the donors feeling in the inner circle with access to the director. Gaining entry to exhibitions before the general public plays a key part in attracting donors, as well as invitations to attend talks and behind-the-scenes tours. The National Portrait Gallery has developed reciprocal arrangements with other galleries so it can offer Patrons (at an extra cost to Patrons) opportunities to attend events such as a breakfast view at the Royal Academy or the National Gallery. Pim feels strongly that co-operating with wider colleagues in the arts world increases the benefit to everyone and encourages more giving to the arts in general.

Hayward Gallery

- **Visual arts**
- **London**
- **Income figures unavailable separately from the South Bank Centre**

By Janet Reeve

Karen Whitehouse, director of development at the South Bank Centre, introduced the "Director's Circle" to the Hayward Gallery five years ago. It has around 20 members paying £1,100 each (the first £95 of which accounts for benefits). Its distinctive features include the feeling of being part of a discrete group of like-minded supporters. The number of members is at an optimum level if the group is to retain a feeling of intimacy and connection with the Gallery. The director asks the donors for their support and keeps the link and motivation for the support close to his vision for the Gallery. This is a clever way to ensure a feeling of connection in a large arts centre environment and donor retention rates are high.

The involvement of the director, the CEO and members of the board is crucial to the success of the scheme. The Director's Circle members gain access to exhibitions before the general public and, at an additional cost, can use facilities for entertaining. The head of individual giving oversees the scheme with the membership manager responsible for delivery. The department's researcher has proved very helpful in providing background information about donors and identifying new prospects. The scheme generates around £20,000 a year plus Gift Aid, a tidy sum of reliable unrestricted income. The Director's Circle members are also a useful group of advisors and the sort of network from which other forms of support frequently grow.

Directors' Circles are an example of groups of people coming together, in this case on a permanent basis although membership may change. Another approach is that of a temporary association, such as patronage of an exhibition of the works of a particular artist or a production syndicate for a play or an opera. The Welsh National Opera production syndicate for *Don Carlos* in Autumn 2005 enabled the company to draw in opera-lovers, mainly London-based, who had no previous relationship with WNO. Supported by a London-based member of the development team, volunteers hosted private events in London offering opportunities to learn about plans for the production as they developed and to meet the creative team. The first night in the new Wales Millennium Centre provided the opportunity to showcase the company and the venue, and to create the foundations for possible involvement in other syndicates in the future.

Another area where people may feel undervalued is that of legacies. We do not yet have in the UK a tax-efficient mechanism whereby the donor can make an irrevocable commitment of a gift of capital, to be received by the beneficiary on the donor's death. The donor benefits from income tax relief at the time of making the commitment, and the beneficiary is confident of the gift. A detailed description of this US-style approach is in Additional Information.

This poses a delicate challenge for organisations in the UK about how to treat donors who perceive themselves to have made a major commitment from their estate, but which the beneficiary cannot rely upon under the current UK regime. They can only use their own judgment of the sincerity of the donor, but, by noting their pledges and nurturing a relationship with such people, should be able on a case-by-case basis to ensure appropriate participation.

What not to do! – a true story

Betty H supports a number of arts organisations. She is not significantly wealthy but has no children and expects to leave most of her assets on death to charitable causes. BH was a board member of a regional lottery-funded venue for six years and contributed significantly to the challenging capital campaign for matching funds in nurturing relationships, supporting the development team and giving £10,000 – her largest single donation to any organisation. Legacies are discussed in Chapter Eight.

A few months after the new venue was opened BH retired from the board, pleased at the splendid new building and expecting to be kept in touch with the activities of the organisation. But within two years there were several changes, including a new chief executive and a new head of development. The organisation appeared to lose touch with her. Then a new chairman (HG) was appointed.

BH was delighted to receive a letter from HG telling her of his pleasure in being asked to lead this splendid local asset, and inviting her to a performance, preceded by a reception. However, her pleasure faded when it became clear that HG evidently had no idea of BH's previous involvement. She was being invited to be "introduced" to this wonderful organisation. Furthermore, the invitation was to an show for which she had already bought two tickets. Although her name was on a donor list in the foyer she felt air-brushed out of its history.

In a call to the development office she was told that there had been two versions of the invitation letter; BH had received the wrong one. The right one would have referred to past support. And no, they hadn't checked with the box office. It later transpired that everyone had received the same letter; this was blamed on HG's PA, who, it was said, had not prepared separate sets of letters. HG had just signed the letters without checking against the lists.

BH decided to accept the invitation. She wanted to attend the show anyway and thought that in spite of the mix-up it would be nice to meet HG and perhaps become involved again; after all, she had cared very much about it. She arrived at the reception early, anticipating (as the development office assured her would happen) meeting HG. She expected to receive a rueful apology, be thanked for her past contribution and encouraged to be involved as a supporter again in some way. She planned to respond positively: everyone makes mistakes, and it was the organisation she cared about. But although she saw herself being pointed out to HG by the head of development, and it was a small room, he decided there were more important people to meet. There was no introduction or meeting, nor an apology.

BH decided not to bother with this organisation any more. She may attend performances but there are other places in the region offering the same art form, other opportunities for engagement with artists, other venues where she can share her enthusiasm and knowledge with fellow supporters where her commitment is respected. And she will certainly not be leaving it a legacy!

Many of the "horror stories" heard in the course of writing this book relate to cavalier treatment of donors – some major – all of whom might have given more, or might have left a legacy, and may have recounted their disappointment to wealthy friends.

Tracking and recognising loyalty

With a facility that enables the organisation to track what people come to, and how often, and what they plan to come to, the way is open for a number of imaginative ways to tell people that you know about and appreciate their support, and to invite them to become more involved, including asking for their views – a tactic adopted by the ENO as we see in the case study in the section on wealth screening in Chapter Eight. The essential nature of this course of action is that it is not only about asking for money. (The use of the audience and visitor database for donor development is explored in detail in Chapter Six.) We have already noted that few organisations recognise loyalty effectively; this is one way to develop this approach and mindset.

Examples might be:

We are so pleased that you came to the new production of Othello last week. We see that you have attended all three of our Othello productions over the past ten years. We know this one has been controversial, especially the fact that some of the actors had hidden microphones. As you know we are experimenting with this and as you are a frequent member of our audience we would be interested in your views.
Sent by email from the development office

We're delighted that you are coming to Aida next week and see that this is the fifth production you are attending this season. To celebrate we enclose a voucher you may exchange for drinks for you both at any bar.
Sent by the development office with a card featuring a photograph of the venue

We realise that you have now attended nine performances in the past two years and note that you are coming to your 10th for the production of Pygmalion *on Saturday week. We would love it if you would join me (artistic director, play director) in the XYZ bar in the interval.*

Signed letter

We know that you have now been a gold circle patron for five years. With the tax we have been able to reclaim the company has received nearly £6,500 over that period. We are deeply grateful for your loyalty and generosity. To show our appreciation I enclose a signed photograph of our leading lady and hope you will enjoy the flowers that are being sent separately.

Letter signed by chair

We note not only have you been a Friend of the Sullivan Hall for over 20 years but that you nearly always attend concerts of English music, and have come to all the concerts conducted by Luke Younger in the last 3 years. As you may already have heard on the grapevine, we are planning a major celebration of English music in 2008, to be directed by Luke Younger. We would be delighted if you would like to join myself and others from the Sullivan Hall, and Luke himself, together with other interested supporters, to hear about our plans for the 2008 English Music Festival. The event will be in the Elgar room at 6.00pm on X date, to be followed by a reception which will be attended by some of the musicians involved.

Letter from the chief executive/director

All these should be sent to the person on the database and their partner.

And do you send Christmas cards or email messages to all your loyal supporters? Do you mark their birthdays?

It is essential to strike the right balance between conveying informed appreciation and a sense that Big Brother is watching them. But with carefully chosen words supporters should feel noticed and thanked for their continuing commitment.

This kind of attention requires an excellent database system and mindset in the development office which asks the right questions to elicit the kind of information on which these approaches are based. Apart from staff time the outlay is minimal; it is the database management and staff input which is all-important.

What about recognition?

In addition to appreciation, some want some form of recognition of the significance of their contributions. This is not about names on walls but about being taken seriously.

"It's not about recognition, but if people treat donors so carelessly do they really need the money? A three-line hand-written letter would have been better. I even wrote to [the director] offering constructive help. I got a reply from someone else – not encouraging."

Recognition by whom?

It could be argued that there is a difference between recognition by posterity, in terms of leaving an impact on society, and current recognition with the family name on a building or plaque, for example. For some, the concern was approval of their family, while for others the audience for their philanthropy was their peer group: members of their community, other major donors, or others in the same profession or business (important to some who had made money). Relatively few were concerned by the posthumous approval of later generations outside the family.

The question of how public any recognition needs to be is a very personal and individual matter. In some cases, donors interviewed had taken active steps to avoid publicity or recognition for some or all of their donations. Many had sought anonymity in certain cases, and a few channelled their giving through a trust whose name could not be associated with the family name. Others saw quiet giving as a private family matter or as part of their values.

For others, a good report of the work of the organisation in the media provided the kind of recognition they required.

However, in many cases the situation is more complex than a simple denial of interest in recognition. Several people are already nationally known, either as business or City leaders and/or as donors, and many are known locally. A few have an international reputation. Many of these pointed out that they "don't need it". As one well-known donor to the cultural sector said: *"the curse of the name – they keep coming back"*. Others pointed out that the leading givers would be identified in some way anyway.

Those with experience of supporting both social welfare and cultural or educational organisations pointed out that venues visited by the general public provide opportunities for the recognition of a range of gifts, as do guidebooks, exhibition catalogues and programmes for performing arts events. Among those who see the plaques and list of donors are peers and fellow donors. Such recognition is reinforced and recurring. Similarly, fundraisers will try to persuade donors to allow their name to be publicised, as an endorsement and to encourage others.

A comparable or much bigger gift to a social welfare institution is quite different. Even with a capital project such as equipment or a specialist unit at a hospital, those who use the scanner, for example, are unrelated to the donor community, and the motivation of the donor (for example, family experience of cancer) is quite different. With organisations such as children's charities, public recognition may be thought inappropriate by both donor and beneficiary.

Recognition for what – how much was the gift?

A related and important point concerns the level of gift for which donors are recognised. Some organisations promote Gift Aid to donors, particularly those in the higher tax rate bracket, with examples demonstrating that the net cost to them of a donation worth £10,000 to the recipient will "only" cost them £6,000. At the level of major donations the matter is usually resolved, but when the time comes not all who give, say, £500 receive "credit" for the gross amount of £640, which is what the beneficiary receives when the tax is reclaimed.

On the other hand, some organisations are now distinguishing the amount requested depending on the mechanism used by the donor, so that the gross amount received is broadly similar; gifts from a donor using a charitable trust, for example, may be sought at £2,500 for a certain tier of support whereas a donor using Gift Aid may be asked for £2,000 if the recipient can reclaim £560.

Does it influence the decision?

A number said that while public recognition would not influence a giving decision, it was a bonus – rather like a courtesy present wrapping service for an expensive gift. For some, it is evidence for posterity (within and sometimes beyond the family) which acts as a motivator, a factor touched on in Chapter Three.

"It's not a deciding factor, having one's name on a building, but it would be nice to leave something more permanent."

"I like the odd plaque. It's very nice – especially for the children. I want to be independent so I don't go for honours. The children will see their father's name on things and feel proud. They will give when they are older."

People also did not want to be left out of the lists of donors. This was not so much for recognition by the general public as a desire that their peers should not think that they (alone) had not contributed. They didn't necessarily like this characteristic in themselves, but saw it as having positive aspects: providing an example to others.

"The ABC Room at X art gallery encourages others and clearly denotes the room. It is setting an example. Of course, people see the name on the board and it produces other applications but there is a feeling of warmth."

It was noted that invariably nowadays it is the organisations seeking funds which incorporate "naming opportunities" and other benefits and options for recognition into their proposals requesting support. They are an integral element of the shopping list. Some people appeared almost to resent the implicit assumption that these factors, rather than a passion for the cause, would be decisive. Others suggested that while they were not themselves interested, public acknowledgement might be attractive to some people.

The Jerwood Foundation has generously supported many organisations. Although not strictly the direct testimony of an individual donor, its perspective is relevant.

Giving and naming

During the last 10 years or more the arts world in particular has benefited from substantial capital grants. And although these have come mainly from the Lottery, some major foundations and trusts have also been involved in making such grants. It is also the case that potential beneficiaries of grants understand well, or pay heed to, the difference between a request for capital and an expectation of revenue support.

CASE STUDY

The Jerwood Foundation

By Alan Grieve CBE, chairman

In the case of the Jerwood Foundation, there is clear water between the Jerwood Foundation which is mainly, but not exclusively, concerned with capital grants and the Jerwood Charitable Foundation which develops and undertakes major revenue grants in the performing and visual arts. These go under the banner of the Jerwood Visual Arts following the Jerwood mission to support young people and their careers in the arts.

At the time the Lottery was developing its guidelines through the Arts Council, the recipient was usually obliged to find at least 25% of the capital from other sources. For some projects this caused problems; with fundraising taking two years or more the original costings would almost certainly have escalated by the time the complete partnership funding was in place. There was then a new burden to refinance the "inflationary" element. To meet these pressures the Jerwood Foundation decided to support capital schemes within the arts which required a capital grant to "unlock" the Arts Council Lottery Funding.

"Looking back over the last 10 years or more, I can say that each project has its own individual factors, problems, aspirations and hoped-for outcome," says chairman Alan Grieve. *"There is no standard approach. My own view is that if there are too many names it can dilute the identity of the building and they become no more than signage.*

"All donors should review every aspect of an application before deciding on whether the naming of the whole or part of the building should be considered. For me, naming would certainly never be a major consideration in whether to make a capital grant. Just as with a commercial venue, until a project has been studied, understood and assessed it would be entirely premature to think of the advantages or disadvantages of suggesting a naming of the whole or part of a project.

"In the case of the Jerwood Foundation, it has more often than not been the case that I have wanted to see the name Jerwood as part of the capital scheme if it is a reasonable, proportionate and rational request. This has certainly been true where we have had a previous relationship with the recipient as was the case, for example, with the Royal Court, Glyndebourne and Wordsworth; we were already supporting the activities of the applicant and wished to enhance and continue the relationship by assisting in a capital project which would carry our name. I believe that in the case of Jerwood we have demonstrated high standards, achievements and excellence and we would be guarded about adding our name to any project where we felt these might not be reflected now or in the future. There are many examples, such as the Jerwood Centre within the Wordsworth Trust and the Jerwood Hall within the LSO UBS Centre at St Luke's, where we are proud to have our name carried within the building and believe that we have enhanced their offering.

"Some trusts or foundations might want to consider naming as a primary requirement, for example, in memory of someone, and this approach has its place. However, I would want, on behalf of the Jerwood Foundation, to look at the purpose of the capital grant. Naming would be discussed in the context of the negotiations of the conditions of the full grant framework. I believe that this individual approach works to the benefit of donor and recipient.

"There can be no set rules as to when it might be appropriate or inappropriate to consider a naming and there is certainly no mathematical formula as

to whether the donor has any right to suggest a naming based upon the percentage of the grant to the total cost.

"We have also been asked whether, as a grantor, the Jerwood Foundation would have any objection to being set alongside other donors who may wish to have their name carried within the project. In general terms, there can be no absolute rule but it seems to me confusion can be caused if there is a proliferation of names. In a major project, there is usually no problem with a major donor being the named principal benefactor with other donors equally acknowledged in some other way. The Jerwood Hall which is the prime space within the UBS & LSO Music Education Centre at St Luke's is an example of this. I know that this gave no problem to UBS and it certainly gave no problem to Jerwood.

"However, the benefactor should have the right to veto the positioning of their name alongside current or proposed donors whose objectives or values may conflict with those of the main benefactor.

"I have no doubt that if a major donor agrees to make an early decision on a grant to support a major capital project then it influences others, especially if the donor has a reputation for knowledge, care and understanding within a particular field. If the Jerwood Foundation decides to support a capital project with a substantial grant within the arts field, then it might sway the judgment of other potential donors whether or not there is a naming opportunity."

In this context it is interesting to look at The Wordsworth Trust, which in May 2000 received £500,000 for the Collections Centre from the Jerwood Foundation. At that time the original project cost was estimated at £2 million. This was followed by grants from the Heritage Lottery Fund (£2.25 million, of which £1.575 million was later transferred into endowment), the North West Development Agency (£1.575 million) and European Regional Development Fund (£0.4 million). Michael McGregor, the development director, reports that the Jerwood grant was the catalyst for all subsequent gifts. There is a case study about the Trust in Chapter Eight.

It should be noted, however, that there can be a downside, particularly where the donor is perceived as extremely wealthy.

Nichola Johnson, director of The Sainsbury Centre for Visual Arts, University of East Anglia, says that while it is tremendous to have had the support of a major family trust, there is a perception that there is no further requirement for funds from other sources. The naming of the Centre can be a barrier to other potential donors attaching their name to projects and activities. She points out that over time this perception diminishes and cites as examples the Wallace Collection or the Getty Museum.

In conclusion, the interest in recognition is entirely a matter of personal style, character and preference. Even for those who wish others to be aware of their major gifts, the audience for their philanthropy is usually confined to their family, peers and community, rather than the general public. However, people do want to feel appreciated and acknowledged, and if the recipient makes a habit of recognising major donors in some way, and offers such recognition as part of the asking process, then most do not want to be left out. Recognition is a means to an end – a validation of the donor's own actions which sustains their self-esteem and gains approval by those whose opinion they value. It is noteworthy that so many who have been great achievers in business want their children to be proud of their contribution to the public good, and their reputational legacy to be based on their philanthropy. Perhaps, as one person suggested, they see themselves as the new Medici – for more details on the Medici see Additional Information.

Consultation and influence

As a corollary to recognition there is a fear among some recipients that donors will want to "have a say" in how their donations are allocated. However, in every case where this was mentioned the focus of the donation was outside the arts or heritage sector. And in none of the cases discussed was expenditure donor-driven, beyond responding to the core mission or project or "shopping list" provided by the beneficiary. What was important was the feeling of involvement or being asked for advice.

Being an investor

Many compared their position in relation to a charity with that of being an investor in a business. Those making this point included experienced donors from a range of sources of wealth as well as new donors with new money. It is very important to recognise and understand the rise of the donor-investor, and to remember that many of the people arts and heritage organisations are trying to reach have experience in other sectors.

"With ARK [Absolute Return for Kids, the charity established by the hedge fund industry] there is complete involvement in how the money is spent – choosing the recipient, evaluating needs, measuring impact and outcome, being cost-effective. Guys in the City are concerned about administration costs. They want to feel that they can meet the director but in fact they may not have time. Board seats shouldn't be bought but there must be an understanding that a donation is an investment and that one wants to be involved in governance. There is also the importance of the

symbolism of giving being equivalent to being a major shareholder. Major donors should want to be involved and charities should want them to be involved. If you are a major shareholder in a start-up you have a lot to say. Most of these things are about sensible governance – fiscal probity, periodic reporting, openness in how you treat employees and a known budget and investment policy."

Although ARK is a particular case, this contributor who was involved in the establishment of ARK echoes the thoughts of donors from a range of backgrounds. First, we see that the donation is viewed as an investment and the donor as a partner in the enterprise – something which the recipient should see as a positive factor. There are concerns about administrative costs, a desire to meet those who deliver the mission, as well as for other involvement, and at the same time a recognition that there may be a lack of time. It also reinforces the evidence that the areas in which donors want some kind of involvement are to do with governance and reporting, not the methodology for the delivery of the core mission.

Messages that attract donor-investors

There are very clear indications about how to attract and retain a following of donor-investors. What is important is that the potential return on their investment is expressed in a way which is linked to what the individual donor-investor cares about. This is about making the contact as personal as possible. It means getting to know people over a period, learning about their values and concerns, sharing your vision and gradually showing how your programmes and projects resonate with their own passions. It is important to remember that you are trying to demonstrate a return on investment that will ensure repeated and increased investment. So the messages and methods must be designed to produce the highest level of engagement from your donor-investors, and a relationship with them that will be loyal and lasting. What does this mean for the way relationships are managed?

Practical aspects of managing relationships are discussed in more detail in Chapter Seven; here we note that crucially, it means taking it seriously. It is about understanding that looking after donors – often called "stewardship" – is not an optional extra. Every opportunity, including the use of email and the website, should be taken to remind people that they are involved with an excellent organisation which reflects their own values, passions and expectations.

Technology offers the opportunity to be spontaneous, opportunistic and focused. Organisations can send reviews of shows or performances drawing attention to an artist individuals particularly like; you can report on a key development in a project people have supported; you can tell them about some exciting plan soon to be announced, so that they feel they are "on the inside".

Indeed, no opportunity should be missed to connect donor-investors with the mission, and to tell stories in all the materials. We have already mentioned annual reviews, which as well as providing an opportunity for financial feedback – essential for donor-investors – can demonstrate, through photographs, charts, case studies and explanations, the impact and effectiveness of what you do.

This advice is not only for large and mainstream organisations. Take the example of National Life Stories (NLS), established in 1987 to "record first hand experiences of as wide a cross-section of present-day society as possible". The key focus is oral history fieldwork. Donation income was just over £160,000 in 2005. Core funding comes from the British Library but recognising that other support is needed, NLS has modernised its name and redesigned its literature and letterhead with the intention of "attracting more notice and support". As part of this strategy it has invested in a professional comprehensive full colour annual report and accounts – not a dry series of financial statements (although these are there) but a compelling account of the work of the NLS, descriptions of partnership and alliances, reflective articles, reports of projects past and present and, of course, explanations of how to support the NLS and a list of those who have already done so, in the year reported on and previously. It is a highly successful cross between a formal annual report, a brochure and a magazine with a long shelf-life.

Key points

- Understand the mindset of the donor – transaction or philanthropy.

- Ensure impeccable communications, including appropriate appreciation, recognition, information and engagement.

- Those who give through a personal charitable trust should be treated as any other individual donor.

- Recognise loyalty.

- Ensure there are relationships at a number of levels, including with other donors.

- Lose no opportunity to remind donors of the mission and how it is being achieved.

Of course, a key asset of the culture sector is that the mission is there for all to see and share – on the walls, on the stage, on the screen, on the page, in the garden. There is no shortage of opportunities to engage with donors and prospects. But how to draw people in? We have seen from the Hallé story that donors may be recruited who are introduced as clients of a sponsor. Is that usual? In the next chapter we explore how people decide to give.

Chapter Five

Encouraging people to give

n the previous chapter we explored the expectations of the wealthier or higher-level donor in their relationship with the cultural organisations they support, particularly if their motivations are primarily philanthropic rather than transactional. In this chapter we look at how people decide to give.

As we have seen, first-class relationship management and appropriate recognition by the recipient organisations together underpin and reinforce the philanthropic inclination. They transform what might start as a one-off impulsive response to a request into an integral and important part of people's discretionary expenditure. More than that, they validate the choices people have made and ensure that charitable commitments continue because the donor gets such pleasure from the experience. They address the five key motivating triggers identified in Chapter Three and are the most important factors in sustaining a culture of giving.

The research on which *Why Rich People Give* was focused on wealthy individuals engaged (usually) at a very personal level with an organisation. It does not necessarily correspond to the experience or cover all the motivations of people solicited and engaged through direct marketing, whether mail, phone or internet. But many of those who commit to a £10 per month direct debit or make a one-off gift of £30 are equally motivated by civic pride, putting something back into an organisation that has given them great pleasure and a desire for the offered benefits. And we know that these are the overwhelming majority of donors to arts and heritage organisations (by number although not by value).

With audience fundraising (explored in Chapter Six), giving is clearly linked to frequency of attendance. This is an aspect of a relationship, but it is a marketing rather than a personal one. Any sense of engagement or involvement is usually initially mediated by a mass-marketing medium, most commonly mail. Although in principle the direct marketer is trying to replicate the personal quality of a face-to-face conversation, in practice it is qualitatively different. (However, in many case studies, the telephone is increasingly important in encouraging repeat donations, committed giving and increasing the level of support; it is suggested that one reason for the success of this approach is that it does indeed provide the opportunity for a personal exchange.)

It should be recognised that there are many regular donors at a modest level who have no wish to be "involved" with the organisation. They are happy to give a certain amount but have no desire to meet the artistic director, attend drinks events or "join" anything. (Opera North commissioned research which clearly showed that for some people who, on the face of it, looked just like members of its Friends scheme, the idea of joining was a strong disincentive to donation through the Friends.) As we have seen, another factor is that people may feel they support two opera companies or art galleries or local attractions already; they wish others well, and donate at a small level to provide some encouragement, but are never going to become involved in a major way because of the desire for focus, and limited time for in-depth relationships. In other words, one size does not fit all.

But how do people become involved in the first place? This chapter is about how donors decide to give, with a particular focus on larger gifts. Of course, what constitutes a "larger gift" depends not only on the absolute amount but on its position in the philanthropic portfolio of the donor and on what is thought to be appropriate for the beneficiary. One donor giving £1,000 a year may regard it as a very significant donation if that represents, say, 50% of their charitable giving and their income is £75,000 a year. This might also be the largest sum received by some smaller niche or local cultural organisations.

This is not the same issue as that faced by some regional organisations who find it hard to persuade prospects of an appropriate level of gift. Several such organisations have reported that a donor might give, say, £25,000 or £50,000, or even a six- or seven-figure sum to a national institution, probably based in London, but just £5,000 to an entity based in the regions, even if it has a national remit, world-class reputation and a vision and mission that resonates with the donor's passions. In these cases a major gift from a board member, to set the "level" of what might be expected from major donors, can have a significant influence.

And there are the cases of wealthier people who have the capacity to give and an interest in the art form, but for one reason or another have never been asked in a way which unlocks significant support.

Response to unsolicited requests

"There needs to be a personal approach or the cause must be very compelling."

Most well-off people receive a large number of unsolicited requests every year. Well-established personal trusts or well-known philanthropists can expect up to 1,000 letters a year – indeed, one person said they received 10 requests a day. Some people review every request they receive. More commonly, unsolicited applications are not considered. For those with established foundations and an administrative infrastructure, the requests may be filtered by a lawyer or administrator, on the basis of known criteria.

Most people who give regularly have a clearly defined set of priorities. However, many are not regular or strategic givers, and may be in the process of developing their approach to philanthropy. But in assessing requests for significant support two criteria are central – who asks and the nature of the cause.

The importance of a personal and appropriate approach

In this section we focus on unsolicited and unplanned requests from organisations not previously supported, or from those with which there may have been limited contact.

Donors interviewed for *Why Rich People Give* and subsequently report huge irritation at unsolicited (and other) mailings which are incorrectly spelt or addressed, have been clearly produced by a mail-merge programme, cannot cope with titles and honours ("Dear Sir Jones", "Dear Dame CBE") or, even worse, open with "dear friend", or "dear [first name]" from a stranger or junior staff member. Having a donor or supporter number quoted by a charity they had supported in the past was seen by some to belie the individuality of the relationship. People expect a personalised approach, with some understanding as to why the project or cause or organisation may be of interest. A hand-written covering letter is desirable but at the very least a hand-written note was expected to complement and reinforce a standard mailing.

Who should make the approach

"A major factor is where people I know are asking for money. It's about respect, and their involvement endorses the cause and the relationship."

Virtually everyone will at least review and respond to a request or invitation that comes from a person or organisation they know and respect. The endorsement of someone known is important because some reliance can be placed on the diligence of the asker. In the research, this was particularly the case where the request was from a respected professional or business colleague, or someone who had a track record as a leader in the world of the particular charity. If the asker has also given money, so much the better; many people alluded to this.

"I get 10 requests a day. The question of who asks counts more than anything else. Is the person who asks a giver? The asker must be a lay/volunteer leader, not a professional. Is it someone who has given to charities I want to support?"

These comments are entirely consistent with the views of askers, whose experience is discussed later in this chapter. The additional factors that emerge here include the implication of potential reciprocity and the importance of the asker being a "lay" person – that is, not a paid member of staff, and by implication a peer of the prospect. Peer-to-peer fundraising is an essential component for really major gifts.

This does not mean that there is no role for the development office; on the contrary, such asking (for major gifts) will usually follow detailed research (see Chapter Eight for an article about research) and a period of engagement and cultivation over many months or even years, all carefully planned by the development office.

A few people claim not to be influenced even if it is a friend or known contact who asks. For them the most important factor is the cause, the extent to which it fits pre-existing criteria and the quality of the specific project. But even then, the request is more likely to at least be considered if a known intermediary is involved. A recurring comment was the perception that money is wasted on unsolicited approaches, especially if they appear unnecessarily glossy or expensive.

The nature of the cause

"The main focus of my support is already decided... the area of work, for example, health and so on, is considered, as is the geographic basis of the work and the performance of the recipient in using grants wisely and economically."

Most people who are thoughtful about their philanthropy have already decided their broad areas of interest. This is not surprising as we know the impetus in early giving is to do with being moved to a particular cause or interest. So while people may look at causes outside their area of interest if the proposal comes from a respected contact, most people who have already decided on their priorities ask whether it fits within their criteria and chosen focus.

Many have also determined the main sectors or charities they want to support. Older people are also more likely to have decided their priorities and preferences, as are those who have set up a regular mechanism for giving such as a trust or Charities Aid Foundation (CAF) account. Information about giving mechanisms can be found in *The Guide To Giving* – see Bibliography on page 298 for details.

Having said this, a few admit that sometimes irrational factors influence as well, including whim and mood. Such factors may lead to a more reactive and immediate response to a newspaper report or an unsolicited mailing, but not usually in the culture sector. However, this highlights a most important point; philanthropy combines intellectual understanding, the imagination, the capacity to give and the heart.

Most people will consider a request for support for a cause operating in a sector to which they are committed. They want to know how their money will be used and how it will make a difference. We have seen that making a difference, expressed in varying ways, is a key factor in both motivating a donor and sustaining continued interest. We also know that many "investor-donors" ask about effectiveness and the impact on the community, and may be interested in the application of their own expertise and influence.

"[I ask myself] Is it making a real difference if I give or not? Many organisations have lots of money and are able to raise it from elsewhere; the money I put in must make a real difference. It's not just money: I may be able to help with fundraising and make suggestions of other funders and endorse the project."

Whether or not people have decided on a few chosen causes, or are still in the process of considering how to focus their giving, most people give where they feel they can make a bigger difference and have a recognisable effect. This desire to focus on impact and obtain "value for money" can sometimes militate against larger organisations. Associated with large charities were perceptions of unnecessary bureaucracy and the idea that a donation would be a drop in the ocean. A reluctance to fund core costs, for small as well as large organisations, was mentioned frequently. This was seen as the responsibility of institutional grant-makers or government (where applicable), even by experienced donors who understand the complexities of managing a charity.

If the cause is of interest, the donors may have made significant longer-term commitments to one or more charities operating in the field. An apparently sizeable trust with objectives entirely consistent with those of the charity soliciting support may have very limited uncommitted funds. Indeed, from the perspective of the applicant there may be a paradox: the more involved and engaged the donor, the less likely, in some cases, they are to be able to make substantial commitments to a new recipient, however deserving.

One challenge and opportunity for the culture sector is to present its mission in a way which draws in those who think that they don't like the arts, or are afraid that they won't know what to do. The whole question of the impact of the arts on wider society was explored in Chapter Two. The case study of Trevor and Lyn Shears in Chapter Three highlights their response both to the arts and heritage that they love and how it reaches out into the community. There are various possible starting points. Several case studies highlight the excitement and response felt when people actually see what goes on behind the scenes; prospects may be interested in technical aspects such as paper conservation, the logistics of touring with an orchestra, the process of training a young dancer, the technology behind the showing of rare books and manuscripts on screen. It would be very sad if the combination of first-class prospect research on the one hand and creative flair on the other could not find in most organisations in the culture sector an aspect of the work where interests meet.

Other factors

Potential donors consider a number of other factors once the nature of the cause is seen as relevant to their interests: whether it represents value for money; the competence of the organisation and who is leading the initiative; and the kinds of involvement it will require from them. Information to help them decide is therefore crucial, particularly as they may be considering many such requests. The challenge for culture organisations is to present creativity, innovation, risk and the development of talent in a way that resonates with the donor.

CASE STUDY

Royal Academy of Arts – development of Patrons scheme 1996 to 2004

- **Visual arts**
- **London**
- **Total income: £20m**

By Theresa Lloyd

The Royal Academy of Arts is an independent fine arts institution that promotes interest in the visual arts through a comprehensive and ambitious exhibition programme, education, and the Royal Academy Schools, to ensure that the skills and knowledge of today's most talented artists are passed on to the next generation. The Royal Academy is completely autonomous and receives no public funding. The Friends organisation – the third largest in the world – numbers more than 88,000 members. The Royal Academy is governed by the 80 Royal Academicians, who are all eminent practising painters, print-makers, sculptors and architects. It has been at the heart of the cultural life of the UK since its foundation in 1768.

The challenge

In 1986, when John Nickson arrived at the Royal Academy from English National Opera, two points stood out: there was huge potential for a proactive director of development. Furthermore, there never had been, and would not be, public funding. At that time:

- Few people were recorded as having given more than £1,000.
- The Royal Academy had raised significant capital for development projects but there was no programme in place to ensure regular support.
- Members of the Friends scheme – which was the market-leader – were only asked to give their subscription fee.

The Royal Academy needed to plug the financial gap, and one element in the new portfolio of mechanisms would be to develop a scheme for major new support. It was decided to set up an Exhibition Patrons Group, starting with a pilot scheme to test the response. The results were very positive, and in the first year (1996) 33 people contributed £800,000; gifts ranged from £1,000 to £250,000.

This pilot worked because it was started with the trustees, because a trustee and John Nickson went to see everyone, and because the people concerned knew and cared about the Royal Academy. These donors became the founder members of the Exhibitions Patrons Group.

Development of Exhibition Patrons Scheme

It was decided to structure a scheme with people giving at three levels – £1,000, £2,500 and £5,000. A briefing meeting with senior supporters was arranged, and the volunteer leadership was organised by the chair of the Royal Academy Trust who gave money himself and supported the scheme.

In 1997 the Exhibition Patrons Scheme was formally launched. By 2004 the revenue amounted to more than £1 million a year, drawn from almost 500 members contributing at four levels: £1,250, £2,500, £5,000 and £10,000. In addition, the Royal Academy was encouraging people to give £10,000 and above to be patrons of specific exhibitions. Some of the donations are likely to be made just once, but some are expected to be renewed.

It should be noted that over the same period the Royal Academy Trust Office and the Friends were brought into the development department and the number of Friends increased from 67,000 to 87,000 in 2004. The gross income from Friends is £5 million. In addition, Friends gave £1.3 million to the capital project of £18 million.

During this period (from end 1999), capital donation and pledges amounting to £18 million were received.

The whole focus was an endeavour to change the relationship from one of subscriber to supporter to donor.

How was it done?

The Royal Academy invested in a new team and allocated resources to developing higher-level donors. In due course it recruited an excellent person, who demonstrated charm and leadership and was very methodical. Nevertheless, all this took time and some trustees were impatient.

A development board was therefore established as a sub-committee of the Trust. The development board helped to design and polish the scheme.

Broadly speaking, Patrons receive exclusivity and early access. They have a menu of options, and at £10,000 they enjoy the right to allocate their donation to a preferred project, access to curators, lectures, private views and lenders, the opportunity to be invited to dinner after a formal exhibition opening and other intimate small gatherings.

The opportunity to participate in exclusive private art tours is a major additional benefit. These are now regular events for Gold partners. An example was a visit to Rome, over a long weekend (Thursday to Sunday). The cost is £3,500 to £4,000 a person. The tour is accompanied by the chair or another trustee, an art historian and a senior member of the development team, together with a local expert and experienced guide and a tour manager. The key elements of the tour include private guided visits, meals at exclusive venues, and flawless support arrangements.

As a result, the Royal Academy knows that if people are offered the best they will pay for it. There is a stronger network of donors who know and respect each other and look forward to meeting again, and deeper understanding by the development director and head of individual giving of the interests and concerns of some of the major donors.

Resources and success factors

The Royal Academy believes that it is essential that the staff are highly professional and empathise with the vision and mission of the cultural organisation, and with the passions of the donors. The management of the relationship with donors must be on a bespoke and not a production-line basis. The development team attends a large number of morning and evening events for patrons and servicing costs are high.

Furthermore, the director of development spent most of his time with people able to give £10,000 or more in revenue support. (During this period the team also worked on major capital campaigns and to support the US and Japanese organisations supporting the Royal Academy.)

There are 36 people in the development office. Staff includes the corporate fundraising and the trusts and foundations team as well as the events team which organises the fundraising events, and also services the rest of the Royal Academy and arranges all the non-revenue-earning events such as exhibition openings. It is not straightforward or even possible to allocate fundraising costs against income.

Royal Academy of Arts, Annenberg Courtyard

Other points
Events
In the early years there was some resistance to the idea that those who attend exhibition openings and related events must be givers, and it took three to four years to move to this position. Many cultural organisations

give away too much in benefits, for historical reasons. While opportunities to strengthen links are crucial, there is a point above which organisations should not attempt to give more and more benefits. Support should be seen as moving beyond a transaction to a partnership and mutually beneficial relationship. This is explored at length in Chapter Four.

Development board

John Nickson, as newly-appointed director of development, inherited the Royal Academy Trust Advisory Board. However, although members wanted to be helpful they were not raising money. Under a new chair they made good progress, including:

(a) Persuading the Academy that the Opening Gala of the Summer Exhibition should be the first buying opportunity (not, as hitherto, the buyers' day the next day). This means that high-level donors have an initial opportunity to buy.

(b) Developing the Patrons scheme.

However, they found that although one-to-one relationships with board members were excellent, the meetings were not always productive. Too much time was being spent supporting board meetings. The board stopped meeting as a group and development found other roles for most of the members. (Other organisations, not only in the culture sector, have had similar experiences. However, others have made the development board structure work well. See the item on volunteer leadership in Chapter Eight and various case studies throughout this book.)

What are the lessons? What made it work in this case?

A key factor was the acceptance of advice given by the hugely experienced John Nickson during his early months that requirements were essential: investment in development, reorganisation and the support of trustees.

The essential elements were the right staff and resources, coupled with the involvement of an active and dynamic director of development in getting new money, and trustee support and engagement – as supporters of the judgment and strategy put forward by the development director, as donors and as ambassadors.

Small gifts

The pilot scheme in the Royal Academy case was successful because it started with people who knew the organisation well. But what happens if they have never visited? People may well be persuaded to attend an event or show because they respond to a friend or someone they respect asks. Many of the wealthier among those interviewed will consider this as a "small gift" – usually defined as less than £1,000.

"When people I know ask for help I give £1,000 or less. In 90% of the cases the cause is almost immaterial."

It is clear that being asked by the right person is never a sufficient condition for a significant donation. Nevertheless, being asked by "someone I know" is often the key determinant for small gifts by the wealthy, although there are other factors in play as well.

Unlike most major donations, smaller gifts – apart from membership contributions, especially in the arts and heritage fields, as discussed in the previous chapter – are often made to causes outside the donor's main field of interest. For many of the wealthier a donation at the level of £1,000 or below was "a token gift" and there was a mix of pressures and influences on a decision to give. These are briefly considered below.

Sponsorship

"I haven't given anything below that threshold [£1,000], unless you count charity tickets or marathon sponsorship."

Much small gift support is for events and sponsorship, although many did not really count supporting fundraising events as serious giving. A significant minority cited sponsorship of activities such as marathons as examples of small donations. The cause is often immaterial and in many cases the respondent could not remember what it was.

Social giving

Social giving – that is giving when relatives, friends, colleagues or perhaps another donor asks – is quite different from an engaged commitment. Generally sums are small (to the donor), causes are diverse and it was sometimes felt to be part of what is expected within the donor "network".

"If a friend asks I give. I don't enjoy the social side but I recognise that it's part of the role of mixing with the great and the good. Part of the role is to give. A lot of it is

pocket money giving – £500 here, £1,000 there. This probably amounts to £25,000 a year. My primary giving areas are education and health."

Small gifts can be appropriate

"I do when a friend asks or because sometimes that's what's asked for. For a small organisation that size of gift may be very important."

Many small donations are made to support specific activities of individuals or organisations. Mainly, this is where a small donation is perceived to be all that is necessary or appropriate for the recipient. This includes support of students, local causes and unplanned giving, such as disaster appeals.

Many pointed out that for a small or new organisation, a gift at or below £1,000 could be very encouraging, and would encourage others. More than one person gave donations at this level to projects in their place of birth or upbringing. Some people were fairly strategic about the process for such giving. Just as people had set aside money for requests from friends, some allocated money for small amounts for local causes.

"I give... 10 to 20 small grants to self-help regional or local groups with low overheads, volunteer-run. These will be one-offs from between £100-£500. It's less than 5% of my total giving and I don't monitor the effectiveness."

Committed resources

In more specific circumstances, donors said they might make such a small gift if they had already allocated their charitable giving for the year, but felt the cause was worth supporting.

"I make such gifts to a good cause I know nothing about, or to a tiny charity, or when I am short of money but I want to give something. I sometimes give money to individuals through another trust: for example, a student at an art college."

Some who wish to support causes or people outside the focus of their trusts may give through a separate mechanism.

"If a friend is involved and it doesn't fit the criteria I might give personally and not through the foundation."

Like this contributor, others set aside specific budgets for supporting friends and other unplanned giving, and might, for example, use a CAF account for such purposes.

"I have a pot for small gifts. It always gives income. At the start the limit was £500 and occasionally £1,000. One gets appeals one can't resist: for example the [local] music festival."

Large charities

Whereas many donors focus small gifts on individuals or small charities, they and others might also give small amounts to major organisations. This may be because they feel that it will be easier for these to raise money elsewhere – or because the impact of a major gift has not been effectively explained.

Key points

● Everyone makes what they regard as small donations. When they do so it is usually in response to requests from people they know. Nearly all the sponsorships and tickets for events were in response to requests from friends. Many recognise the element of reciprocity here.

● A few set aside a pot for gifts to causes or projects where a gift below £1,000 will be appropriate – local causes, support of gap years and travel scholarships, hardship cases and disaster appeals.

● In many cases of requests made by friends for small amounts, the cause is almost immaterial. But it can certainly not be assumed that because a friend has asked, what starts as a small one-off gift will become a bigger gift.

● The nature of feedback and involvement expected from "small" donations is quite different, and minimal, compared with that for giving to causes where there is a real commitment. With very few exceptions, this type of giving does not lead to a major engagement, unless the passion or interests of the donor has been aroused.

● The most important lesson for the development team is that it is essential to understand the motivation of the donor.

● If someone has attended an event or performance because a friend has invited them, they may come, enjoy the show and, at best, make a small donation. But unless they are really enthused with the art form, whatever their capacity to give and even philanthropic values, they will never become a major donor.

This is also true for those who become members at a certain level, in order to obtain benefits such as priority booking, as we explored in the previous chapter.

Major gifts

"I work it out with each one. I think I am a fair person and can see both sides. I wouldn't give money if I thought they couldn't manage the project. It's very important to feel appreciated. I expect to be listened to."

"I don't believe in strings being attached, but as the sums increase I would want more of a say."

Requests for major gifts are be considered very differently, and in nearly every case the prospect will know the organisation and its leadership well, even if this is to be the first sizeable donation. There will have been an extended courtship period.

"I look at every project. There is a contract with every charity based on experience. It covers standards, recognition, the timing of payments, what the gift will cover and feedback. One gets embroiled in affairs. The more embroiled, the more one gives."

This comment was made by a very experienced major donor to arts and heritage organisations around the country.

For major gifts there may be a desire for influence, not on the core programme but on factors affecting the likely success of the project. Those with family businesses consider influence on project design or management as protecting the family name; if the family business is associated with best practice, then the organisations they endow or support should be too. They are willing to be flexible about arrangements but also want them clarified in advance.

In more than one case a large gift led to the donor not so much wanting a say but asking fairly fundamental questions. The following example was someone who supported and raised money for a performing arts organisation outside London. This was their first major gift.

"I don't expect to have a say – except perhaps where I have made a huge donation like to [ABC theatre]. When I had raised the money I asked how it had got into that state in the first place and looked at the weak board."

Experienced donors were sensitive to the accusation that they expected to influence activities outside their expertise. But where they had such expertise they believed they had a right to be heard. Having been targeted and motivated to make a difference, they see – as in their business lives – that the difference may be made not only with money, but with the application of the skills which are the source of the wealth. This is very important. Some organisations are seen to solicit money but appear to reject expertise. This is viewed as a lack of the respect which is crucial to a successful partnership.

However, while the responsibility and experience of the involvement brings pleasure from the relationship with those running the organisation – a factor we have seen as important in motivating recurring giving – some donors also noted that it was important for themselves and other donors not to patronise the recipients or to influence the design of the core activities. It must be recognised that the leaders and senior staff of the organisations they support bring their own expertise and commitment.

What this tells us is that major donors, and those with the potential to become major donors or leave a significant bequest, believe they merit an individual programme of engagement. It is important for recipients and donors to take time getting to know each other. For major gifts there should be agreement in advance on how the relationship is to work.

Sharing the giving decision

An additional element in the decision-making process is the fact that most donors involve their partner and in some cases other members of the family in their philanthropic activity. It is essential to involve partners throughout the cultivation process. And it is essential that those who give through a family charitable trust should be treated as individuals and not dealt with by a "trust fundraiser" whose role is to deal with institutional foundations. The administrative mechanism may be a trust but that has nothing to do with the personal decision-making process. Too many organisations behave as though they have no understanding of the benefits of establishing a family trust and do not treat the prospect or donor as an individual.

Asking others for money

There is no doubt that most of those who have experience of asking others for donations find limited enjoyment in it. Essentially, the reasons are a combination of not knowing where to start, not believing themselves to be socially adept or a good networker, embarrassment, not feeling properly briefed about the prospect and unsatisfactory past experience. The basis of the disappointment in past encounters lay either with the response of the prospects or with the inadequate level of support provided by the organisation seeking funds.

In many cases, lack of preparation and knowledge of the prospect, particularly of their financial circumstances, led to embarrassment and fear of "getting it wrong". Many recognised that if they did ask, people might give for the "wrong" reasons – not for the cause but because of the asker. This gives little satisfaction to the asker, and not much to the donor. This was particularly the case with events and small gifts. Some refuse to engage in this kind of approach and say they would *"rather write a cheque myself"*.

A few, including experienced askers, reported examples of lack of adequate professional support from the fundraising staff, lack of research and appropriate targeting, lack of involvement from senior management and lack of flexibility about visiting projects.

However, where people do care passionately for a particular organisation or cause, they may overcome their reluctance. This is much more likely to happen where people have a formal relationship, such as board or committee membership.

The analysis of what makes donor asking effective was similar across the range of experiences and attitudes to asking for money. Several factors were seen as contributing to a successful outcome to requests.

Being a donor as well

"Peer pressure is essential. I have given, why don't you? The fact that we have given to our maximum is impressive and we can endorse the work of [major charity]. Donor get donor is the best mechanism for charities to use."

Styles of asking

Various suggestions were made as to how to "get the message across" and "capture the imagination". For many with experience it was essential to find a way to involve people. One approach is to show them the actual work on the ground, or on the stage or on the walls; the involvement of young people in creating the art or demonstrating the craft can be particularly compelling. The challenge is that many prospects do not have time, at least in the working day. For those in the culture sector this may not be a constraint.

Targeting and timing

"One should never just ask one's friends; one should start with a project and be transparent. Good fundraising is about matching people, timing and knowing the project. It's a question of finding the right people, they are there."

Building on that, several with knowledge of high earners such as those in the high-tech sector or hedge fund industry suggested that it was a matter of stage in life. Many were not ready for major philanthropy, and particularly not the support of

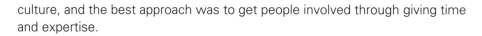
culture, and the best approach was to get people involved through giving time
and expertise.

Awakening an interest

Everyone recognised that major gifts come from those who are fired by the project.
The challenge is to awaken the interest. They also made the point that this kind of
fundraising is hard work and very demanding. In the Jewish community in particular
this was seen as a burden which should be shared. This is more akin to the
American approach.

Some causes have prospered because of the application of marketing and PR skills
learned in commerce and entertainment, often given as a gift in kind. These were
implemented in projects and causes which had harnessed celebrity involvement.

*"I use the same skills to get people to care about [cause] as for selling a movie or
celebrity."*

Offering public recognition

Although, as we have seen, there are virtually no cases in which recognition is
reported as a primary motivator, more than one asker suggested that, together with
the nature of the cause, recognition is an important trigger. It is as though people are
saying *"I am not influenced by this, but others may be"*.

Strategic support from the recipient organisation

A key success factor mentioned by several interviewees was the quality and nature
of support received from the charity. This was about staff competence, preparatory
research and prospect information, and information about the charity itself.

Time after time three related points were made in various ways by those with
experience in asking, and in being asked:

● The need to invest in high calibre development professionals.

● The need for peer-to-peer asking.

● The need to ask for large sums of money.

Training can help trustees, senior staff and donors who are willing to be askers to be
more effective in asking their peers. This is discussed in Chapter Eight.

Key points

- The management of the relationship with the donor is the most important element in creating and sustaining a commitment to philanthropy. An incompetent or insensitive approach to communications can have a seriously adverse impact on future giving. Someone interested in a particular art form, but who has had a disappointing experience with a specific recipient, could nearly always find an alternative beneficiary – or could decide to give less, or not at all.

- At major donor levels the links should be with director, artistic leaders and senior management, not only the fundraising staff. High-level givers expect a personal programme of information, feedback and engagement which demonstrates respect and desire for a genuine partnership in delivering the mission. They do not expect to influence the programme of the charity, but want to be able to share their expertise in, for example, governance, financial management, IT or property maintenance. Many, particularly younger donors, see their position as analogous to that of investors in a business.

- The extent to which donors desire public recognition, as opposed to private expressions of appreciation, very much depends on personal preference. However, where recognition is offered by the recipient charity, few wish to be left out. But the recognition is like "gift-wrapping", a confirmation for those whose good opinion they value – themselves, their family, their peers and, very occasionally, the general public – that they are making a difference.

- The significance of the source and method of approach of the request varies – for some it is all-important, and few claim not to be influenced in any way by the person soliciting support or the design and focus of the proposal. Those who claimed not to be influenced had all established charitable trusts, and developed a clear framework for their philanthropy. For some the filter of the office provides a protection from the importuning of personal contacts.

- In the cultural sector it is less likely than for causes related to social welfare that prospects will receive unsolicited appeals for organisations with which they have no connection whatsoever: where they have never bought a ticket or attended an exhibition and know no-one connected with the institution.

- However, too often people, particularly, it has to be said, volunteer leaders, behave as though they forget that people give significantly because of a passion for the cause. They seem to assume that one invitation to an exhibition or a show, coupled with drinks and something to eat, will be sufficient to awaken that passionate interest. But as any experienced development professional will tell you, nurturing such engagement takes months and years of cultivation – and may never be awakened.

● People may be introduced to an arts or heritage organisation through a friend, but they decide to give because they care about the mission of the organisation, want to see it flourish and, often, want the buzz and rewards of sharing their enthusiasm with like-minded supporters and those who deliver the mission. Effective asking shows them how their support can achieve all those goals.

In the next chapter we explore the mass-market approach to effective asking.

Chapter Six

Chapter Six

Fundraising from audiences and visitors

By David Dixon

This chapter discusses large-scale donor programmes using direct marketing techniques such as mail and telephone. Some may question the necessity for an audience fundraising programme involving a large number of relatively small gifts when they could instead focus on soliciting support from a relatively few wealthy individuals, trusts or businesses. The question is easily answered:

- Depending on the organisation, the income from an audience/visitor fundraising programme could be higher than from any other single source of income.

- With statutory funding on a downward course in real terms and sponsorship apparently stagnant, organisations need to investigate all possible sources of funds.

- Once established, the Return on Investment (ROI) on an audience/visitor fundraising programme can be higher than for other sources – it depends on your organisation and the duration of the programme. It is important to do the sums to make a proper comparison but it is not always the case that larger donations bring better cost-income ratios.

- Donors giving through a regular mechanism such as direct debit give for many years – the average across all charities is around nine years and there is evidence that in the arts it is higher.

- This means that the ROI, when measured over the "lifetime" of the donor, can be very high, even when compared with quite large single donations.

- Because an audience/visitor fundraising programme involves hundreds, or perhaps thousands, of individuals, it can be relied on to generate income for several years ahead (it isn't known which individuals will drop out, but assumptions can safely be made about how many will stay on average).

This is wonderful news to boards, directors and programmers who can pencil in at least part of their budget for several years hence, as long as they maintain the investment in the looking after, or "stewardship" of these donors.

● By the same token, because future income from regular donors is to some extent guaranteed, investment can be justified in relationship-development tools such as events and newsletters, increasing the likelihood of upgrades and additional gifts.

● Research in the US and the UK has demonstrated clearly that a majority of all major donors first give a small amount to get to know the organisation. An audience/visitor fundraising programme should feed into a major gift programme as well as helping to uncover potential business supporters and trustees of trust funds.

● It can also provide a springboard for legacy promotion (see Chapter Eight for a section on legacy promotion).

● Fundraising from audiences and visitors strengthens relationships and increases overall loyalty to the organisation, benefiting long-term ticket sales and visits.

Arts and heritage organisations are perfect for large-scale individual donor fundraising

I began my fundraising career working for Oxfam where I learned all the tools of the trade, including direct marketing, major donors and corporate sponsorship. In fact, Oxfam was one of the pioneers of direct mail (and later telephone) fundraising in the UK and over the years it has built up a database of hundreds of thousands of donors. Other household-name charities have followed suit so that today, tens of millions of us in the UK donate to charity as a result of mail or telephone solicitation.

Yet most arts and heritage organisations have an enormous advantage over Oxfam and almost all other charities – donors to arts organisations walk through their doors!

Most charity fundraisers in the UK have to spend vast amounts of money to acquire new donors. Given that the most expensive part of a donor programme is getting the first contact with the prospective donor, in this sense arts and heritage organisations have it made!

There are other ways, too, in which cultural organisations have a headstart over most other charities:

- Cultural attenders are, on average, middle-class and middle-aged. Whilst this may bring other problems, it is perfect for fundraising.

- Many of these attenders are passionate about "their" museum, opera house, theatre etc and all are at least mildly interested (otherwise, why did they come?).

- Attenders at performing arts venues, in particular, gladly give their name and address details to be stored on a database.

- This database also records a wealth of transactional information which can be used to segment donors into different groups, for example, by attendance patterns, type of show, postcode, value of donations and tickets etc.

- Even organisations which do not sell tickets or capture customer data (such as free museums) have every opportunity to offer products that will strengthen the relationship with visitors when they come to the building, such as memberships, mailing lists, catalogues and donation opportunities .

- Cultural attenders are usually very happy to hear from their organisations by post, phone or email – they rarely regard communications from "their" organisations as "junk".

It has been suggested that "real" charities have an advantage because their causes are more emotional. The question posed here is: "Who would donate to an orchestra when children are starving in Africa?" In reality, of course, people simply don't choose in that way – otherwise only very few charities would exist, all of them dealing with children in the developing world. Many people also support more than one charity in several sectors, including the arts, social welfare and the environment, for example. Millions of people care passionately about the arts and heritage and donate accordingly.

If cultural organisations have so many advantages, why don't more people make donations to them? Time and again research demonstrates that the main reason why audience members do not donate to the organisations they visit is that nobody ever asks them to! (And as we see in the article on legacies in Chapter Eight, many people do not think of their local theatre or art gallery as a charity at all.)

People can be asked by letter, by phone, on a website, face-to-face, in a leaflet, by an announcement from the stage… but they must be asked.

The most successful fundraisers ask for the right amount of money from the right people at the best time and in an appropriate way, and these important technical matters are covered elsewhere in this book.

As the funding of UK and European arts organisations moves away from reliance on grants from the state towards a more mixed portfolio of income sources, asking supporters for money becomes ever more important. Many, perhaps most, cultural organisations in the UK now have some sort of audience or visitor fundraising programme. The question is, how can they be most effective? This is where we really can learn from other charity sectors.

Donation mechanisms

Donations can be made by audience members in a variety of ways, some well known and others – for example, gifts of shares – less well used. Some mechanisms are relevant only to certain target groups – only shareholders can give shares, only employees of certain organisations can use the Give as You Earn scheme – while others can be used virtually by everyone.

Most donors will use different mechanisms at different times, from dropping coins into a bucket to entering into a direct debit. The choice of giving mechanism rests, ultimately, with the donor, but fundraising charities should consider carefully which mechanisms should be promoted to be most effective in attracting donations from audiences and visitors. These include:

- Cheque, credit card and cash receipts.
- Direct debits (Paperless Direct Debits should be set up for internet and phone gifts, see below).
- Standing orders (if direct debits cannot be used).

And possibly:
- Give as you Earn through local employers.
- Gifts of shares.

Committed giving

The core of any large-scale individual fundraising programme is committed giving. A donor commits to a regular donation by authorising a regular payment from a bank account or credit card. In the UK there are only three possibilities:

- Direct debit, where the donor authorises the charity to take money from their account at a specified frequency (the recipient's bank pulls money from the donor's bank).

- Standing order, where the donor tells their bank to send a set amount each period (their bank pushes the money to the recipient's bank).

- Standing credit card authorisation, where the donor tells their credit card company to send a set amount each period.

Of these, direct debit is by far the best option, for the organisation and for most donors, for various reasons:

- If an existing direct debit donor wishes to change the amount they give in each period, whether spontaneously or as a result of a suggestion from the organisation, it is not necessary for them to confirm in writing. A verbal agreement is enough for the charity to take the money from their account. However, the charity must send a confirmation letter to make sure there is no misunderstanding. See below for further information on direct debits.The same is true for fixed payment schemes such as memberships. Of course the donor or member can choose to cancel at this or any other time.

- By contrast, a standing order donor needs to fill out a new form each time they change their donation or membership amount. This is a hassle for them and for the charity – donors are lost through simple inertia on their part and organisations incur additional costs in sending out forms and chasing lapsers.

- Standing credit card payments have the additional headache that a credit card expires every few years, at which point you have to contact each donor again to set up a new authorisation. Few UK charities now allow giving by standing credit card payment because of this additional cost.

Whilst there are initial costs in establishing a procedure with your bank to allow direct debits, the benefits in donor retention and cost savings in renewing or upgrading donors far outweigh the small additional costs.

The Gold Standard for committed giving is Paperless Direct Debit (PDD) which allows new donors to authorise a direct debit without actually signing a form. There are strict regulations on how the organisation should confirm the donor's wishes and it must be approved by the bank as a PDD originator. Once that hoop is jumped through, the charity can take direct debit sign-up over the phone or on a website, with obvious benefits. Once established, the same PDD system can also be used for memberships, subscriptions and so on, as well as for fundraising.

Note that, under this definition, a series of single donations, for example, by cheque, is not a committed giving programme. In the US this promise of future cheque donations is known as a "pledge", and is used because US banks do not commonly operate direct debits or similar electronic fund transfers (EFTs). This is one area where Europe is well ahead of North America.

CASE STUDY

National Galleries of Scotland – capital appeal

- **Visual arts**
- **Scotland**
- **Total income: £16 million**

By David Dixon

Vision

In 2000 the National Galleries of Scotland (NGS) unveiled an ambitious project to refurbish the Royal Scottish Academy Building and to build an underground link adjacent to the National Gallery of Scotland, in the centre of Edinburgh. The Playfair Project, named after the original architect of the two buildings William Henry Playfair (1790 – 1857), was a £32 million project of which £10 million had been pledged by the Scottish Executive and £7,390,000 million by the Heritage Lottery Fund, with the remaining £14 million to be generated through fundraising.

Private phase

With the appointment of the first director of development, Victoria Dickie, in 1998 the groundwork for the quiet or planning phase of the Playfair Project began to take shape. This was extended with the appointment of the first capital projects manager, Claire Beattie, who was to focus exclusively on the Playfair Project. At this time the development department established a Friends scheme to encourage a broad base of support and a corporate hire initiative, and continued with a successful corporate sponsorship programme.

As the private phase of the campaign was launched in 2000, the Playfair Campaign Council was established, charged with the task of making contact with wealthy prospective donors, business leaders and trustees of foundations. By 2003 just over 100 individuals had provided generous lead donations totalling £10 million.

Public phase

The public phase of the campaign involved raising the final £4 million through the widening of the identification, research, and solicitation processes. In 2003 a new fundraising team of three people was introduced to complete the fundraising project. This comprised Catrin Tilley (director of development), Peter Thierfeldt (head of fundraising) and Sam Lagneau (Playfair campaign officer).

Research and data management

The need for research and database administration grew rapidly during the public phase as the number of donations being made increased. The department changed databases to Raiser's Edge, a well-known fundraising management software system, and hired a database manager to assist in the introduction of prospect tracking and overall management of the database. Data from the Friends and donors was transferred without difficulty whilst the external mailing list database was imported and the data de-duplicated and cleaned. This database was used as the basis of donor and prospect management for the remainder of the campaign.

Donor prospects

An initial prospect list of over 500 potential major and middle-sized donors was refined by desk research and discussion with contacts of the prospects, leaving a "hot" major gift prospect list of 151 individuals. By the time the campaign concluded in 2005, 80 of these individuals had given, many at substantial levels. Geo-demographic data obtained from Experian was used in refining the prospect list but NGS did not use conventional wealth screening as most of the relatively small number of prospects were known personally by the Campaign Council (see below) or NGS.

Campaign Council

During both the private and public phases, the Playfair Campaign Council was central to the success of the Appeal. The Hon. Ranald Noel-Paton chaired the Campaign Council and other prominent members included Professor Ewan Brown CBE, chairman of Lloyds TSB Scotland, Gavin Gemmell CBE, chairman of Scottish Widows and the previous chairman of the trustees of the NGS, The Rt. Hon the Countess of Airlie DCVO. The Campaign Council, facilitated by the head of fundraising, generated many mid-sized gifts in the range of £1,000 to £40,000 and a number of major donations over £50,000.

Individual giving

Most of the individual donations came from individuals in Scotland, but some fundraising was also carried out abroad. For example, an event in Hong Kong in November 2003 attended by the chairman of the Campaign Council, director of the National Galleries of Scotland and head of fundraising, raised over £50,000 as a result of a drinks reception and a number of meetings with fewer than 50 prospects.

Fundraising scheme

A main fundraising scheme and theme was developed for the public phase of the Playfair Project fundraising campaign. This was to help restore the landmarks that helped to earn Edinburgh the name "Athens of The North". This innovative scheme encouraged donations not for the interior of the gallery, but for the exterior architectural features of the Royal Scottish Academy Building. Individuals could help restore an acanthus leaf for £500, a wreath for £1,000, support a column for £5,000, adopt a sphinx for £15,000 or give to the general Playfair Project fundraising fund. One of the lead donations to the public phase was as a result of this initiative. The statue of Queen Victoria by sculptor Sir John Steele which crowns the north entrance of the Royal Scottish Academy Building was sponsored by a donor who gave on the first day of the telemarketing campaign seeking wider support for the project.

Telemarketing campaign

Much of the fundraising effort was devoted to personal relationship development with prospective major and middle-sized donors, but NGS also utilised the telephone and mail to contact approximately 2,000 members of the Friends scheme. Although these contacts had not been identified as prospects for major donations (as defined by NGS), it was expected that they could make gifts of some thousands of pounds. The Phone Room was engaged to carry out a special campaign whose opening 'ask' was for £5,000 with discussions around that amount relating to supporting a pillar or a wreath. With Gift Aid, the telephone campaign generated £190,000 (at a cost of £9,000), including a gift of £100,000, which NGS believes is one of the highest-ever solicited by telephone in the UK. Mail and personal approaches added a further £36,000 from the Friends of the National Galleries of Scotland.

Friends & Patrons

The Friends of the National Galleries of Scotland were very helpful and many gave several times individually and some through group initiatives. The Patrons of the National Galleries of Scotland, which is a separate charity supporting NGS, had been established specifically to focus on acquisition of works of art. The appeal office worked closely with individual patrons, many of whom became major donors. Prior to the opening of the first phase of the Playfair Project in August 2003, all Patrons who had not contributed during the private phase were invited to do so by a personalised letter from the Campaign Council chairman and over £180,000 was raised from 51 patrons.

Difficulties

The Playfair Project Fundraising Campaign eventually exceeded expectations, but there were two particularly demanding periods. In March 2004, following a long and thorough application process, The Kresge Foundation in Detroit awarded a Challenge Grant of $600,000 to NGS. This time-limited challenge was to help raise the remainder of the project total from individuals by December 2004 in order to release the Challenge Grant. This opportunity re-ignited the major gift solicitation programme with a first-time gift of £200,000 from an individual in America and a £100,000 gift from a European individual, along with two upgraded gifts from Scottish individuals of £500,000 and £150,000. Many past donors also upgraded their support at this time and took features at £5,000, £1,000 and £500. Overall, 454 gave to the direct mail and telemarketing campaign and an additional 50 gifts were secured through the major gift programme. The true challenge came following the launch of the final phase of the Playfair Project in August 2004 when the facility had already opened.

Knowing that donors might not want to give following the opening of the building, the Appeal Office was anxious to secure a final major gift prior before that date. In the end, the donor only agreed two days prior to the official opening! This £500,000 gift was received from Sir Tom Farmer (the founder of Kwik Fit), who had originally contributed at the start of the campaign. NGS had been in discussion with Sir Tom for some time; he has a great interest in younger people, especially in encouraging them to embrace wealth creation and entrepreneurship, and wanted his naming of the main concourse of the newly-created underground area of the gallery to act as an inspiration to the many young people who use the new facilities (which include a specially designed education area).

Conclusion

Since the opening of the refurbished Royal Scottish Academy Building and Weston Link there has been a significant increase in visitors, leading to an award from Visit Scotland. The public campaign which ran from June 2003 to February 2005 was so successful that it received two awards from the Institute of Fundraising (Scotland) – the Campaign Award and the Telephone Campaign Award.

The Campaign Council was dissolved in February 2005 after the successful conclusion of the appeal. There was some regret that the Council was not restructured to assist with the challenge of revenue fundraising, although a new committee is now under consideration. The Playfair Project benefited from a willing partnership between the public and private realms. The Scottish Executive and the Heritage Lottery Fund came up with over £17 million but it was private donations of over £14 million which delivered Scotland's biggest-ever fundraising effort in the arts to date.

The private campaign ran from Autumn 2000 to May 2003 and raised £10 million from over 100 individuals, trusts and companies. The public campaign, which ran from April 2003 to February 2005, strategically raised almost £4 million from individuals, trusts and companies in an innovative manner, meeting all of its objectives. This effort marked many "firsts" for the National Galleries of Scotland: the first direct mail campaign, the first telemarketing campaign, the first-ever Scottish recipient of a Kresge Foundation Challenge Grant, and the first time funds were raised from abroad. Sound planning, project management and a strong communication strategy enabled this ambitious project to flourish. Over 2,400 contributions were received over the total campaign, with 2,300 during the public phase. Gifts ranged from £2 to over £2,000,000. A small appeal campaign team of three delivered the public campaign just in time for the opening of the Weston Link in July 2004, which was itself eight months ahead of schedule. The building project and the fundraising campaign were lauded as "determined, quiet and efficient" by an editorial in *The Scotsman* on 4 August 2004 – but also as setting a benchmark for future fundraising campaigns in Scotland.

Fundraising and marketing working together

The techniques used in acquiring new donors and developing long-term relationships with them are derived from marketing. Their aim differs from the sales and/or visitor results which marketers are looking for but, quite literally, fundraising from individuals *is* marketing.

In the context of an arts organisation this means that the people in the development department are doing the same sorts of things on a daily basis as their colleagues in marketing. For example, both:

- Usually rely on a database to manage their actual and prospective "customers" (i.e. ticket-buyers, visitors, donors, purchasers, sponsors, members etc).
- Use direct marketing such as mail, phone and email.
- Also use indirect media such as free leaflets, paid-for adverts and PR.
- Are rapidly colonising the internet as a space for publicity, communication and transaction.
- Measure success using Return on Investment (ROI) calculations.
- Develop personal relationships with a small number of key "customers" and more remote, but nevertheless managed, relationships with a large number of smaller customers/donors.
- Work strategically but have fierce short-term targets to meet.

And, in the end, the success of both fundraisers and marketers is measured, directly or indirectly, in terms of money.

However, the most important way in which their work overlaps is that, by and large, they are talking to the same people. Existing audiences buy most tickets (or make most visits) and are also the source of most individual donations. A database of attenders or visitors is the goldmine for both fundraisers and marketers.

Do fundraising and marketing compete for these people? Will they spend less on tickets if they give a donation, or vice versa? Exactly the opposite; anything that strengthens the relationship of an individual with an organisation is good for everyone, including the individual concerned. This has been proved time and again by research in the commercial sector and more recently in the charity sector. The greater the number of relationships a person has with an organisation, the longer they stay involved and the more they are worth to the organisation. Whether regular givers should also be part of a Friends scheme is discussed in Chapter Eight.

It is well known that a more frequent customer is more valuable in terms of sales or visits. In addition to the extra purchases they make, by definition frequent customers are more loyal and therefore spend dramatically more over the lifetime of their involvement with the organisation.

The table below shows real figures from a UK regional theatre and shows how customer retention rate (from one year to the next) increases with frequency.

Frequency (visits in one year)	Retention rate (from one year to the next)	Lapse rate
1	47.68%	52.32%
2	91.78%	8.22%
3	97.86%	2.14%
4	99.31%	0.69%
5	99.69%	0.31%
6	99.89%	0.11%
7	99.93%	0.07%
8	99.94%	0.06%

Even people who attend just twice in one year are very loyal. This is why so many organisations use loyalty marketing schemes such as subscriptions, two-for-one offers, memberships, points accrued as people buy tickets or visit etc. Just a small improvement in frequency improves loyalty which has a dramatic and disproportionate effect on sales and visits over the longer-term.

Frequent visitors are also more valuable in terms of donations. Large-scale audience fundraising has been undertaken in the UK for at least 15 years, a great deal of it by telephone, and the evidence is crystal-clear that one of the key indicators of propensity to donate is frequency of attendance. The following table illustrates this:

SEGMENT	Number contacted	Pledge rate (%)	Total donated (4 year value)	Average per phone contact	Average per gift	ROI
Friends	442	33.94	£27,625	£62.50	£184.17	10:1
Stage 2	470	25.32	£14,943	£31.79	£125.57	5:1
T5+	304	22.70	£11,040	£36	£160	6:1
T3-4	237	17.30	£5,793	£24.44	£141.28	4:1
T2	250	16.40	£3,978	£15.91	£97.03	2.5:1
TOTAL	1,703	24.66	£63,379	£37.22	£150.90	6:1

The codes T5+, T3-4 etc. show the number of attendances by the people in that database segment over the preceding two years. Note that the members of the Friends scheme performed well too; in fact, this Friends programme is designed to appeal to frequent attenders, so the group already contained many of the most regular attenders.

The "Stage 2" group were donors to a previous appeal and contained a mix of frequent and infrequent attenders. The direct cost of the campaign was around £16,500, plus some small ongoing costs of mailing to help secure the long-term donations (see below under donor development).

These figures come from a telephone fundraising campaign for a regional theatre but the same pattern is found across all types of arts organisations, irrespective of whether solicitation is by mail or by telephone. As well as helping to analyse results, the coding allowed the data to be segmented so that some groups received a slightly different approach e.g. Friends were acknowledged as such and ask levels were higher.

The illustration overleaf shows the effect of increased frequency in increasing fundraising income:

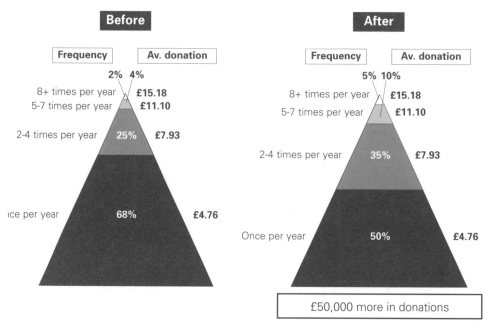

Before

| Frequency | | Av. donation |

2% 4%

8+ times per year £15.18
5-7 times per year £11.10

2-4 times per year **25%** £7.93

ice per year **68%** £4.76

After

| Frequency | | Av. donation |

5% 10%

8+ times per year £15.18
5-7 times per year £11.10

2-4 times per year **35%** £7.93

Once per year **50%** £4.76

£50,000 more in donations

In this idealised scenario, based on real examples, the organisation achieves average donations shown on the right of each pyramid which increase, as we have already seen, with frequency. Now look what happens if the organisation is able to make small improvements in frequency, so that now 5% (rather than 2%) of visitors come five times or more, 10% (rather than 4%) five to seven times per year and so on. Only the frequency of visit has changed – with the same number of visitors in total, and the same average gift values by frequency band, the organisation is £50,000 better off in donations.

This should not really be a surprise. Loyalty in terms of visits suggests a deeper relationship, more support for what the organisation does, more communication (two-way), and more opportunity for the organisation to put its case. Better gifts come from more regular visitors.

At many points in this book we emphasise that relationships are absolutely key to successful fundraising. When considering a relatively small number of major donors, large trust funds and corporates, these relationships can and must be quite personal; they really do feel like "relationships" in the usual sense of the word. But when dealing with thousands of audience members or visitors, we have to communicate using less personal media such as the telephone, mail or email. The strength of the relationship is nevertheless just as important, and the skill of the fundraiser lies in managing and developing these multiple relationships using the tools of direct marketing. Marketers talk about customer relationship management (CRM) whilst fundraisers talk of donor development; both are based on exactly the same principles.

This leads to the interesting conclusion that fundraisers want as many frequent ticketbuyers or visitors as possible. Frequent visitors are developed from first-time visitors, so fundraisers also want as many new people through the door as possible. These are the same aims as marketers'.

At the very least, marketers and fundraisers must coordinate their planning. This goes for practical matters such as mailing schedules, database coding, management of benefits (such as priority mailings or free tickets) etc. But it is even more important to coordinate the development of longer-term relationships. Does the subscription scheme sit well with the regular-giving programme? Is the language you are using to encourage donors consistent with overall branding? Is your membership scheme working for marketing or for fundraising (it probably can't do both) and are you providing development paths that will assist both marketing and fundraising? These are strategic issues which need to be addressed across departments. For more analysis on marketing and fundraising, see Chapter Eight.

Some arts organisations and many other types of not-for-profit organisations have combined the marketing and fundraising departments into one team whose focus is customer relationship management (CRM) i.e. the development of long-term relationships with individuals. The basic premise is that long-term marketing and fundraising is much more cost-effective than constant re-invention of the wheel. This may not be appropriate for all organisations – partly because there are not many managers who are experienced in the detail of both marketing and fundraising – but it is worth considering.

CASE STUDY

Welsh National Opera – large-scale individual giving

- **Opera**
- **Wales and touring**
- **Total income: £14.6m**
- **Development income: £1.6m**

By David Dixon

Welsh National Opera (WNO) is Europe's largest touring opera company, regularly touring Wales and central and southern England from its base in Cardiff. As well as this "core" UK touring, WNO performs around the world and has established an enviable reputation for its artistic standards, a reputation maintained and strengthened in recent years by its music director, Carlo Rizzi.

Photo: Bill Cooper

WNO's 2005 Don Carlos.

Under the leadership of its director of development, Lucy Stout, WNO has generated substantial fundraising income, especially from corporate sponsorship and from trust funds. However, despite some successes, a lack of resources prevented the organisation from committing to a consistent programme of fundraising from individuals, whether major donors or large-scale committed giving from audiences.

All that changed in 2004 as WNO prepared to move into the magnificent new Wales Millennium Centre (WMC) in the regenerated former docklands of Cardiff Bay. WNO realised that the high-profile opening of its new home would bring an unparalleled opportunity to reach large numbers of potential new audience members (the WMC has 85% more seats than the New Theatre, its previous home in Cardiff – a formidable marketing challenge!). WNO was also determined to seize the moment and establish a long-term individual giving programme, something it had considered embarking on for some years.

The simultaneous aims of achieving a dramatic increase in audience numbers and in recruiting large numbers of new donors from the audience required the marketing and development departments of WNO to work closely together. Both departmental directors (Lucy Shorrocks is director of marketing) also wanted to ensure that the initial enthusiasm for WNO in its new home was not just a flash in the pan, but the start of a long-term increase in ticket sales and in individual donations. To this end the departments jointly engaged an external consultancy which had experience of both marketing and fundraising and could offer strategic advice on long-term income generation from audiences through both sales and philanthropic gifts.

Following this, the marketing department created a new subscription programme which has proved extremely effective, not only in the first year of WNO at the WMC, but for subsequent seasons too. Meanwhile, the development department embarked on a programme of donor recruitment using telephone and mail. Key to this twin-track approach was that, with support from the consultants, a combined communication plan was created which ensures that marketing and fundraising approaches to individual audience members are coordinated. This plan allows the development department to schedule phone and mail campaigns away from the main ticket selling periods, to coordinate donation approaches to subscribers, and to agree prioritisation of access to cultivation events. The plan covers WNO's performances in Cardiff and throughout the UK.

The development director required support at the highest level for her strategy, not least because the recruitment process using phone and mail would require an investment of over £110,000 (and a new member of staff to manage the project), the largest single investment in a fundraising initiative in the company's history. Supported by her opposite number in marketing, she was able to demonstrate to the board and senior management colleagues that the communications plan ensured a joined-up approach which would strengthen WNO's audience relationships. She also presented an investment plan and a projected cashflow for a three-year cycle of donor development and recruitment which included testing and regular analysis of results. Lucy Stout says that her colleagues *"were not sceptical, but did need to see the proof that this investment was justified"*.

The campaign began in 2005 with a test of telephone fundraising run by an external agency using data from Cardiff (previous New Theatre bookers) and a touring venue, the Birmingham Hippodrome, to check that the initial projections were realistic and could be replicated away from home. This was followed throughout 2005 and 2006 by a rolling programme of telephone fundraising taking in all of WNO's touring venues and concluding with Cardiff again, this time using data on new attenders at the WMC.

From September 2006 a further 20,000 people who could not be contacted by telephone will be sent an innovative mailing pack created in-house and designed and printed as part of an in-kind sponsorship. The results of the mailing are not known at the time of writing, but the estimates are for a minimum 3% response and an income of around £50,000 including Gift Aid.

The initial recruitment process from phone fundraising finishes in Autumn 2006 and will have generated an estimated £150,000 including Gift Aid in the first 12 months of the campaign.

More importantly, WNO will have recruited over 1,000 regular donors whose monthly or quarterly gifts by direct debit will provide around £100,000 including Gift Aid each year, at little additional cost. Experience from general charities and from within the arts suggests that the average "lifetime" of such regular donations is around nine years. This suggests that, even if WNO were to do nothing else with these donors, other than replace the small numbers who lapse, the initial investment will generate around £900,000 at a Return on Investment (ROI) of 8:1.

This new income from regular donors will add to income from the mid- and high-donor Partnership programme and the Friends scheme to create a stream of around £500,000 each year of "first development income" i.e. it can be put first into budgets for future plans as it is the most reliable fundraising income.

Naturally, WNO has no intention of stopping there. From late 2006/early 2007 it will begin a process of donor development consisting of a) contacting people who initially made a single gift and asking them to convert to a regular gift, and b) contacting regular donors and requesting them to increase their contribution. In this way the number and value of donations will increase over time. The intention of this programme is to provide an underpinning of guaranteed income each year to complement other fundraising which can be less secure.

WNO will also use the base of donors generated by the direct marketing process to build its legacy fundraising programme, an activity it has already begun to develop with no little success. Lucy Stout cites an example to show how this can work:

"In Spring 2006, The Phone Room spoke with a gentleman as part of the test of telephone fundraising. He told the caller that he was unwilling to make a gift but would consider making a bequest to WNO. A note of this conversation was passed the next morning to WNO's development department who immediately sent a letter referring to the telephone conversation, together with legacy information i.e. he received a personal approach within 48 hours of the initial conversation. He made changes to his

Will almost at once and WNO received his bequest of £50,000 just a few months later."

Lucy does not expect all legacy fundraising to be as quick and direct as this! But, as she says, *"what it does illustrate is that if you don't ask, you don't get."* She describes the success of the audience fundraising programme as a big boost to the morale of the organisation as a whole since it demonstrates in a very concrete fashion the loyalty and support of audiences at all the venues where they perform.

The decision was made early on that no benefits would be offered to donors in exchange for their gift. This made the "ask" very straightforward and saves a great deal of time on administration as well as saving costs on the benefits themselves. It also makes the entire amount eligible for Gift Aid. WNO already has a benefit-led Friends programme and wished to keep a clear distinction. In fact, many Friends also became donors. WNO is confident that offering benefits would have added cost and complexity without increasing the number or level of gifts.

Key points

- Fundraising from audiences requires close cooperation between development and marketing colleagues.

- Large-scale fundraising from individuals is a strategic matter, requiring commitment from the organisation over several years.

- Expenditure on this kind of fundraising (indeed on all kinds of fundraising) is a long-term investment which needs careful management through forecasting, testing and regular monitoring.

- Fundraising from audiences strengthens relationships overall.

- There is no need to offer benefits in exchange for donations.

- Good administration and attention to detail are vital when dealing with large-scale individual giving programmes.

- Committed giving can produce stable, long-term income which complements other fundraising.

The donor development process

Just as the customer is more important than the sale, the donor is more important than the gift. The process of managing the donor from first gift onwards (and upwards!) is called donor development. It is usually presented as having three main elements, to which I have added a fourth.

● **Donor acquisition (recruitment)** is the task of soliciting the very first gift from prospective donors and is the least cost-effective part of the programme. Mainstream charities who earn most of their – sometimes very substantial – income from individual donors are content if their donor-recruitment activities break even or even make a small loss in the first year of the donor's lifetime (of involvement), because they know that they will generate very large amounts of income from future gifts from these new donors.

● **Donor retention** is finding ways to keep the donor and get them back if they lapse. Most single donors lapse because they are not asked soon enough for a further gift – more than six months is too long – or because they are not communicated with effectively; many regular donors lapse accidentally for simple reasons like changing their bank.

● **Donor upgrade** is simply asking for further and higher gifts – ideally regular gifts by direct debit. This is an extremely cost-effective operation if handled properly and sensitively, and the more donors available on a database ("donorbase"), the more cost-effective and profitable it should be. Contrary to popular belief, asking for further gifts from existing donors strengthens relationships – the concept of "not bothering" donors is misguided.

● **Donor relationship management** is the job of communicating with donors to improve their understanding of what an organisation does and to increase an organisation's knowledge of them, i.e. it is about deepening and strengthening relationships. Naturally, this should involve retention and upgrade at some stage, but it is a wider issue.

There will always be some falling away or attrition in a donorbase as donors die, move away, or as their circumstances change. A long-term donor development programme therefore requires ongoing donor acquisition as well as retention and upgrade to replace those who are lost and ideally to grow the donorbase over time.

The ideal sequence of donor development is often shown as:
Recruitment as single donor ➤ regular donor ➤ increased regular donor ➤ advocate ➤ legacy donor.

Fundraising databases

The task of a fundraiser is made significantly easier if they have access to appropriate fundraising software. When dealing with major donors, sponsors and trust funds it is a matter of keeping a large amount of information on a smaller number of people and organisations – although this could easily amount to several hundred records. When dealing with an audience or visitor fundraising programme a fundraiser may need to keep track of contacts with and donations from several thousand prospects and donors.

Whilst it is not literally impossible to do without a fundraising database (see Watermill Theatre case study in Chapter Seven), it is very difficult and wastes valuable time while risking the kind of poor administration which may lose donors.

A good fundraising database will keep track of donors and donations, allowing speedy and accurate administration of Gift Aid, benefits, memberships, communications, solicitations and gifts. The system will allow for segmentation, for example, by how recently they have donated, frequency, and value of previous gifts. This can make a big difference to the effectiveness of mail and telephone programmes. It will also timetable trust fund deadlines and help ensure sponsor benefits are delivered as promised. Last but not least, the database will provide for accurate reporting and analysis.

There are many companies offering fundraising software, of which the best known in the UK are probably Raiser's Edge, Progress and VisualAlms. An internet search will reveal these and more and many provide free demonstrations. They are often also keen to visit to explain their products, free of charge. The cost varies, but the cheapest are within the reach of even small organisations, while the more expensive systems cope with the demands of the most complex and wide-ranging fundraising operations.

The dedicated fundraising software packages described above are sold throughout the charity sector, but the cultural and heritage sector have an added possibility not open to other charities – fundraising modules linked with ticketing systems. This trend towards integration of ticketing and fundraising systems developed in North America where fundraising is a part of life for all cultural organisations.

New products of this kind are becoming available all the time, but at the time of writing Tessitura, ProVenue Max, AudienceView and SRO (formerly sold in the UK by Artifax) all offer good fundraising functionality. An interesting development is that the distribution rights for SRO in the UK and North America were acquired in 2005 by Blackbaud, maker of Raiser's Edge, one of the world's best-selling fundraising systems. This move demonstrates the level of interest in the cultural and heritage sectors. Suppliers of all ticketing systems know it is necessary to offer some level of fundraising management, although their capability varies – simply allowing a single donation to be taken at the point of ticket sale is not a fundraising system!

Earlier we looked at how development and marketing departments need to work together if an organisation is to develop strong long-term relationships with audiences and visitors. Clearly, combining information on one database is desirable, since the alternative is to have duplicate records on the ticketing and the fundraising systems. This raises the likelihood of errors creeping in on one or the other record, clashing communications and an inability for fundraisers and marketers to see the "whole" picture for an individual record, segments or the customers/supporters as a whole.

Telephone fundraising

The first telephone fundraising campaign for a cultural organisation in the UK that I know of was by the The Royal Liverpool Philharmonic Orchestra in 1989. I am told that the orchestra was in deep financial trouble and orchestra members themselves got on the phones to members of the audience to ask for support. The campaign met with great success. Not long afterwards, The Oxford Playhouse ran the first planned telephone fundraising campaign, repeated every year over the next decade. Nowadays, there are relatively few performing arts organisations in the UK which have not tested telephone fundraising and for many it is a major component of revenue and/or capital fundraising. The South Bank Centre, the Royal Academy of Arts, Welsh National Opera (see the case study earlier in this chapter) and the Royal Albert Hall are among the major organisations which have recently run telephone fundraising campaigns of tens of thousands of contacts each. Even smaller bodies such as the Watermill Theatre (see case study in Chapter Seven), Tyneside Cinema (see below), Norwich Theatre Royal and Northern Ballet Theatre have found telephone fundraising effective.

Note that most of the organisations on the list above (to which many others could be added) are from the performing arts, simply because they gather data on their customers at the point of ticketing. Without an audience or visitor database of some sort, fundraising by telephone or mail is much more difficult (see Chapter Eight).

Not all telephone fundraising campaigns are successful, of course, although most are. However, feedback from many organisations suggests strongly that the majority of donors (by number) to arts organisations in the UK have been recruited by telephone. The phone works well because it is a very personal medium, allowing real people to talk with each other about something about which the prospective donor is already passionate, or at least interested in.

Most arts organisations (in common with most charities in general) find it cost-effective to outsource telephone fundraising, although some (see Tyneside Cinema case study below) have organised their own campaigns with outside help.

CASE STUDY

Tyneside Cinema – capital appeal

- **Cinema**
- **North East**
- **Total income: £1.7m**
- **Development income: £870,000**

By David Dixon

For 70 years Tyneside Cinema has occupied a unique role in the cultural life of the North East and of the UK as a whole. It is an arthouse cinema showing the best films from around the world and also acts as a showcase for regional film-makers, as well as training upwards of 6,000 adults and children each year in film-making skills. It is the last surviving News Theatre cinema still showing films in the UK so has a historical and architectural value as a building, as well as being an important element of the cultural and social history of Tyneside.

The age of the building and its constant use by film-makers, trainees and filmgoers led, inevitably, to a slow deterioration in the fabric and equipment of the cinema. Moreover, rapid development in the technology of film production and presentation threatened to leave the Tyneside behind unless it could substantially update its technical equipment.

Rather than adopt a piecemeal approach, the Tyneside decided on the big bang option involving a complete restoration and installation of the latest digital technology in the cinema, an extra screen in a modern roof-top extension and a new lift to facilitate patrons with physical disabilities. Naturally, it only took this course of action after extensive consultation with current and potential funding partners and, by the time the public stage of the appeal was launched in April 2006, £6 million of the total £6.5 million target had already been identified from sources such as the Heritage Lottery Fund,

Regional Development Agency, EU funds and several local trust funds, including the Northern Rock Foundation and the Shears Foundation (see case study in Chapter Three).

Of course, raising this much money behind closed doors represented a triumph in its own right. Nevertheless, for a small organisation with virtually no track record of public fundraising and little spare budget, raising the remaining £500,000 was a challenge. Failure would risk some of the funding already in place and jeopardise important elements of the project.

Mark Dobson, chief executive of the cinema and Gillian Spry, director of fundraising, worked out a further programme of trust fundraising where it was felt more money could be raised relatively cost-effectively. However, individual giving would not be neglected and a twin-track approach was adopted involving potential major donors on the one hand and the cinema's audience and Friends on the other.

Customer details are not captured from door sales (a common problem with cinemas) but the cinema has a total of 5,200 people on its mailing list out of which nearly 2,000 are in the paid-for Friends scheme. First, the Cinema's database was wealth-screened to identify potential major donors. The resulting prospect list formed the basis of personal approaches which, at the time of writing, are still ongoing. Secondly, the cinema decided to approach the remaining individuals on its database (the great majority) for support.

The database was segmented by recency and by strength of relationship (Friends at the top, members of the mailing list for less than two years at the bottom). The whole database received a specially prepared mailing pack and, in the case of the Friends, a DVD. The most promising prospects were to be phoned, since the cinema was confident that the phone would yield the best returns. The remainder received a donation form with their packs. Cost for the mail and telephone campaigns (excluding DVD production costs) was estimated at £11,000 and an income target of over £60,000 set. Costs of the campaign were covered by funds raised locally - in particular the production of the DVD which was supported by Northern Film and Media.

It was decided that this initial campaign would focus on pure donations – either standing orders or single gifts. The cinema website has also been re-launched and offers an online donation facility administered through CAF. The cinema has held back other offers such as seat sponsorship for later in its campaign.

Organising a telephone campaign proved a challenge for the Tyneside, since none of the outside telephone agencies would take on such a small number of contacts. Instead, the possibility of running a campaign internally was investigated. At this point the cinema used part of its small budget to hire a consultant specialising in this area who was able to confirm the viability of this approach and who helped in setting the strategy and structure of the campaign and in preparing the creative materials needed. Later, a specialist trainer was brought in to train the callers and supervisors.

Image: Fletcher Priest Architects

Cut-away section of the proposed building showing fully restored classic auditorium, restored Tyneside coffee rooms, Mike Figgis digital Lounge, brand new Electra and a brand new third screen.

The cinema utilised its events manager to recruit call-centre staff from amongst a pool of volunteers who had worked at recent festivals. A team of three supervisors and 12 callers were assembled to work paid shifts across a five-week period. For a campaign of approximately 2,300 contacts a small room with a few telephones was sufficient, and paper forms giving prospect information on which gift details and comments could be recorded were used. The first night of the campaign was a nervous moment for the volunteers as well as for Gillian and her colleagues, but it soon became apparent that the call was welcomed by all who were phoned and the staff soon began to enjoy the work and the surrounding social element. The mail campaign also worked well, in fact producing better average donations than the phone, although at lower percentage response.

The cinema is very pleased with the results so far (fundraising continues). To date the campaign has raised £35,000 (including Gift Aid) from a total of 535 donors. The sums raised are useful contributions towards the target and it is felt to be very important that the Tyneside's Friends and attenders are able to contribute to the renaissance of their cinema.

Key points

- Even a small database can be wealth-screened and produce useful prospects.

- Mail is a valuable tool for fundraising and can produce more cost-effective results for some segments of a database.

- Telephone campaigns organised in-house can be very effective at low volumes of contacts, although professional technical advice and call-centre skills training is essential.

- Involving audiences in an appeal has a psychological benefit for both audiences and staff, as well as raising funds and securing relationships.

What are the main ingredients of a telephone fundraising campaign?

- **Data segmentation** A starting database of members, ticket-buyers, subscribers, former donors etc requires an initial division into appropriate groups ('segments'), firstly to identify the best prospects and secondly to allow different segments to receive slightly different approaches or ask levels. The key points to consider when segmenting are evidence of loyalty and evidence of affluence.

- **Telephone number tracing** Even if you have good phone number records it is worth the very small cost of "tracing" your data against the BT telephone directory, a process which finds new numbers and corrects wrong ones. Many data agencies can do this for you.

- **Telephone Preference Service (TPS)** It is illegal to call people on the TPS register with whom you do not already have a relationship. This law, which is part of the UK's data protection legislation, is designed to stamp out unsolicited sales calls. Happily, cultural organisations already generally have a relationship with the people whose data they access (ticket-buyers, members etc), so the TPS should not be an issue, but fundraisers should be sure of their ground here.

- **Creative** What will be said during the call? A script is needed which sets out the key features of the appeal and the organisation, together with supporting information in case the prospect asks additional questions.

- **Ask levels** How much money will be asked for? This is crucial – if no amount is suggested the prospect has nothing to react to and will feel lost. Is £50 too much or too little? Is a cheque better than a regular gift? The caller should make an opening suggestion and discuss from there. The ask level will vary between organisations and between segments (see National Galleries of Scotland case study earlier in this chapter where the opening ask was for £10,000). However, a "typical" attender or visitor to a cultural organisation should have no problem discussing a £10 per month direct debit.

● **Script** Taken together, the creative and ask levels form the script (see sample in Additional Information). Telephone fundraising without a script is a catastrophe, although this does not mean that the agent should be kept in a straitjacket by the script – rather, it provides a direction of travel and a destination, but with plenty of scope for meandering and stop-offs along the way.

● **Pre-call letter** Many cultural and heritage organisations send a letter in advance of a call to let the prospect know something about the appeal in writing and give them the chance to opt out of the campaign. This is by no means essential and does add to the cost, but it is often thought to be necessary to avoid complaints from the small proportion (perhaps 10%) of people who hate the phone.

● **Calling agents** These need careful selection, training and support. Working on the phones is not for everyone, but some people love it. There needs to be a schedule to ensure enough people are available at the right times to make the number of calls anticipated.

● **Equipment** The Phone Room uses sophisticated software and hardware which cost over £250,000 to install and can handle campaigns of tens or hundreds of thousands of calls. A small campaign of just a few hundred calls needs no more than some desks, phones and sheets of paper with prospect details.

● **Administration** The systems need to be in place before anyone picks up a telephone! Who made a gift? How much? Credit card or cheque? Whose address has changed? Whose husband died last week? All of these need careful recording and appropriate action taken.

● **Fulfilment** Many (probably most) calls lead to some sort of follow-up by post or email, a process called "fulfilment". The main possibilities are:
  o Donation form and accompanying letter.
  o Confirmation letter for PDD or credit card donations.
  o "Maybe" letter with a donation form.

Response to mail is dramatically increased if a freepost (or pre-stamped) envelope is included.

- **Reminders** Many people who offered a gift do not return the form (which is one reason why Paperless Direct Debit and credit card gifts are so useful). Most mean to do so but it languishes in the "to do" pile. A reminder call or letter is probably needed.

- **Reporting** How well is the campaign going? Are changes needed to the script or ask levels? Are any of the calling agents struggling? Are any of the data segments unprofitable? Daily reports are an essential part of any telephone campaign, as are end-of-campaign summary reports (see sample in Additional Information).

- **Evaluation** When the dust has settled it is obviously necessary to sit down with all involved and work out what went well and what not so well, particularly in relation to the income (short-term and long-term) and costs.

How not to do it! – a true story

In the late 1990s a well-respected regional theatre engaged The Phone Room to undertake a test of telephone fundraising from their audience. The test was successful and several other campaigns were commissioned, leaving the theatre with a healthy net profit in the first year from donors and a continuing stream of income from gifts made by standing order. The Phone Room advised the theatre that the likely average lifetime of donations by standing order (or direct debit) would be many years.

In 1999 the fundraiser who had commissioned the campaign left the theatre and her replacement did not stay long, leaving the theatre without a fundraiser, although senior managers did stay in post.

In 2001 the theatre needed to raise £1 million for a capital project but elected not to engage a fundraiser. Instead the theatre's marketing office wrote an appeal letter featuring the director and a star name associated with the theatre. The mailing was sent to all of the theatre's database, including former donors, and failed to generate significant income.

In 2006 the theatre told a fundraising consultancy it was considering engaging that it was still receiving £23,000 per annum from standing orders from over 300 donors recruited in the 1990s by telephone. A quick calculation showed that in the intervening 10 years these donors had contributed over £250,000 between them to the theatre at no cost at all (after the initial telephone recruitment campaigns which paid for themselves within 12 months). The donors had not been invited to events or received any communication other than the appeal letter. There had been no attempt to increase the level of giving or to retain donors who had stopped giving.

The theatre has a Friends scheme with, coincidentally, roughly the same number of members as the standing order donors discussed above. The Friends scheme generates around £5,000 per annum for the theatre and is described by the theatre (including in its public literature) as the main way for the audience to give to the theatre.

What the theatre did wrong:

- It failed to keep in touch with donors who doggedly continued to give despite the silence from the theatre.

- Within two years it had forgotten its own experience of the success of telephone fundraising and reverted to mail, with very poor results.

- It failed to build on the success of the initial recruitment of donors by repeating the process annually – losing out on many thousands of pounds of un-tied annual income guaranteed for years ahead.

- It thought it could do without investment in professional in-house or external fundraising input and saw its fundraising income fall steadily over the years.

- It failed to make the most of its loyal donors by suggesting increased giving or even noticing when they stopped giving.

- Nobody did a calculation about the cost-effectiveness of the Friends scheme versus a donation request.

How strange the change from major to minor

The distinction between major and "minor" donors is entirely pragmatic i.e. there is no magic formula or cut-off point. The question is one of internal capacity of the development department versus the amount each donor has given (or might give).

Major

A major donor is someone in whom the organisation is prepared to invest a significant amount of effort to build up a good relationship. Major donor fundraising is very personal and requires special skills – in larger organisations often a dedicated manager or even a whole department. These skills are quite different to those needed for database-driven direct marketing.

How many of these personal, often quite quirky, relationships can the development department realistically manage? A few hundred at most, possibly fewer. When we count from the top, in terms of actual or potential gifts, when we reach the number of relationships which can be managed, that sets the cut-off amount for major donors – anyone below that mark will have to go into a less tailored fundraising programme.

Core

At the opposite extreme are the several thousand donors who give relatively small amounts, but ideally on a regular basis, which nevertheless add up to significant income and which, over time, can often be more relied on than many individual major donors. It seems unfair to refer to them as "minor" donors – "core" donors seems more appropriate. Gifts of a few hundred pounds, or direct debits of some tens of pounds each month, certainly fall into that category. With such a large number of people there is no alternative but to use a database and mass communication techniques using mail, phone and email. Organisations must strive to create the semblance of a relationship and never lose sight of the fact that these are people and not just bits of data.

Midi

In between these two extremes is a group of people who give substantial amounts of money but are not really major donors. For example, few cultural organisations are likely to categorise a donor of £500 to £1,000 a year (by single gift or regular gift) as a major donor, unless there is reason to believe they could give a lot more. However, £1,000 is still a lot of money and it would be a shame to put them into the same programme as the £50 or £5 per month donors. The obvious solution is to create a halfway-house approach. Contact with midi-donors still requires a database, mail and phone, but it is not difficult to create a more intense programme with different events, a different mailing programme and more use of the phone for this group.

Moving up the ladder

The typical donor ladder suggests that donors can be moved up from core to midi and then to major. This is a poor representation of what happens in reality. Certainly, donors can and should be substantially upgraded (see above under donor development), but very few people are in a position to make a major gift, or even a midi gift. Most upgrading is done within each "band" i.e. people move up a step or two on the ladder.

Having said that, a core regular donor programme is essential for major gift fundraising. Why? Because within any large-scale database of donors there are always some very wealthy people who have not yet been recognised as such.

Some major donor prospects are already well-known and others give immediately at high levels. But many others give first at lower levels and only later identify themselves (or are identified) as potential major donors. These people are not so much upgraded as picked out.

There are several ways of identifying as yet unknown major donor prospects from a donor database:

● Identification by board members, other major donors, fundraising staff etc.

● Postcode analysis to pick out wealthy addresses.

● Wealth screening i.e. comparison with a database of wealthy and influential individuals gathered from public sources (see article and ENO case study in Chapter Eight).

● Information gathered from the donor during contact with the organisation (over the phone, at an event etc).

Research on the database should be carried out fairly often and staff managing the core fundraising programme specifically instructed to look for signs of major donors in their database. (For a more detailed discussion on research see Chapter Eight.)

Once a suspected major donor is identified, they should be discussed between relevant staff members to ensure that they are followed up appropriately. What action is appropriate will vary case by case.

Once identified, major and midi donors must be flagged meticulously on the database to avoid them receiving the regular mailings, invitations etc unless it is consciously decided that they should be included in certain general activities.

Checklist

● Are you offering a simple mechanism for people to make a philanthropic gift to your organisation?

● Are you offering a scheme for people to receive benefits in exchange for a fee?

- Are you marketing both possibilities separately and assertively? (Why have a scheme and not market it properly?)

- Have you listed all the possible reasons why audience members might give you more money?

- Are you trying to speak with individuals to find out what motivates them personally?

- Are you trying to identify groups on your database who respond to certain types of approach (education supporters, art lovers, club joiners, benefit-buyers, exclusivity-lovers and so on)?

- Have you varied your marketing to focus on different aspects of your work and evaluated the results?

- Have you actually asked your audience for money?

Chapter Seven

Managing an effective development strategy

By David Dixon and Theresa Lloyd

This book provides a guide to developing individual giving. The challenge is for boards and senior management to have the confidence to invest wisely, to understand their role and that of the professional development office, and to be able to oversee and assess the competence of the development office.

How to manage individual giving

The role of the board and senior management is two-fold. On the one hand it is, with the guidance and support of the development team, to participate in the cultivation and involvement of prospects and donors, and on the other to ensure that the investment in the development activities they have approved is value for money for the organisation. It is the role of the development office to implement the strategy.

The purpose of this chapter is to bring together the various tools for measurement and assessment of effectiveness, some of which have already been mentioned.

Allocation of responsibilities

The division of responsibilities may vary considerably between organisations, but a typical division of labour could be:

● The board retains overall supervisory responsibility for fundraising, as it does for all aspects of the organisation, and trustees can expect to be asked to support the development activities directly in appropriate ways.

● A separate development committee may sometimes be appropriate, bringing as ambassadors well-connected volunteers who do not have to take on the legal responsibilities of board membership. Their role is to lead other donors and volunteers. In effect they look outwards to secure support, not inwards to manage staff. Membership of the board and such a committee would probably overlap.

In some cases a separate foundation is established. In this case the development director and team may report to the chair of the separate foundation, and that board will in principle approve the strategic direction of the fundraising activities. These options are explored in detail in Chapter Eight.

- The chief executive takes overall management responsibility and is heavily involved with aspects of budget approval, target setting and agreeing priorities.

- The development or fundraising director or manager takes day-to-day management responsibility, reporting to the chief executive and providing professional advice and practical support to the chief executive, the board and development committee.

Other departments with a part to play in supporting fundraising from individuals are:

Marketing, which has an important role in preparing marketing materials, press and PR, and database selections. It also has a coordinating role in ensuring that fundraising is carried out in a way which enhances the organisation's relationship with its audience.

Finance is ultimately responsible for accounting for income and expenditure on any fundraising, and usually for administering donations through several mechanisms, dealing with VAT and Gift Aid, and reporting.

Front of house and box office (for ticketing organisations) engage with the public who are the main source of individual donations, and front-of-house staff may well be the people donors meet most often; it is their task to make people feel "part of the family".

Technical staff such as IT support may be involved in providing back-up to the database systems, and it is essential they understand the importance of an integrated approach involving marketing, box-office and development systems.

Catering staff may be asked to undertake some activities in relation to events; we see in the horror story in Chapter Eight the impact of subcontracted staff engaged by an out-sourced catering organisation having no idea of the significance of a major donor.

Perhaps most importantly of all, **curators, artists and performers** should be involved as appropriate in meeting current and potential donors and enthusing them with the organisation's work. It is not sustainable for this to happen as a "favour" to the development office. It should be recognised that their time is very valuable, that their involvement should not be engaged lightly, but that such participation is part of their role. How each organisation manages this process varies, but at the very least there must be a lead from the top so that it is seen as an integral part of their responsibilities.

In practice, many performers and artists enjoy meeting those who are passionate and knowledgeable about their art form, as shown, for example, in the case study of the OAE Chair Patrons scheme in Chapter Four and the comment from Richard Cordery of the Royal Shakespeare Company in Chapter Eight.

In order to create and sustain this corporate culture it is essential that all staff and volunteer leaders are briefed regularly to ensure they are fully aware of what is going on with fundraising, particularly successes which have involved participation from outside the development office. All communications which support any fundraising (see Chapter Eight for more on communications) should be distributed internally. Email bulletins and regular staff meetings provide ready media for reports of development activities.

The whole issue of a corporate culture of engagement with development is discussed in Chapter Eight.

Setting targets – what not to do

It is essential to set targets for fundraising. The challenge is the basis on which they are agreed. Clearly, it is inappropriate for the development office to set its own targets without reference to the organisation's overall budgets and plans. It is equally problematic if a target is handed down from on high without reference to the fundraisers!

There are several inappropriate ways in which a target for the development fundraising may be set, all of which have been observed by these authors. It should be added that in all cases these tactics were put forward by boards including business people who strongly advocated the adoption of "business-like practices" in the management of cultural organisations, and who would not have contemplated such an approach in the commercial organisations with which they were involved.

a) To fill a funding gap

The organisation pulls together its plans and budgets, and even a wish-list, calculates its revenue sources (public funding and box-office) and tells the development office that the target is the difference between the total expenditure on that basis and the anticipated income. Not only does this bear no relationship to the realities of the marketplace or the level of investment in development, but as there is no responsibility for this target taken by the development team, measuring performance against this figure is an empty exercise.

b) Add a percentage to the previous year's achievement

This approach appears more reasonable, but takes no account of special factors which may have affected last year's result. Were there particularly popular or unpopular shows? Was there charismatic leadership which is no longer involved? Were there competitor activities which distorted the marketplace? Is the development team consistently under-performing i.e. should targets be much higher?

c) We should raise as much as organisation X

The major difficulties involved in benchmarking are explored in Chapter Eight. There are so many factors influencing success in development that setting a target in relation to the perceived success of others, operating in very different circumstances, is always inadvisable.

d) At cost plus a mark-up

At least this approach should guarantee a surplus, but over what period are the figures being measured? We know that development is about investment, and that donors have a value over their lifetime. We also know that the shape of the fundraising portfolio has a major impact on the ratio of cost to income; a high proportion of legacy income significantly reduces the average cost, while corporate relationships may be relatively expensive to service.

The ratio of investment to income is discussed in detail in Chapter Eight.

Setting targets – a possible approach

Because these approaches are so unsatisfactory, it is essential that the development office takes control of, or at least is deeply involved in, the process of setting the targets for its own performance. This means developing a deep understanding or how it should be done, and sharing that expertise with others, especially the board and senior management. The fundamental question when setting targets is not how much the organisation wants or "needs" to raise, or has raised in the past; it is a matter of setting a budget on the basis of how much money is out there to be raised – what is the "market" for the organisation, given the nature and range of its activities and the amount it is prepared to invest.

Once an estimate has been made of the overall potential size of the market, the next question is how much it would cost to raise a given sum, and over what period. At this point, assuming budgets are limited, priorities must be agreed and targets and associated costs built up. (And since cultural organisations often take a short-term view, this is the point at which so often legacy marketing is postponed, as it is assumed that the pay-back for the investment will be long-deferred – an attitude challenged in the article in Chapter Eight.)

For individual giving, target-setting starts with the prospective donors. But how can an assessment be made of possible income from individuals? How is the size of the "market" to be estimated? This is not an exact science, but a few techniques can help to establish at least a "ballpark" for potential donations. These include:

a) **Wealth screening** This is reviewed in detail in Chapter Eight; in brief, matching information on visitors and supporters (Friends, donors, ticket-buyers, members, shop customers and so on) against wealth lists can establish a crude figure for the pool of wealthy people associated with the organisation and even an estimate of their potential for giving. This information can be matched against indications of the strength of their relationship with the organisation (for example, one can assume that on average members have a much stronger relationship than shop customers, and those who attend frequently a greater affinity than occasional visitors). It is important to include lapsed donors and Friends in such screenings.

b) **Peer group interviews** Private interviews with people who are already closely involved with the organisation and who have contacts in the social and business groups where your potential major donors are to be found can be very helpful. The purpose of such interviews is to get opinions about the likelihood and potential size of gifts from named individuals (names which interviewees may suggest and/or arising from wealth screening) and, at the same time, an opinion on how well the organisation is equipped to cultivate the potential donors. Opinions may vary, but an overall picture is likely to emerge which will help in setting targets and assessing the size of the task in reaching the targets. Interviewees might include board members, current donors, long-standing members and prospects suggested and introduced by such people.

This approach is akin to that involved in a feasibility study for a capital campaign, which is discussed in Chapter Eight.

c) **Database analysis** If the organisation has a database of audience, visitors, Friends and so on then it is possible to build up a picture of potential donations step by step:
    1) Segment the database by relationship in a hierarchy, for example, donors first, then members, then subscribers, then frequent visitors, less frequent and infrequent (or a similar structure).

2) Estimate how much a person in each group might give in one year and what percentage they might donate if asked directly (if you have no figures to base this on, ask other organisations who have undertaken this exercise). Multiply this by the number of people in each segment and add up the figures.

d) Testing Fundraising from major donors cannot easily be tested, but it is quite possible to run small phone or mail campaigns to test the response from different segments of the database. The results will allow the estimates from the database analysis to be corrected and a more robust target to be established. Undertaking a pilot programme of this type is usually a very good idea – a successful outcome supports a bid for investment resources, while a disappointing result enables the design or focus or targeting to be reviewed. Several of the case studies in this book are based on testing the market first.

Comparison with previous performance and audit by outside specialists of particular techniques can be added at this stage as further evidence to help build realistic targets.

If these methods are new to the organisation, there are professional fundraising advisers available who can provide expertise.

Developing an expenditure budget

Once market estimates have been established, the cost of raising the money also needs to be calculated. Capital campaigns in particular may have major cash flow implications. Wealth screening may identify a number of major prospects, but since major donor development is labour-intensive and funds for investment may be limited, there is a need for prioritising. The situation is more acute if the potential income is likely to be earmarked but the fundraising costs, particularly staff, come out of the core budget. The more restricted funds are raised, the more the pressure on the core operating costs. This is a major argument for "educating" donors about the need for core costs to run an effective organisation, including investment in current donor support and future income generation. The challenges of restricted donations are explored in Chapter Eight.

Similarly, and at the other end of the gift spectrum, a telephone campaign to the hundreds or thousands of people on the database could yield high rewards, but it is still essential to calculate the costs and the timing of the break-even point, let alone revenue surplus.

The challenge in fundraising is that, like commercial investment in developing a customer database, the costs are heavily weighted at the start. It is therefore important to review the estimates both of income and cost over several years in order to put expenditure for the first year in context, and to substantiate recommendations for investment. We return to this later in this chapter. The reality is that, however tantalising the opportunities, there will usually be a constraint on investment: hence the need to rank the options. Once priorities have been set and some opportunities left, with regret, to later years, the income target for the year and an associated cost budget can be finalised.

This target can then be entered with some confidence into the organisation's general budgets. The income target may be less than the organisation would like it to be, but it is important that a realistic target, and the rationale behind it, are understood and accepted by the organisation's management and board, and plans made accordingly. It is possible that it will be higher than anticipated, if the organisation is willing to invest. It is extremely unlikely that it will match the "funding gap".

This is one reason why it is important that development is represented on the senior management team – it is likely that budget-setting will often be reviewed, not because the market will change, but because different options for the use of funding will produce different income patterns over the long-term.

Opportunity cost

One interesting side-benefit of building up income estimates in this way is that it also creates an estimate of potential income that is not being sought: i.e. opportunities that are not being pursued because of perceived practical and cost issues. This "opportunity cost" is real income foregone, and an actual loss to the organisation. If the size of this opportunity cost is known then the fundraiser has a basis for a serious budgeting discussion along the lines of *"If my budget were increased by £X then it seems likely I could raise £2X this year and then £4X for the next three years"*.

Conversely, if budget problems lead senior managers to propose a cut in fundraising budgets, they should understand that this will inevitably lead to a loss of income greater than the budget savings. This should be important information for the board and senior management.

Thinking about the longer-term and measuring effectiveness

So how does an organisation start thinking about the likely long-term value of a donor? The techniques described here are now completely intrinsic to the approach of major social welfare charities that rely on "direct marketing" for their donor recruitment. They provide both an approach to budgeting and a way of measuring effectiveness.

The key commonly-used measures relevant here are:

● Return on Investment (ROI), which evaluates the cost and income of a marketing activity over time.

● Net Lifetime Value (NLV), which evaluates the cost and income of a customer or donor over the period during which they support the organisation.

Return on Investment (ROI) is a simple way of measuring the effectiveness of each fundraising activity undertaken by the organisation, whether it be a mailing or phone campaign, a major-gift programme, a corporate membership scheme or a series of events. The formula simply compares the costs with the income:

ROI = income divided by costs

The result can be expressed as a percentage or as a ratio. This simple formula allows the comparison of different activities to assess which has worked best – the higher the ROI the better. ROI can be used retrospectively, to evaluate all or part of the fundraising activity, or in advance, using estimates of cost and income to decide how to invest resources.

Using an ROI calculation also helps to target activities more effectively. For example, a mailing may work best for one segment of the database, but the phone may be more effective – have a higher ROI – for a different segment.

And ROI will allow the head of development to compare different types of fundraising as well; for example, business sponsorship with individual giving, to establish a true comparison across activities with very different cost and income structures. This is essential when planning investment across a fundraising programme.

The challenge is to include all of the relevant costs and income.

Costs

These might include:
● Direct costs e.g. print, mailing, design, advertising agency support.
● Overhead costs e.g. staff time (including non-fundraising staff).
● Cost of any benefits promised or planned (e.g. tickets, programmes, entertaining).
● The cost of future servicing of the relationship – perhaps for a number of years.

The last three items on this list are often inadequately accounted for when evaluating fundraising, but must be included.

Income

This might include:
- Direct income.
- Additional income e.g. from Gift Aid.
- Guaranteed future income e.g. from direct debits.
- Pledged income (calculated separately, however, since it is not yet guaranteed).
- The probability of a legacy.

We see that the last item on the cost list and the last two items on the income list introduce a new element to ROI calculations: the concept of future costs and an associated income stream. It is essential to incorporate these if the investment activity is designed to bring income over several years. Examples include a membership scheme or committed giving programme, where simply looking at first-year cost and income does not give an accurate picture. It can be a challenge to estimate how many years on average a new member or donor will support the organisation, but there are various techniques.

Net Lifetime Value

This is the value of the donor to the organisation over the period of support.

> NLV = lifetime income minus lifetime costs

Clearly, there are three factors to assess: income, costs and, crucially, the likely length of the relationship.

"Lifetime" in this context means the anticipated length of the donor's donation history, from first gift to last. Usually, since future costs and income are less valuable than cost and income today, a discounted value (linked to the bank interest rate) is applied to the expected future income.

So how might an organisation obtain a reliable estimate for the "lifetime" of a donor? Some charities have had donor-bases for many years. Their records show how much "typical" donors of different types have donated over the years, and for how long they have supported the organisation. By grouping people together in a number of segments (how they were recruited, type and level of donation, postcode, age etc), a reasonable estimate can be made of the costs incurred in acquiring, retaining, servicing and developing them. Of course, such information cannot help identify the likelihood of any particular donor behaving in a certain way, but it does establish averages across groups of donors in terms of income levels and the likely proportion who will stay with the organisation – called the retention rate;

the drop-out rate is sometimes called "attrition". This will provide some very useful data that can help guide the focus of the fundraising activities.

Many arts organisations now have the benefit of a long-standing database of donors and an associated fundraising programme, with evidence going back 10 years and more. Some have provided case studies for this guide. They and others may be willing to share their experience, and charities in other sectors may be happy to help. Direct marketing in particular is a very mature technique and there are a number of publications, Institute of Fundraising training courses, and conferences devoted to the subject.

However, because the component parts of the calculations of Net Lifetime Value are estimates only, caution needs to be exercised when projecting forward more than, say, three years. It may be that, carefully nurtured, half of the current donors will still be giving in 10 years' time, but it would be unwise to make a major investment on that basis. For a shorter period, however, such estimates indicate likely income and investment can be made accordingly.

Calculating Lifetime Value

It is hoped that the reader will not look ahead and skip over the next section. Not only is fundraising about money, but it is essential that all those who are responsible for raising it – trustees, senior management and development offices – understand the principles behind this concept, even if they leave the calculations to others. For a group of people (a whole database or a segment) the formula for calculating lifetime value is:

> Gross Lifetime Value = (V/N x L) x (X x R)
> *Where*
> V = total annual value of the group
> N = number in the group
> L = estimated lifetime of involvement in years
> X = number of new recruits each year
> R = retention rate (% of people who stay with you each year)

Estimated costs over the same lifetime (costs of donor recruitment and servicing) are subtracted to give Net Lifetime Value.

How much is a donor database worth?

As well as providing a management and budgeting tool, calculating Net Lifetime Value enables an organisation to estimate the value of its entire database and of different types of donors within it. This in turn indicates how best to invest to increase its value.

The value of the database can be estimated by applying the formula to the entire list. This will, of course, require significant guesswork, especially on the more major donors, where the challenge will be even greater because relatively small percentage variations will have a significant impact on the overall value, and these in turn will depend on the level of investment. The process needs to be repeated regularly.

Possibilities for increasing the value can be thought about in terms of the factors in the formula set out below:

V (annual value) could be more	– ask for more money
N (number of people) could increase	– attract more donors
L (lifetime) could increase	– develop relationships to encourage people to give for longer
X (new donors) could increase	– improve the rate at which new donors are acquired
R (retention rate) could improve	– find ways of reducing the proportion of donors who lapse each year

In an ideal world, an organisation will wish to achieve all of these, but in fact, the figure which makes the biggest difference to the overall lifetime value is the retention rate (R). In other words, taking care of donors and making an effort to get them back into the fold if they stop giving is a very cost-effective activity.

And looking at matters in this way is a good approach to including legacies in the fundraising mix. As we see in the article in Chapter Eight, legacy marketing usually appears to start to pay back after three to four years. Donor servicing for people who have pledged legacies is relatively cheap. It makes sense to take a longer view, and to support investment in bringing in more legacies.

Monitoring and measuring effective investment

This approach to assessing database value and therefore setting a target for potential income over time can only work if these concepts or "key indicators" are monitored regularly. In charities which depend on effective direct marketing, key performance indicators (KPIs) are set and measured for indicators such as the retention rate, average value, new donors in one year, proportion of donors on regular giving schemes, and total number on the database.

It is perhaps more difficult to undertake these calculations for higher-level donors but the principle is the same. As well as looking at financial reports, the development team, senior management and trustees should look regularly at these figures and take action if, for example, the retention rate drops, or the number of new donors falls, or if the average donation is static. Adopting this logical and analytical approach also means that when the development strategy is succeeding, it should be easier to make the case for further investment.

Fundraising costs as investment

However, many fundraisers and consultants have experienced boards which cut the fundraising budget when there is a budget shortfall. The argument seems to be that the development department must take its share of the pain, but a moment's reflection should reveal that this is not a sensible course to pursue. A well-run fundraising department is not a net drain on resources since it will be raising several times its costs in income each year – cutting costs will therefore reduce income even more, leaving the organisation in a bigger crisis! At the very least it should be covering its own costs, even if all the additional income generated is earmarked for budget-relieving projects and programme activities. Of course, if it is thought that fundraising is badly run, then that is a different question. But the rational response to a financial crisis is to increase expenditure on fundraising, not to cut it, perhaps even transferring cash from elsewhere to allow this to happen, even though this may not be popular.

Often the true reason is a failure of nerve; in fact, a leadership failure. The board or senior management is not willing or able to explain to those delivering the core mission why at this time investment in fundraising should be sustained, and that department "protected" from the cuts which are falling elsewhere. The truth is that the period of pain would be much less if investment in development were increased.

Taking the long view

It also has to be recognised that investment in fundraising needs to be managed over a number of years. There are few fundraising activities which can be started from scratch and yield substantial income in the first year. (Perhaps events fall into this category but even then they need some momentum to develop a reputation and captive marketplace – see the article in Chapter Eight.) Even existing programmes may need to wait for some time before new investment brings in the expected return.

This situation is very common in the commercial world. An example is insurance; companies have to spend a considerable amount in marketing and sales costs to recruit a new policyholder, but once that person is signed up they will continue to pay premiums for many years. Insurance companies know they have to accept considerable losses in the first years for new policyholders, but that they will recover this and far more in the future. The insurance companies regard their customers as an asset.

In the same way, donors (and sponsors) are an asset to a charity, and the value of this asset can be calculated going forward. Indeed, there has been discussion in the wider charity sector of putting fundraising expenditure on the balance sheet, rather than in the Profit & Loss account, and writing it down over a number of years, much as one would do with other investments (installing a new bar or ticketing software, for example). This approach is fraught with obvious pitfalls and has been resisted, probably rightly, by accountants. However, even if the organisation's official books cannot capitalise fundraising costs, they should nevertheless be managed and analysed over some years if their true impact is to be properly measured.

In order to manage fundraising investment effectively it is necessary to have accurate figures on costs, returns and cash flow. In many cases these will be estimates (see the section on target-setting above) which must be monitored carefully and adjusted as real results come in.

The whole issue of cost to income ratios is explored in more detail in Chapter Eight.

Risk management

Managing investment also requires the organisation to have due regard to risk management. This is not the same as risk avoidance. All investment carries some element of risk, but not investing at all is certain to produce nothing – the riskiest thing an organisation can do is to take no risks.

The key questions are:

- How big are the risks?
- What could the organisation afford to lose if it all went wrong?
- How can uncertainty be reduced?
- What are the key decision points and the cost of abandoning an activity at any of those points?
- Can these risks be hedged against?
- How does this all compare to the potential return if it works out well?

An organisation contemplating individual giving might think about these questions in the following way:

- We have never run a programme like this before. However, many organisations like ours have done so with great success, so we rate the risk as "medium".

- If we put £x into the programme this year and get nothing at all back (even though that is highly unlikely) it would be uncomfortable but not disastrous. However, to invest £Y would be foolhardy until we have more experience and can reduce our uncertainty levels.

- We can reduce uncertainty by undertaking tests of some elements of the programme and by hiring outside advisors to give us the benefit of their experience.

- We would need to invest £x at first, and then another £x each six months. We will gain more information as we go along but will always retain the option of abandoning the programme or amending it substantially at each investment point. We will not chase sunk costs!

- We can't easily hedge against the risk of this innovative project not working, but the upside is very attractive. Could we find a current or new entrepreneurial donor who might underwrite the possible loss (or even lend the money to make the investment)? They might want to keep an eye on their investment and our progress, and we are comfortable with that.

- The potential return in this year is moderate but excellent in future years.

These are just examples, of course, but they show the kind of thinking required. It is important to note that the organisation can quickly reduce its levels of uncertainty and therefore be more confident of its investment as it gains experience of running such programmes.

All of these management approaches indicate some of the success factors in individual giving. Another is about recruiting first-class staff. Recruitment is discussed in detail in Chapter Eight. These and other requirements for success are reviewed in Chapter Ten.

This guide is not intended as a counsel of perfection, but to alert boards and senior management to the complexities of development, and provide examples of best practice. We have included a range of techniques and mechanisms.

But it is recognised that in reality some elements will be missing and yet, because of a compelling mission, inspirational leadership and extremely hard work, the organisation will achieve its goals, at least in the short- and medium-term. The Watermill is one example.

CASE STUDY

The Watermill Theatre, Newbury – fundraising on a shoestring

- Theatre
- South East
- Total income: £1.5m
- Development income: £250,000

By David Dixon

Mack & Mabel 2005, Watermill Theatre production.

"This rural idyll has quietly become one of the most admired and influential theatres in the country. In the past five years it has transferred more shows to the West End than any other theatre in Britain." Daily Telegraph

This rural theatre of just 220 seats in the countryside outside Newbury, Berkshire is one of the powerhouses of British theatre production and touring which in 2005 was awarded two Tonys for its Broadway production of *Sweeney Todd*.

The theatre was converted in the early 1960s from a former watermill on the banks of the River Lambourn, surrounded by the Berkshire countryside. The energy for its development as a producing organisation came from its founders, Jill Fraser MBE and her husband James Sargant.

The Watermill manages to achieve its worldwide theatrical success, organise an ambitious educational programme and run the theatre itself with Arts Council and local authority grant support amounting to just 20% of its £1.5 million annual turnover. The rest is earned from ticket sales, income from touring, other sales (it has a lovely restaurant) and, of course, from fundraising.

The fundraising story of The Watermill was, until recently, not as impressive as the rest of its achievements. Susan Foster was appointed as the theatre's first professional fundraiser in 2000 (she had previously been director of development at the Oxford Playhouse), at a time when corporate sponsorship amounted to around £40,000 per annum, mainly from small local businesses, with little other fundraising. The Phone Room had run a small telephone fundraising campaign in 1999 directed at the theatre's audience which proved very successful, but the response overwhelmed the theatre's small administrative team and, when Susan arrived the following year, she found piles of unacknowledged and unrecorded donation forms and letters. In fact, the telephone campaign led the theatre to the twin realisations that fundraising for The Watermill could be very effective but that it could not be managed properly without professional input.

When she began with The Watermill in 2000, Susan set her sights on putting proper systems in place for administering donors and donations, on increasing sponsorship and on telephone fundraising to secure individual donations. Recently, trust fund research and applications were stepped up with the help of a small local agency.

Administration was sorted out by recording all donations on a comprehensive spreadsheet and by flagging donors on the theatre's ticketing system. Regular donations are checked bi-annually against bank accounts and problems discussed with the donors concerned. Gift Aid is reclaimed annually by the finance department after liaison with development. This system works, but is rather inefficient and wastes a great deal of time in administration. Susan is in no doubt that the best solution would be to install a dedicated fundraising software package such as Raiser's Edge or Progress.

By 2006 corporate income had increased to over £100,000 per annum including a corporate club, training, Arts & Business awards, and support for touring as well as presentations in the theatre itself. There is a much wider range of companies involved. In the same period, regular giving increased to £35,000 per annum with additional single gifts amounting to around £10,000 raised by each telephone fundraising campaign (run more or less annually) of around 1,500 telephone contacts. Trust fund income for revenue has risen to around £30,000 per annum and overall the target for revenue fundraising is £250,000 in the financial year 2006-07 (just under 17% of total turnover).

This five-fold increase in revenue income is impressive in itself, but it has been achieved at the same time as The Watermill has been running a £3 million capital appeal. This appeal has been the focus of a great deal of high-level individual fundraising which is described below.

The Watermill's appeal is unusual in that it involves the sale of the theatre building by its owners to The Watermill Theatre Trust which runs the theatre's operations. The dilemma was that, having put all their own money into buying The Watermill in the early 1980s, Jill and James needed to sell the building in order to be able to release their life savings so they could retire. Of the £3 million appeal target, the agreed sale price was £1.7 million with a further £1.3 million for capital improvements.

The appeal was first discussed in 2003 and work began in earnest in 2004. The theatre initially took advice from Iain McMullan, a fundraising consultant specialising in capital appeals. Susan Foster explained that the consultant's advice was helpful, especially in relation to the structure of an appeal board, but that his main value had been in persuading the rather anxious members of the theatre's main board that the appeal could and probably would succeed. Susan explained, rather wryly, that the board felt more confident hearing this from a man in a suit. After the board agreed the strategy for the appeal, the consultant withdrew, as agreed, and Susan took on the running of the appeal.

As a first step, the theatre's ticketing database was wealth-screened by The Factary and, later, by Charity Consultants (the same raw data was screened through two different systems since the organisations use different data sets and, although there is a strong overlap, more prospects in total can be identified). Prospects uncovered by the screening fed into private meetings during 2004 designed to uncover potential members of the appeal board and/or major donors.

Many of the names brought out by the wealth screening were already known to The Watermill, but by no means all. In fact, the person who eventually became chair of the appeal board was discovered in this way. Ralph Bernard is CEO of GCap Media (formed by a merger of Capital Radio and Great Western Radio) and had formerly led the appeal to build the new Great Western Hospital in Swindon and had been involved with plans to build a new theatre in Marlborough, Wiltshire, where he lives.

Although he had attended The Watermill as a paying customer (and it transpired his daughter had appeared in Watermill Youth Theatre shows), he was not known to The Watermill and initially did not attend cultivation events. Eventually, however, a meeting was arranged and it became apparent that he would make an ideal chair for the appeal board. In his turn, he persuaded his friend Andrew Tuckey, formerly deputy chairman of Barings plc, a former director of the Royal Opera House, trustee of the Esmée Fairbairn Foundation and now director of Bridgewater Finance, to become deputy chair of the appeal board. Together these two recruited the remaining members of the appeal board, some from existing Watermill contacts and some from the prospect list generated by wealth screening.

The appeal was formally launched in 2005 and is planned to finish in 2007. There are no benefits in exchange for donations, but there are opportunities for recognition; donors of over £150,000 are offered a small plaque in the area where their donation is directed and those who give over £300,000 are offered a naming opportunity. The development office does make a point of ensuring donors and prospects are well serviced, keeping in touch with regular mailings and occasionally inviting donors to a special pre- or post-show reception.

Donors of £20 or more are automatically enrolled in the Friends programme, the theatre's main audience-relationship programme. There are no ticket-related or other financial benefits to the Friends (so there are no Gift Aid problems), but its members receive information and invitations to tours, talks and similar events. The intention is that, once enrolled in the scheme, donors will be encouraged to renew and so maintain an involvement with The Watermill well beyond the end of the appeal.

The theatre is committed to a high level of donor care and is keen on donor recognition, but Susan Foster describes a prescribed benefit system or tiering as "a recipe for disaster". She does not believe these systems attract more or higher gifts and they bring administrative and Gift Aid problems, as well as adding unnecessary cost.

The development director is clear that the key to the success of the appeal so far (it is on target) is the network of personal relationships which she and the appeal board have developed. She makes no distinction between corporates, trusts and individual donors in this respect; a private donor may also help to unlock funds from the company they chair, or may be friendly with the trustees of a family trust fund. Personal relationships underpin the bulk of the income for the appeal, supported by "routine" trust applications and audience fundraising by telephone.

One unusual aspect of The Watermill's appeal is that development director Susan Foster has taken a much more active role in developing relationships than would normally be the case, or than she expected. Because the appeal will financially benefit the founders and leaders of the theatre, Jill Fraser and James Sargant, they felt unable to involve themselves fully in fundraising. In their absence Susan became the personal face of The Watermill in dealings with potential and current supporters. She feels this was inevitable but not desirable, although she does not feel it has hindered the appeal since everyone can understand the unusual position of the theatre's founders.

Not all members of the appeal board are large-gift donors, but all are involved in making links with wealthy individuals, and with personal contacts at companies and trust funds. Some people who are very active and helpful in the fundraising effort do not wish to become members of the appeal board. An exclusive event to be held at a private country house in the autumn of 2006 is designed to bring on more major donors. There will be a performance of a Watermill new-writing production to emphasise the theatre's commitment to nurturing new talent. Invitations will be issued personally by the appeal board and other well-connected supporters.

The appeal is mentioned in every season brochure, in every programme, on the theatre's website (where a donation can be taken by credit card), and there are separate leaflets available in the foyer. The plan is to continue fundraising into 2007 and finish with a "last push" including a telephone campaign to all audience members and to previous lower-level donors. There have been no mail campaigns due to lack of resources. So far around 2,500 people have made donations to the appeal.

"Lack of resources" is somewhat of an understatement. Susan Foster had no assistant until Spring 2006, there is no fundraising software, leading to the wasting of a great deal of her time, and the development office is itself little bigger than a cupboard in what looks like a garden shed (all staff suffer the same lack of space and new offices are a crucial part of the improvements to be paid for by the appeal). That the theatre can maintain a revenue fundraising programme of £250,000 per annum and at the same time run a £3 million capital appeal under these circumstances is little short of miraculous!

There is a sad note to add to this story: in February 2006 Jill Fraser, the theatre's artist director and executive director and, as we have seen, its co-founder and co-owner, died, leaving a gap in the lives of those who knew her and in the management of the theatre. The appeal continues.

Key points from this case study

● It is possible to raise large amounts of money with limited budgets.

● However, a strategic approach is needed, taking a view over several years.

● The key to fundraising success lies in the development and management of personal relationships.

● Good administration is essential for any kind of fundraising.

● Some elements of fundraising can be outsourced, in this case telephone fundraising and "routine" trust applications.

● The main board of The Watermill was hesitant over the appeal and a separate appeal board was essential. Members of the appeal board are now joining the main board which lends authority to the appeal board and increases the confidence of the main board.

● The lack of investment in a fundraising database and assistance in the development department were financially unnecessary, given the sums being raised, and have made fundraising more difficult.

● Wealth screening was extremely useful, but only when the prospects uncovered were then followed up appropriately and rigorously.

● Benefits other than excellent communications are not necessary to secure gifts.

Chapter Eight

Analysis and advice

n this chapter we cover a wide range of specialist topics. Some sections have been written by leading experts and practitioners in their field and these are clearly credited. In other cases I have drawn on my own experience and that of others to emphasise specific issues. The subjects chosen have all been identified in one way or another in the other chapters, and are thought to merit closer examination. They cover strategic and technical advice, and, as elsewhere, the sections include illustrative case studies and practical guidance.

Topic index

Black and minority ethnic arts

In one sense the challenges for minority ethnic cultural organisations are the same as for any small or medium-sized niche organisation promoting activities of interest to a special interest group; to identify and involve those who share the passions who have the capacity and propensity to give, and to demonstrate that the organisation is effective in what it does, and that the money will be well-spent and will really make a difference.

However, a discussion with Jatinder Verma, artistic director of Tara Arts, reveals a very different mind-set among those who might be thought to be his natural constituency. This is a reflection of fundamentally different attitudes to culture and its role in the expression of faith and in society. To draw an analogy from music: Western music, in its emphasis on harmony, is about the orchestration of a variety of themes and instruments to the service of a single idea; Indian music relies on a very small number of instruments in support of the single artist. William Blake's vision of "the world in a grain of sand" is curiously more applicable to Indian thought than Western. According to Jatinder, it is part of the European tradition to focus on culture, innovation and risk, because the self can only be realised in the world (cf., "man is a social animal"), of which the arts are an integral part. For the Indian, the world around is fundamentally illusory, so the focus of human development is necessarily internalised.

To this philosophical bent of the heart is added, through the experience of migration, the instinctive desire for reassurance of identity, to hark back to "traditions" – which are, for the South Asian, inextricably bound with faith. Coupled with the desire to "make it" in the new country, this results in immigrants viewing artistic endeavour as purely individual indulgence, rather than a contribution to familial or communal welfare.

Added to this very private approach are demographic influences. Businesspeople may support their home village because of their emotional ties, because the needs are great, and because they may go "home" to be buried. They may support commercial activities which have a cultural focus – for example, investing in shows such as *The Far Pavilions*. But according to Jatinder, Asian immigration has been far less diverse in terms of religion and language than the Jewish diaspora: proportionately fewer South Asian immigrants to Britain come from a class or tradition in which it was customary to patronise culture, and the great majority of the cultural experience comes through religion and the cinema.

Successful Asian entrepreneurs may support national charities and organisations in the UK, as much as others do, because they are seen as excellent, for social acceptance and to be part of a network. *"People make mega gifts for good karma."* But hitherto at least, organisations such as Tara Arts have found it very hard to make the case to wealthier individuals from the Asian community that awareness of Asian art in its many forms, and of its practitioners, is potentially an important aspect of UK life. Audiences for Asian artistic endeavour – from theatre to film – are drawn from within and beyond the Asian community; they affirm a sense of being part of the general British cultural landscape and therefore are an eloquent testimony of being "native"; and, in supporting such artistic endeavour, Asian businesses are investing in their own futures, by helping in the formation of a healthy multi-cultural society.

Tara Arts was founded in 1977, in the wake of the racist murder of a young Asian boy in Southall. The company's mission is to build bridges of the imagination across cultures. It produces four theatre productions each year, touring theatres and junior schools across the country. The company has a full-time staff of five, employing performers and other staff on a project-by-project basis. In 2005-06, its annual income was £535,000, of which 36% came from box-office and fundraising activities, less than 1% from individuals and none from Asian business. The remainder of the income came from Arts Council England.

Board development and training

There are various ways of strengthening current boards and identifying potential new trustees who have the mix of skills needed at any particular time.

A good start is to work out what those needs are. In order to address the question of board development, and the desired role, structure and membership profile of board and other volunteer leadership, it is useful to undertake a board audit or review, with the purpose of:

○ Knowing what the current members are able and willing to contribute in terms of time, professional expertise, opening of networks and money.
○ Matching these with the organisation's needs on the basis of its current plans.
○ Identifying the gaps.
○ Identifying the means of addressing them.

It is often helpful to start by considering both what is required from board members and how well those needs are currently being met.

The requirements may include:
○ Definition and agreement on what the organisation needs and can reasonably expect from board members – linked to clear terms of reference.

O Identification of the networks (cultural, academic, policy-makers, institutional, business, wealthy individuals, media etc) which the organisation seeks to penetrate (not only for fundraising purposes).
O The range of skills the organisation would like to have available.

There are two elements to what board members bring – their skills and networks, and what they are willing to do.

In most cases the basis of this audit is a standard questionnaire, coupled with a confidential interview with each board member. The interview is also an opportunity to explore ideas of how the board might develop, and what an individual needs from the organisation to make their board membership more effective, particularly (but of course not only) in fundraising. At the same time, senior management should be invited to contribute to the audit, and encouraged to provide confidential input about their expectations from the board.

In considering gaps it is also important to look at terms of office and plan for future requirements when someone with known expertise is going to retire. It is recommended that this work is undertaken by an external consultant in order to ensure objectivity, confidentiality and confidence in a dispassionate analysis.

How to find trustees

Once the board has considered the audit report, it may then consider strengthening itself through recruitment. The Charity Commission publication *Finding New Trustees – What charities need to know* may be of interest and can be downloaded free from **www.charity-commission.gov.uk/publications/cc30.asp**. It covers finding potential trustees from a range of sources and using a variety of methods. Charity Commission experience and research shows that the traditional methods for recruiting new trustees – by personal recommendation and word of mouth – remain the most popular. However, its research work has shown that whilst these methods are still widely used, they are not necessarily the most effective ways of finding the people with the skills required as they limit the field from which trustees can be drawn. Using wider and more inclusive methods of searching for new trustees, such as advertising and using trustee brokerage services, can access a wider range of applicants and the Commission recommends that trustees consider these methods. The paper includes details of a number of organisations that maintain registers of potential trustees, or offer a trustee brokerage service, matching potential trustees with vacancies on the boards of charities.

The National Council of Voluntary Organisations (**www.ncvo-vol.org.uk**) has a trustee bank directory, and one of the organisations very relevant to the culture sector is the Arts & Business Board Bank. The Board Bank programme places trained senior business executives as trustees for arts and cultural charities. The programme is available across the UK and is a very useful resource for arts organisations interested in ensuring that they have the appropriate skills and expertise within their boards. The arts organisation does not pay for a new board member; the search is currently free of charge, but there is a cost for additional board training and development.

Board review

Having found trustees, what next? The Charity Commission says: *"In an effectively-run charity the induction process marks the beginning of an ongoing process of trustee training and development, to ensure that trustees can continue to make an effective contribution to the charity. The level of training and support which trustees need will vary depending on the size and nature of the charity, but trustees may wish to consider some of the following:*
○ *Individual training courses.*
○ *Away days for the whole trustee board, with or without staff.*
○ *Briefings or workshops as part of trustee meetings.*
○ *Visiting other charities which carry out similar work.*
Trustees should periodically review procedures for the recruitment, induction and ongoing development of trustees to ensure they remain effective."

The appropriate induction process will vary for each organisation but all trustees should be provided with key documents such as:
○ The charity's governing document.
○ The charity's latest annual report and accounts.
○ Minutes of recent trustee meetings.
○ The charity's policy on dealing with conflicts of interest.
○ Any other key documents that trustees will need, for example, the charity's strategic plan and its vision and values or mission statement.

In addition, all trustees should receive copies of the Commission publications *The Essential Trustee: What you need to know (CC3)*, and *Hallmarks of an Effective Charity*. Many established charities now engage in a regular (annual) review involving an assessment of the contribution of individual members against the set terms of reference and responsibilities agreed to when trustees join the board.

Another source of guidance recommended by the Charity Commission is *The Code of Governance for the Voluntary and Community Sector*, published by the National Governance Hub (a partnership of organisations working to improve governance of charities and other voluntary and community organisations). The Commission has contributed to the development of the Code in partnership with NCVO, ACEVO (Association of Chief Executives of Voluntary Organisations), Charity Trustee Networks and ICSA (Institute of Chartered Secretaries and Administrators).

The Code is a practical and easy-to-use guide to help charities to develop good practice. It is based on seven key principles designed to apply to any charity:

- ○ Board leadership.
- ○ The board in control.
- ○ The high performance board.
- ○ Board review and renewal.
- ○ Board delegation.
- ○ Board and trustee integrity.
- ○ Board openness.

You can download copies of the code from **www.governancehub.org.uk**. There is also a summary version of the code, and a leaflet called *Learning to Fly* (for local voluntary and community organisations).

The emphasis in this guide on good governance is not only because it makes a difference to how organisations thrive, but because increasingly, donors care about this. And as charities, cultural organisations are subject to the scrutiny of the Charity Commission, as we have seen in the recent case of Tate and the acquisition of works of art by its trustees[1].

Board training

Nowadays, there are many opportunities for board training, including those provided by NCVO and ACEVO (**www.acevo.org.uk**.) NCVO provides a wealth of documentary advice as well as a range of courses. ACEVO provides a number of training and support services, including for organisations with fewer than five employees. As with NCVO, part of its training involves directors and chairs attending together.

A number of organisations, including Arts & Business, provide off-the-shelf training for boards on all aspects on governance as well as bespoke training for individual board members and organisations across the sector. Arts & Business bills its training as a comprehensive overview of the roles and responsibilities of trustees, including support materials and information on other useful organisations and bodies. There is

1. In July 2006 the Commission published a report that Tate had purchased art from serving trustees without permission. The Commission found that the acquisitions were in the interests of the charity and should stand, but highlighted deficiencies in Tate's policies and called for significant improvements to be made.

also ongoing support for the trustee and the arts organisation and the relationship is monitored and evaluated at regular intervals.

Some legal and accounting firms with charity practices devise programmes for trustees. Advisers who really understand the specific challenges of engaging trustees and artists in donor relationships can also provide very focused and sensitive training. A few specialist consultants have the experience and seniority to provide bespoke and practical guidance to trustees who wish to strengthen and broaden the base of their capital and future revenue income from the private sector, and who recognise that they must invest in a professional approach to solicit support in the form of major gifts. There is more detail about board membership and fundraising in the next section.

Artistic leaders also need training, and some pioneering organisations such as the Clore Leadership Programme provide this. For more detail see Additional Information.

Training for fundraising should bring together volunteer leaders and senior staff and experts in a shared learning process. Afterwards those involved should understand:

❍ The nature and importance of major donor fundraising.
❍ The marketplace.
❍ The role of the development office - processes and techniques.
❍ What they can expect from and how to work with the development team.
❍ The range of reasons why people might support their organisation, and what they look for.
❍ The importance of prospect research.
❍ The importance of developing long-term relationships with prospects and donors, and their role in this.
❍ The various ways people can give to charities.
❍ That actually asking for money is just a step in a long and continuing process of developing and nurturing a partnership.
❍ That links with major donors can and should be mutually rewarding relationships – fundraising can be fun.

Such knowledge will make them more confident in their capacity to solicit financial support for their organisation.

Board membership and fundraising

"They need givers and getters on their boards. If one is composing the board of a money-seeking organisation, then there must be some getters among the mix of skills – preferably some who are giving at the same time."
            (A distinguished chair and former chair of several leading arts organisations)

"The key questions are the quality of the leadership of the organisation and whether they see fundraising as a business and how professional they are at fundraising."

(A major donor)

Board membership and other involvement

Volunteer activities, particularly board membership, are a major part of giving among the wealthy in the US. Among the elite, contributions of money are just part of an overall involvement with non-profit organisations. US elites have played a major role in founding, sustaining and overseeing non-profit organisations[2].

Francie Ostrower found that 75% of her interviewees[3] served on a non-profit board, and 78% raised funds for various organisations. It should be remembered that the sample selection was based entirely on monetary contributions, with no regard for volunteer activities. With striking frequency the largest gifts went to organisations with which the donor has a relationship other than as a giver. Board membership, being a user of the services and having a close relationship with someone linked to the organisation were key factors. This was true for over 90% of all gifts in the areas of health, education, culture and religion.

With the exception of donations to a place of worship, educational institutions and hospitals, board membership was the most frequently cited relationship. For example, some 45% of the largest gifts to cultural organisations went to those where the donor was a board member. The figure was the same in the sector addressing rights, advocacy and policy issues. It was about half that for educational institutions and hospitals, where the key factor was having attended (well over 40%) or the illness of a family member (a third). These findings are echoed by the Boston-based research[4], which found that 71% of those interviewed served on a board, and over 75% engaged in fundraising activities. Over half were involved in event planning.

In the UK research[5], well under 40% of interviewees were on the board of a charity (apart from their own foundation), compared with over 70% in the US research, and only around 10% of UK interviewees engaged in fundraising activities of any kind. The same research found that although many of those who sat on boards or committees of organisations gave a major share of their donations to the same

---

2. For example, in the recent campaign for the Museum of Modern Art in New York, some $500 million of the total $875 million raised came from the board.

3. Ostrower, Francie (1995) Why the Wealthy Give: The Culture of Elite Philanthropy. *Princeton NJ: Princeton University Press.*

4. Schervish, P and Havens, J (2002) The Mind of the Millionaire. *Social Welfare Research Institute, Boston College.*

5. Why Rich People Give.

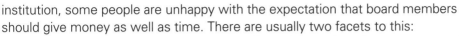

institution, some people are unhappy with the expectation that board members should give money as well as time. There are usually two facets to this:
○ A belief that giving time absolved them from the need to give money as well.
○ A view that the board should not only be made up of the wealthy.

However, there is an exception in one area. A confidential study in August 2006 for an association of Jewish culture providers showed very clearly that the main support came from trustees. Nearly all survey respondents reported that over half of their trustees donate to the organisation, and a fifth or more have raised external funds for its benefit. About half of respondents are reliant on the support of a small number of individuals (five or fewer), with these donors representing 30% to 90% of the organisation's total income.

It is recogised that in the UK the boards of major educational and cultural institutions, and charities generally, have a far broader responsibility than fundraising, and hence a wider range of people serve on them, many of them not rich. But for people to contribute they do not have to be wealthy.

It is the strong view of this author that all board members should be invited to contribute according to their means, and that this expectation should be explicit in the terms of reference of board members. In some cases this may be modest – no more than being a Friend at the most basic level. In other cases it may be substantial, and it should be clear that if someone is a trustee then the organisation should be among their philanthropic priorities.

It is also very clear that people who may be asked for significant sums expect to be asked by those they respect as peers and have themselves given. Organisations seeking funds in the US may be asked to set out what trustees have given (see later in this chapter for more on US giving). For the development office to be able to say on its materials something such as *"every board member has contributed to this project"* is very powerful[6].

But as well as the external positioning, the whole-hearted commitment of trustees to the development process – as givers, identifiers of prospects, ambassadors and as part of the team involved in cultivating donors – is hugely reinforcing to the development office.

However, for many people the giving of time and money is interlinked. They may give time first – formally becoming a member of a board or committee, and

6. The RSC reports (in August 2006) that a significant factor in its capital campaign is the ability to say, to prospects on both sides of the Atlantic, that all board members have contributed.

attending meetings – but do so in the expectation, or at least acceptance of the position, that they will sooner or later make a financial gift as well.

There are various models for the volunteer leadership of fundraising, and it is by no means the case that one size fits all. One approach is to ensure that the board itself is as engaged as possible in the fundraising process. This is the model adopted by The Place.

CASE STUDY

The Place – Board development and strategic planning

- **Dance performance and training**
- **London**
- **Total income: £4.9m**
- **Development income: £361,000**

By Janet Reeve

In the Autumn of 2004 Nigel Hinds, recently appointed executive director of The Place, took professional advice about the feasibility of undertaking a capital campaign to raise around £1.5 million for two new dance studios. He and his executive colleagues felt that the organisation was not yet ready for the increased fundraising activity such a campaign would entail, but they recognised the value of a feasibility study by experienced professionals in giving objective analysis and helpful recommendations.

The study confirmed their view and prompted several important strategic steps forward. Before undertaking a capital campaign, The Place would need to strengthen the fundraising networks and capacity of its board and invest further resources in its fundraising team. In the past, The Place had done little fundraising from individuals and this was identified as a key area that would need building up in preparation for capital fundraising. It would also need to balance carefully the revenue and capital fundraising requirements of the organisation. Changes would take time to implement, but The Place should revisit its plans for capital fundraising in 12 to 18 months.

The current chair, who had successfully steered the organisation through one major redevelopment, had indicated his desire to retire. The Place searched for a new chair stipulating that in addition to strong leadership qualities and enthusiasm for contemporary dance, fundraising ability would be key. The

Photo: Hugo Glendinning

Student dancer Joe Walkling, in training at The Place (2005).

Place used a firm of professional head-hunters to manage the search process. It was a thoroughly consultative process and took six months. This was time well-spent as all members of the executive team and board felt included in the final decision. The Place successfully appointed a new chair (Nicholas Berwin) whose commitment and fundraising ability are outstanding.

Working with Nigel and the executive team, the new chair helped The Place to recruit further members to fill vacant positions on the board. These new members also had the key skills and networks needed for fundraising. The arrival of the new chair precipitated an organisational shift towards a more outward-looking approach, ensuring that those beyond the dance world are aware of the mission and purpose of The Place. This took staff out of their comfort zone, but it created challenging goals and learning opportunities.

Establishing a strong fundraising operation takes time. The Place had secured several major corporate sponsorships and had long-standing support from some major trusts. Before the review, the development department had just two staff. A third person was appointed and the team is becoming more established. The Place has continued to work with advice from one of the consultants involved in the strategic review and is committed to making further investment in the fundraising operation over time.

Working with the director of development and the consultant, the chair introduced a scheme for individuals called The Place Circle which invites donations of £1,000 a year. Donors sign up to a programme of activities and events designed to show them dance and choreography in the making. It is proving popular and as a result The Place is developing an important body of outside supporters. These relationships and networks will prove invaluable as fundraising continues.

Fundraising is now underway for the capital scheme. Although a final commitment to proceed has not yet been taken, some substantial contributions are on the table. In an ideal world, The Place might be advised to continue to build up its fundraising operation for another year before taking on a capital push. The organisation is, however, crying out for more space and with a strong chair at the helm and increased resources in the development department, there is the right kind of energy around to rise to the challenge.

The advantages of this, especially for an organisation in the throes of a major campaign, is that fundraising remains literally and figuratively a key agenda item. Led by the chair, it is clear that there is organisational commitment from the top and he is well placed to encourage other board members to give and be ambassadors for The Place. The job description and background note used by The Place to find its new chair are in Additional Information.

Another way of engaging committed volunteer leadership is to set up a separate committee with delegated authority and responsibility from the board. This is the policy adopted by the National Theatre.

CASE STUDY

National Theatre – National Theatre Development Council

- **Theatre**
- **London**
- **Total income: £42m**
- **Development income: £4m**

By Breda Daly, director of development 1999-2004

The National Theatre Development Council has evolved over nearly 20 years. While it is impossible to separate the fundraising efforts of the council from the organisation, it is nonetheless clear that the council makes an important and real contribution to this effort in terms of ideas, contacts, gifts, energy, encouragement and leadership. Its success relies largely on two factors – the need for a clear structure that is well managed, and the active participation of both its members and all levels of the organisation.

The council has a formidable network and one of its key strengths is its ability to give a first-hand account of the governance and benefits of the National's artistic and educational activities to an important peer group.

To do this the council must be very well briefed, and feel fully engaged and part of the wider organisation.

National Theatre Development Council structure

Objectives
The National Theatre Development Council is a permanent committee of the board exclusively responsible for fundraising and accountable to the board. Currently, two members of the council sit on the board and the chairman of the board is an ex-officio member of the council. Council members carry no legal or management responsibilities.

Council members contribute directly to the National's fundraising success both by encouraging major support from others and by making a personal

Photo: Stephen Cummisky

gift (amount not specified). Furthermore, development strategy and budgets are set in consultation with the council. Council members are encouraged to make the National Theatre the main focus of their arts volunteer involvement and to avoid sitting on other arts councils/boards.

Committees and meetings

The council is a large body with over 30 members. It meets quarterly. These meetings are mainly an opportunity to update and engage all members where reports are made from the National Theatre's director, executive director, chair, development director and team, and invited senior management. Members of the council also report on their activity at working group level.

Each member of the council must sit on a working group. These are mainly sector-based groups focused on individual, corporate, trust and US giving, but also include a planning and strategy group where the chairs of the working groups get together with the chair and vice-chair of the council to discuss future planning, major project responsibility, meeting agendas, budgets, new ideas and council recruitment. These working groups are where the hard work is done and each is supported by the relevant development sector manager and attended by the development director. Meetings are usually quarterly, though some sectors choose to meet more regularly.

Leadership

Active leadership of the council is an important success criterion. It comes in many forms and is a difficult quality to tie down. In essence, a potential chair needs to be deeply committed to the organisation and the role of development within it. They need to have a flair for fundraising strategy, a sphere of influence made available to the organisation and the support and respect of the council members and the organisation.

Membership and recruitment

Tenure for council members is three years, usually renewed once and, in exceptional circumstances, extended beyond that. Some individuals who have made an important contribution to the work of the council and wish to remain involved are then invited to join the Honorary Council. The Honorary Council is sent minutes of all council meetings. It meets twice a year and can be contacted by the development department by telephone.

Recruitment is the ongoing responsibility of the Planning and Strategy Group. This group maintains a list of potential council members based on a needs analysis of required talents and qualities – industry-based, capacity to give, capacity to get, strategic know-how, age, area of influence, etc. This is reviewed every three or so years. Potential new members are then cultivated through an events programme and, if appropriate, invited onto a particular working group where an informal assessment is made by both parties as to whether a closer relationship is desired.

As and when vacancies arise on the council, working group members are invited to join the council. This process takes a minimum of a year and may take longer depending on vacancies.

When an individual joins the council they are given a full induction. This includes a welcome pack with a range of information about the theatre and its needs, an outline of their responsibilities as a council member, contact sheets for the board, council and senior management, and an outline of their entitlements as a council member. They meet the chair of the council and are given a tour of the building and backstage area, and are introduced to key members of the Theatre's team.

Active participation

The fact that the National Theatre board has delegated responsibility for fundraising to the council is a recognition of the huge importance of fundraising to the organisation which needs a clear focus with particular skills and experience. Conversely, members of the council are often happier with a structure that does not give them legal and financial responsibilities but does allow them full participation in and a sense of ownership of the development of the organisation.

In separating this function from the governing body, it is vitally important to ensure that the group receives the same level of transparent briefing and support from the whole organisation. It is not sufficient that this council be managed and serviced by the development department alone, but it is the development department's responsibility to ensure the full buy-in and participation of others within the organisation, particularly at a senior level.

Chair and board
The chair of the board attends council meetings and gives occasional reports of board activities. He or she also plays an active role in the cultivation of most major potential donors and in the strategic development of the fundraising function. Council representatives sit on the board and report to it on council activities, seeking advice and support where appropriate.

Director and executive director
The theatre's artistic director and executive director attend all council meetings and give a confidential and full report of artistic and management planning. They too are actively involved in all strategic development and cultivation. The directors host an annual party to thank all senior volunteers for their invaluable contribution.

Senior management
The general manager and finance director always attend council meetings and regularly report on their activity. Various senior managers are also invited to make guest presentations of their areas of expertise – marketing, production management, catering, scripts, touring, etc – to give the council a deep understanding of how the organisation works as a whole and what challenges it faces. This has the added value of giving senior managers a certain ownership of the development effort and how they can contribute to it.

Development team
The development team is the main day-to-day contact point for the council. The planning and admin team provides support – booking tickets, arranging cultivation opportunities, taking and distributing minutes etc. The sector teams (individual, corporate, trust) work closely with the working groups – brainstorming, problem-solving, and monitoring progress both through the meeting structure and direct contact with members. The development

director works closely with the chair and the Planning and Strategy Group to develop strategy, review progress and processes, and achieve a shared sense of purpose. The development director is also the main liaison point between the council and the executive and senior management team.

Council members
Council members not only attend council meetings (serial non-attendance prompts a phone call from the chair), but actively support the development function through their involvement with the working groups. They also attend a number of cultivation and general National Theatre events.

Clearly, this requires a major investment by the organisation, the development team, other board members and the artistic leadership. But equally clearly this pays off, as the council approach continues to flourish after nearly 20 years.

Another approach is to establish a committee that does not have formal delegated authority, but works closely with the development team to support specific fundraising activities, identify prospects, and help develop and refine particular mechanisms. An example of this is the Young Vic.

This is very much work in progress; at the start of 2006, and in anticipation of moving into its newly-built theatre, it has formed a Development Council. The terms of reference are given in Additional Information. There are two board members (one an actor) on the Development Council, which is chaired by someone who is not on the board. The meetings are monthly and attended by the artistic director and development director. The average age is relatively young – except for the current board members! All members agreed that the council should only be continued if the development team felt it effective, and the measures by which its success will be assessed were agreed at an early meeting. These too are in Additional Information.

This policy of establishing what are essentially committees works well when those involved have no wish to take on the responsibilities and status of trustees. But there are times and organisations for which it might be appropriate to consider the establishment of a separate charity or "foundation" with its own board of trustees. The advantages include:

● The opportunity to establish a prestigious institution focusing on the financial aims of the organisation, particularly the challenge of raising a significant sum of endowment money.

● Clarity of purpose (raising money!).

- To increase the number of active givers and ambassadors with trustee status for the organisation, who can operate on a peer-to-peer basis. (This is particularly useful when the number of trustee ambassadors on the main board may be limited by the constitution of the organisation, for example, where board members are appointed by government, are representatives of membership or are partly drawn from an artist practitioner constituency such as musicians.)

- Holding the reserves in a separate account and balance sheet from that of the organisation, so that prospective funders, whether public or private sector, are not misled about the real financial needs of the operating organisation.

- The opportunity to develop a high level membership structure, linked to a recognised "ladder of giving".

- The possibility of creating the position of president of the foundation.

- The possibility of inviting current prestigious supporters who do not wish to be concerned with direct fundraising, but are prepared to lend their name, open doors and give advice, to be patrons of the foundation.

- The possibility of inviting major benefactors and supporters (including past board members) also to be patrons (too often former board members are forgotten, and their continuing potential as enthusiastic advocates ignored).

- To give a clear message about the organisation's seriousness of intent and the importance attached to income generation activities of all types.

- To involve as volunteers people whose first responsibility, and interest, is to develop relationships with a view to raising money.

Resources and staff would in practice be shared with the main organisation. The independence of the legally separate charity must, however, be maintained in order to preserve its status.

Of course, some of these advantages can accrue without establishing a separate organisation. There is sometimes a risk with this approach: that the values and identity of the fundraising will diverge from those of the institution itself, and that the artistic leadership and senior management will not be engaged in the process, including donor cultivation and management. It is therefore essential to establish trust, and the mechanisms to minimise this risk and coordinate the messages. In practice, this can be managed through the development director, who could become the director or chief executive of the foundation. In any case, it is crucial that new foundation members are in practice, if not formally, approved by the main board, since they are ambassadors for the organisation and must share its values. Members should include "catalysts" or ideas people as well as givers, getters and networkers. It must be seen as, and made to be, prestigious and enjoyable to be involved as a foundation member.

It is also essential to ensure that foundation members are kept informed and involved as to the main mission of the organisation.

One organisation which has followed this model is the Royal Botanic Gardens, Kew. The Foundation and Friends of the Royal Botanic Gardens, Kew, was formally set up in 1995. Following the appointment of Lucy Blythe as chief executive (also known as director of development) in 2002, the remit of the board was clarified to focus on fundraising; it approves the strategy and sets the policies for fundraising management to follow. The chairman and director of Kew are ex officio members of the foundation board, and two other members from the main Kew board also serve on the foundation board.

When people are being recruited the role is spelt out in detail, both for the foundation board as a whole and for the individual members. It is recognised that it is essential that everyone understands that the discussion is a two-way exploration, and that the person being invited must have a face-saving way of declining the opportunity. Equally, having understood and accepted the expectations, the new trustee will be much more likely to embrace the role, and therefore to be successful and happy in it.

As Lucy Blythe says, for this to work there must be a high level of trust and real engagement between both boards and between senior staff in the main organisation and the foundation. The main board must respect the legal independence of the foundation board and the chief executive's legal responsibility to this separate board. Equally, it is the foundation chief executive's responsibility to ensure that the board is fully informed of the needs and priorities of the main organisation, ensuring that the foundation continues to work in alignment and support of its mission and priorities.

In Kew's case, the foundation's efforts in 2005 and 2006 have generated millions, enabling the completion of a new laboratory building – the Wolfson Wing – the architecture award-winning Davies Alpine House, and the Sackler Crossing designed by John Pawson. In addition, among many other conservation and science projects, it has enabled continuing progress on the Millennium Seed Bank Project, which will have saved 10% of the world's flora by 2010 – the largest conservation partnership ever, giving conservationists the raw material with which to restore habitats, and scientists, botanists, nutritionists and other experts precious time to discover the potential of many plants to feed, house and heal future generations.

Capital campaigns, feasibility studies and business plans

This book is not about planning capital campaigns, but since they may be an element in the aspirations of many organisations in the arts and heritage sector, we include a short section on thinking about and preparing for major appeals. Many of the success factors highlighted in Chapter Ten apply particularly to capital campaigns. They are not repeated here. But those campaigns that fail, or need to be re-launched, or raise too little, almost always do so because of lack of planning and investment. Here as much as anywhere in development, *"if you fail to prepare you prepare to fail"*.

And it is particularly relevant to individual giving because the individual donor is nearly always the largest source of private sector support for capital projects.

The planning process is often called the feasibility study. Some organisations just embark on the fundraising process without any market-testing. This is understandable, if regrettable, where there are severe cash-flow problems.

However, such organisations risk appearing naïve and unprepared if they have not done their homework, and do not present their case for support in a form that addresses concerns or highlights attributes to which the donor would respond. It could be argued that it would be a false economy. One rejected application could outweigh the savings. Furthermore, the most common mistake is to ask for too little, too soon. Donors may become "inoculated" against making a bigger gift.

It is much harder to go back to someone who has given £5,000 in response to a very general broadcast appeal and point out that what you were hoping for was more like £100,000, than it is to develop a very focused micro-strategy for that potential major donor. So it is vitally important to understand how best to present a compelling case for support, and how to identify those who might respond to it.

The question of whether a target is realistic depends not only on the conditions in today's market, but also on how that market perceives the organisation or project. It also depends on the nature and amount of the investment trustees are willing to make.

Stage one
Most feasibility studies involve three phases. The first is preparing an initial "case for support" – the presentation of the project, why it matters, what makes it compelling, the track record and impact of the organisation, and the vision and leadership.

It is about shaping the key messages about the organisation, through internal research and discussions which will culminate in a first definition of the case for support. This will provide the basis for testing the marketplace.

Stage two

The second stage is about analysing the potential for success and exploring how the organisation is perceived in the marketplace. In order to design a campaign strategy which is right for the specific project, it is advisable to conduct some market/potential donor research on the basis of the initial case for support. This process will help refine the case statement and give a clear indication of the likely level of interest and support from different constituencies – major donors, trusts and foundations, companies, audiences and visitors. It is usually based on interviews with a selection of people from these different groups. Identification of interviewees and framing an agenda for the discussion is a crucial task.

Using consultants

Organisations usually engage external consultants for this process, even if there is a strong internal development function, as a consultant should bring an understanding of what else is going on in the marketplace, suggest potential interviewees and, most importantly, obtain full and frank feedback about how the organisation and its plans are perceived. An independent and honest analysis may not always be welcome, but it is much better to be in a position to address perceived weaknesses before the fundraising proper starts, and most experienced individual and institutional donors respect the fact that such a process is an appropriate investment in preparing the ground for a capital campaign. Lists of consultants may be obtained from Arts & Business and the Institute of Fundraising. The best approach is probably to ask other organisations who have faced similar challenges for their recommendations.

Information to frame the discussions will be drawn from current materials and the business plan, plus any recent applications to individual and institutional funders. While not being a detailed "shopping list" at this stage, the organisation should be able to highlight a range of achievements and potential funding opportunities and the impact any investment would have. The outcome of this review stage will highlight the strengths and opportunities in the particular case, and the analysis should report, among other things, on how the organisation and its plans are viewed in the marketplace, what perceptions and misconceptions may have to be addressed in the way the case is presented, and any PR messages about the organisation, likely levels of gifts, and the preferred focus of support by different types of donor. In essence, these findings should provide the strategic framework and the key objectives, including target, for the fundraising.

This stage also includes an initial analysis of the organisational capacity, with particular reference to the success factors for a campaign, such as volunteer leadership, membership commitment, a culture of nurturing donors and investment in development. Investment is discussed in more detail later in this chapter.

It is also essential to show how much being sought, and why, and what difference it will make to the organisation. This is particularly important in the case of an endowment (see later in this chapter for more on endowments.)

These elements are usually best drawn from a business plan. The purpose of a business plan is three-fold:

❍ It allows the organisation to describe its core functions and to examine the income generated, and the expenditure incurred, in carrying out those functions.
❍ It provides a mechanism by which to test and demonstrate the way in which capital investment can support and enhance those activities.
❍ It provides a document to support any applications to major funders, whether private or public sector. By undertaking the discipline of articulating the functions and their financial implications, strategic decisions are made and clarified and a context provided for a common and shared forward plan to be developed.

Obviously, business plans can take various forms, and reflect the nature and maturity of the organisation. What they should all contain is a detailed explanation of the "economics" of the institution, including:

❍ A reasoned and robust financial analysis which clearly sets out costs and revenues in all the relevant areas across the campaign for, say, five years.
❍ The assumptions made in reaching those figures, and evidence (from market research or past experience) to support them.
❍ The risks associated with each of the key areas of activity.
❍ The impact on the plans if the income in any of the key areas is significantly less, or the costs significantly more, than planned, and the probability of that happening.

It must show that the organisation will be financially sustainable after the capital project is completed.

A business plan should be regarded as the basis of an eventual prospectus, underpinning the case, and prepared with a view to encouraging investors or partners. And genuine partners are what the organisation should be seeking: those who are enthused with the mission and plans of the organisation, are confident that those running it are going about it in the right way, and who want to be part of it, not just for the immediate development activities, but for the long-term. All of this is about clarifying the mission and activities of the organisation.

Stage three
Stage three is about the development of the framework for a strategy, the likely level, source and timing of gifts, the resources necessary to invest in a campaign,

and the volunteer leadership structure, role and membership profile needed to run the development activities and relate to the key donor constituencies.

It would also include the basis for the development of a communications strategy. See page 166 for more details on that issue.

It could be important to review and evaluate the design and impact of other fundraising initiatives that may have recently happened or be happening at the same time, and which may target similar or overlapping audiences.

Because it is a highly competitive marketplace, and because of the nature of the target group, it is essential that a first-class professional development operation, including detailed prospect research, is in place to support the volunteer leadership. For more on research see page 226. The research for *Why Rich People Give*, and that of others, clearly shows that it is in the management of relationships with major donors that many UK institutions fail.

This whole process means that it will take many months and probably a year or more to put the building blocks in place for a major campaign, and then a period of prospect research, identification and cultivation before significant gifts materialise. At this stage many implementation strategies are distorted because, notwithstanding what research may tell them, people focus on those they perceive as having a major capacity to give, without considering the likelihood that they will give significantly to this particular campaign.

As we have seen, this depends on many factors. Too many, perhaps particularly volunteer leaders, are seduced by the prospect of "landing" a donor who "might" give £1 million, even if there is only a 5% probability of this, and neglect the target with an 80% chance of giving £100,000. An approach to categorising prospects in a way which takes into account the probability that they will support a specific appeal is given under Endowments in Additional Information.

To summarise, the stages of a feasibility study, (some of which may overlap) are:

- Development of the case for support.
- Testing the marketplace.
- Development of a business plan demonstrating the long-term sustainability of the organisation beyond the completion of the capital project.
- Developing organisational capacity, including volunteer leadership, print materials and staff resources.
- Development of the campaign strategy.
- Prospect research, categorisation and involvement.

Communications

This is based on a discussion with Damien Whitmore, who is has been director of public affairs at the V&A since January 2002 and was communications director at Tate from 1992-2001.

A core characteristic of successful fundraising is that it is underpinned by the communication of a clear vision. There needs to be one "big idea" which describes simply and compellingly the unique and excellent nature of the organisation and its work. People give because they are inspired by the reputation and brand; they want to be associated with the values represented by the organisation. So any communications strategy is about telling a concise and persuasive story of success, and carving out a distinctive role from others who may be perceived to be operating in a similar space.

Looked at in this way, communications brings together PR, marketing and fundraising. Indeed, PR can in some cases be a service department for fundraising. The aim of the strategy is to create an environment in which the fundraising can flourish, because people are confident that the institution has a clear vision, knows how to implement it, is led by a highly committed and competent board and is directed by outstanding artistic and professional management. It's all about creating the right climate for success.

Communications is not about changing the "facts on the ground", but presenting them in the best possible light and being prepared for the scrutiny which will ensue. The first step in any PR strategy is often to change the way an organisation thinks about itself, before you can start to change the way the outside world perceives it.

For example, if there has been confusion about goals, or lack of confidence in the leadership, it is crucial to address the underlying problems. People will not be fooled if the messages do not reflect the underlying reality.

The sense of vision has to permeate the organisation, with every person involved being positive about its strategic direction and proud to be associated with it. The buzz of excitement and confidence required in external messages must be embedded internally first. There has to be complete corporate engagement and buy-in – from the board, artists, senior management and all staff – about the goals and priorities of the institution, the implementation processes and the key messages and values.

Once these are agreed they can then be broadcast. There are several possible media but usually the press is key. And it is not a question of a one-off press release. Tate, knowing that it was about to embark on a major fundraising challenge of raising over

£70 million from the private sector for Tate Modern (as it became), knew that a long-term press strategy was necessary and that it wanted to convey several key ideas about the project, including that it was:
- World-class.
- Millennial.
- Essential for London as a world city.
- Building on the great and growing interest in modern art.
- Popular, not elitist.

A number of different ways of spreading these messages were developed, making full use of the high-profile exhibitions programme including partnerships with retail, broadcasting and local organisations; for example, London taxi drivers were invited to see the new museum before it opened. The Turner Prize also provided an opportunity to get modern and contemporary art on the wider cultural agenda and to promote wider interest in it. Of course, there were hitches along the way, and the impact of placing Tate Britain temporarily in the shadows caused some problems, but essentially it was about promoting unity of purpose, progress and success.

To support this approach there was a team of nearly a dozen, strong commitment and engagement from the director, and involvement with a leading external consultant. The responsibilities included information leaflets, event management, presentation of the interpretation of the art, and consistent identity and branding. And now that the galleries are open to the public the success story continues, carefully managed, and preparing the ground for the next major campaign, announced in July 2006.

Work at the V&A is also about growing internal understanding and commitment, improving the physical realities and the pleasure of the visitor experience, and very carefully defining the brand to reflect the fact that it is the world's leading museum of art and design.

Not everyone has or needs the resources of Tate or the V&A, but the principles of a good communications strategy are the same:
- There must be a clear vision, succinctly expressed and shared by all staff.
- There should be some aspect which differentiates the organisation or project from others, and makes it apparent why it matters.
- Reputation must be grounded in reality.
- There must be shared internal confidence, pride and commitment.
- Marketing, PR and fundraising messages must be consistent and mutually reinforcing.

If the messages are not managed by the organisation, they will be managed by someone else!

Community foundations

Community foundations are charitable trusts that support local community causes. Their role is to encourage donors to become involved, manage donor funds and build endowment, as well as to make grants to charities and community groups, linking local donors with local needs. Created by and for local people, they help donors to express their long-term interest in an area and its needs. Community foundations have been active in the UK since the 1980s and a rapidly growing network of approximately 60 foundations is now established across the country. About 90% of the UK population has access to a community foundation.

Community foundations understand their local communities. They identify local needs and mobilise local resources to meet all areas of community need – arts and culture, education, environment, health, community development, children and young people, older people. Their expertise in local grant-making means that many different kinds of donors use them to manage their funds – individuals, companies, charitable trusts and government agencies. Community foundations specialise in personalised giving – donors can specify how, where and over what period of time their gift is spent. Donors can make gifts of cash, shares, trusts, bequests or property. Community foundations offer simple, professional, tax-effective ways to give. As well as managing funds, they build endowment – investing for the future. They pool donations in multi-purpose funds and use the income to make grants.

Too few arts and heritage organisations consider community foundations as potential partners, or explore ways in which community and arts or heritage needs can by mutually met. A case study featured on the Community Foundation Network website (www.communityfoundations.org.uk) concerns Birmingham's Nechells Baths. When it closed in 1995 the building soon became a dilapidated eyesore. Realising its potential, The Birmingham Foundation raised £3.7 million from European and other sources to restore the landmark building and convert it into an enterprise and community centre – combining physical with "people" regeneration. Due to open in 2007, the complex will provide a training centre, crèche, cybercafé and community meeting rooms. The local community has been involved at every stage, from initial planning to learning the traditional craft skills needed for the refurbishment process.

More information about this and many other case studies about community impact is featured on the website which also has donor stories and gives details of community foundations around the country.

We saw in Chapter Three that Trevor and Lyn Shears had been very much guided in the development of their giving by the director of the Community Foundation serving

Tyne & Wear and Northumberland, and it is instructive to look at the relationship with The Sage Gateshead from the perspective of the Community Foundation itself. For the story from the perspective of Trevor and Lyn Shears, see page 38.

CASE STUDY

Community Foundation serving Tyne & Wear and Northumberland and The Sage Gateshead

- Endowment £41m, incl. £11m to support The Sage Gateshead
- Grants last year £10m
- Staff 23
- About 50 individuals and families with funds at the Community Foundation
- Mainly funds social welfare and community causes but with an increasing interest in the arts

By George Hepburn, chief executive

Since it opened in December 2004, The Sage Gateshead has transformed the lives of people throughout the North of England and gained an international reputation for its musical performance and participation programme. Since then, there have been over 650 performances and more than 50,000 learning and participation sessions, encompassing all kinds of music including classical, jazz, popular, folk and world music. Undoubtedly, The Sage Gateshead has already made a very significant contribution to the regeneration of the area and provided a step-change in cultural provision in the North of England. Many of the activities are housed in a spectacular Norman Foster-designed building at the heart of the renaissance of Tyneside's waterfront on Gateshead Quays, but The Sage Gateshead's activities spread throughout the region.

At an early point in its development plans, The Sage Gateshead made a commitment to build an endowment that would support a wide range of artistic and educational activities. By this stage the Community Foundation serving Tyne & Wear and Northumberland, set up in 1988, was already well established, providing philanthropic services for a range of individual and corporate supporters. This led to an initial discussion about whether it was practical to build a substantial endowment managed by the Community Foundation.

The Community Foundation knew that the opportunity to become involved with The Sage Gateshead would be welcomed by many of its supporters and it wanted to support a cultural project that would also make a major contribution to the regeneration of the region.

The Community Foundation team, working closely with the team developing the physical project, enabled a number of private donors to share the vision of The Sage Gateshead through a series of cultivation events – including a superb evening hosted by The Duke of Northumberland at his London home. The guestlist included a number of donors with a background in individual and corporate philanthropy who were attracted by the opportunities at The Sage Gateshead to support the arts for the first time.

A number of these supporters contributed to the endowment fund and form part of a special group who are prominently honoured at The Sage Gateshead. The naming sponsorship is from The Sage Group plc which is based in Newcastle. Private donors include Joan and Margaret Halbert, The Barbour Trust and The Shears Foundation. The David Goldman programme supports a weekend school for outstanding young musicians and The Shears Foundation has named the largest music studio in memory of the late Katharine Shears. Other endowment supporters include the Garfield Weston Foundation and Northern Rock Foundation.

Responsibility for building the endowment was transferred to the staff in the development team at The Sage Gateshead. Their efforts were acknowledged when the director of marketing and development, Lucy Bird, was awarded the Garrett Award for outstanding professional achievement to the arts.

The Community Foundation remains a strong supporter and friend and continues to manage the endowment fund to ensure that the gifts will be invested for long-term benefit to promote music in the region. To date, the total raised is over £11 million.

Although endowments for performing or visual arts are commonplace in the US, this has been a ground-breaking initiative in the UK. It could be a model for the encouragement of major private donations to the arts, particularly for endowment, in other cases.

The above shows the powerful impact of the Community Foundation in the North East. This is based on the combination of a very solid community feeling and the influence of a strong and committed director and support team. We also note from donor research the interest in making a difference, in seeing how the money is spent, in supporting talented or disadvantaged individuals and the powerful influence of being part of a community or network.

There are opportunities to attract donors who feel a connection to the local community when:

○ They can see how their money is spent.
○ It can be used to embellish local facilities.
○ Relatively small sums can make a major difference.
○ There can be rewarding relationships with beneficiaries, other donors and the staff of the community foundation.
○ There is minimal administrative bureaucracy.

However, we noted in *Why Rich People Give* that expressions of feelings of community are minimal in London, although there are a few commitments to individual boroughs.

Corporate culture of engagement

A frequent theme throughout this book is that "development" is not something that the development office does, but something it facilitates or indeed orchestrates. For fundraising from individuals to succeed the entire organisation has to be committed to development. It is a major feature of the story of the enhancement of fundraising in the Royal Opera House.

CASE STUDY

Royal Opera House

● **Opera**
● **London**
● **Total income: £75m**
● **Development income: £16m**

By Ruth Jarratt, development director 2001-2005

In 1999 the Royal Opera House (ROH) re-opened following a successful capital campaign to completely rebuild the theatre. All sources of support had been tapped during the campaign and there was understandably a level of donor fatigue amongst the core supporters.

As part of establishing a "new order" at the Royal Opera House (ROH), the governance was streamlined. The two fundraising arms – the Royal Opera House Trust and the Friends of Covent Garden – were merged and the

Photo: Rob Moore

resulting body, the Royal Opera House Foundation, was put under the direct authority of the ROH board.

With the arrival of its new chief executive Tony Hall, the ROH embarked on another major development programme, focusing on opening up the building and the art to a much wider audience. While there was some scope to finance this ambition through greater cost control and expansion of commercial activity, the challenge fell mainly to the development operation.

I took up my post as development director in May 2001 just weeks after Tony Hall arrived. The remit was to transform the development operation from a capital to a revenue focus and to double the revenue income in three years.

The first job was to build a strong development staff team, merging the previously separate Trust and Friends groups and recruiting new talent. However, after years on the front pages of daily newspapers for the wrong reasons, the ROH was not seen as the place to add to your CV. Moreover, in order to deliver the required growth, there was little or no money to spend on additional headcount.

The solution to the first problem was to recruit a couple of fundraisers who had great potential, and to give them their heads. We solved the second by restructuring the department so that there was a minimum of administrative staff and a maximum number of front-line fundraisers. The development of a culture built on mutual respect, trust and teamwork, with a healthy dose of friendly competition, went a long way to break down the sub-divisions which had existed between the old Trust and Friends teams.

Devolved responsibility and an atmosphere of creativity meant that individual staff members could develop their own distinctive fundraising style, experiment with new fundraising schemes, and develop relationships with their own donors. The emphasis on playing as a team meant that they would know when to "pass the ball" in order to get the best result. In addition, regular reports to and meetings with the chief executive meant that team members received regular recognition at the highest level for their achievements. Within a short period, the department's reputation turned full circle and the ROH became a sought-after employer for fundraisers within, and beyond, the arts sector.

As part of the Trust-Friends merger, a development committee was formed comprising eight new and existing board members, later augmented by additional non-board members. As a new grouping within the ROH, they needed time to find their feet as a group and to establish an effective way of working individually in generating new leads. The arrangement that proved successful was for each member of the committee to be allocated a staff member as their team-mate and gentle pusher. This model ensured in-depth support to the individual throughout the whole process of identifying a prospect, developing the relationship, securing the gift, delivering a programme of involvement and so building the relationship into the future. This model not only produced results, but also provided a vital growth opportunity to a broad group of key fundraising staff. It also enabled the ROH to match person to person and minimised disruption caused by any temporary or permanent staff changes.

Another vital ingredient was the new chief executive himself. Tony had little or no previous experience of fundraising, but was more than willing to learn. He did this by making himself available for any and all activities involving existing and potential donors. Being a natural enthusiast, he had no trouble carrying people with him. He also had a quality essential after all the years of financial insecurity at the ROH – he inspired trust and confidence.

The final element was getting the artists and the wider ROH staff group involved in the development process. Interestingly, it was not lack of willingness on their part which was the obstacle, but an understandable reluctance on the part of some staff to place too many demands on their hardworking and much admired colleagues.

A breakthrough event was a breakfast to which I invited members of the Royal Ballet and members of my own team. The dancers expressed positive enthusiasm for supporting the development effort and a number who had danced with North American companies shared details of fundraising schemes they had been involved in.

Subsequently, a series of fundraisers went on tour with the Royal Ballet, accompanying groups of tour sponsors, and this further built familiarity and trust between the two groups. Similar collaborations followed with the Royal Opera and other performing groups and with the craft departments. Excellent working relationships with senior artistic managers and effective communications within the development team ensured that no single artist or group of artists received too many requests to support the fundraising operation.

The results speak for themselves:

- At the end of four years (if not the three intended) we had doubled the fundraising income and funded a number of projects which were key to transforming the image of the ROH from one of elitism and exclusivity to one of openness and inclusion. And the income continues to grow.
- The proportion of annual development income generated by development committee members from their own gifts, their companies or their introductions, is now running at over 25% annually.
- The ROH development team is acknowledged as one of best in the country.

I have often thought that a good title for a book on fundraising would be Faith, Hope and Charity. "Faith" because one has to believe in the innate generosity of supporters and the essential worth of one's cause. "Hope" because one can't hurry the process of building relationships, of nurturing trust, passion and commitment. And "charity" because that act of giving lies at the centre of fundraising, philanthropy, call it what you will.

As this book goes to press, a wonderful gift has just been promised by a donor whose passion for the ROH has been nurtured by a fundraising team member over the last five years. This reminded me once again of the importance of patience in the whole process. So, for those of you with a more mathematical than theological bent, I offer the following equation as a pretty accurate recipe for successful fundraising: **passion** (theirs) + **patience** (ours) = **pounds**.

From chief executive to dancers, to wigmakers and caterers, there should be an understanding of the role of the development team, and how the involvement of the artistic team and senior management not only supports "development" as an abstract concept, but enables them to achieve their goals in a very practical way.

It is about developing a culture of asking, where this means engaging in nurturing relationships. It can be a slow process, particularly if there is lack of leadership from the board and senior management. But in any case it is worth the development director and team taking time to develop the internal contacts and trust which lead to shared success. An example is cited by Lucy Blythe when she was director of development at the V&A (Victoria & Albert Museum in London). Having cultivated relationships with a number of curators, she was asked to help when one was approached by a donor to discuss giving a collection of objects to the museum. The curator was very keen, but was aware that the gift would cause problems, as the donor wanted the collection to be displayed. This meant funding – in very short supply at the time – would be needed for conservation, cataloguing, display and maintenance.

The issue was discussed and it led to the development of an informal policy on the acceptance of a collection which requires a minimum cash donation to secure its protection and preservation. (There is a separate topic section on gifts in kind – see page 204.) As the curator was also uncomfortable in raising the question of money, the discussion with the donor was led by the director of development, who could bring in the curator on matters of content and conservation of the objects.

This partnership between the curator (who had the subject expertise) and the development director (who could discuss money) led to the negotiation of a six-figure cash donation in addition to the collection. The relationship was led by the key curator who became close to the donor. It wasn't always easy but it worked with the support of the development director and the design of the Deed of Gift to ensure clarity on the nature of the gift and what the institution would be able to deliver. This was particularly pleasing as the donor had had difficult times with previous beneficiaries and the curator really made him feel part of the family. It is understood that the donor and his wife talk about the pleasure of the relationship, and that they have since pledged annual support and a bequest in due course.

From the point of view of the V&A development office, it was a slow process of building trust based on actual experience of working in partnership. The curators who worked with development and succeeded, not only gained resources for their collections, but confidence in dealing with donors, which came in part because they could count on development staff to deal with financial issues, leaving curators to play to their strengths. Their best contribution is to share their expertise and passion with a fellow enthusiast. In due course other curators saw that the original curator had a purchase fund and that participation in donor cultivation and stewardship is a form of enlightened self-interest. There was also real pleasure and fulfilment in a relationship with knowledgeable collectors.

We have also seen the importance of the involvement of performers in the description of the Chair Patrons' scheme at the Orchestra of the Age of Enlightenment, described in Chapter Four. Another organisation that involves artists in developing relationships is the Royal Shakespeare Company.

CASE STUDY

Royal Shakespeare Company

- **Theatre**
- **Midlands, North East and London**
- **Total income: £32m**
- **Development income: £3m, plus a major capital campaign**

By Kirstin Irvine, head of development (revenue), RSC

One of the core principles of the Royal Shakespeare Company (RSC) is "Ensemble", the belief in collective theatre making. Throughout the RSC's history we have seen that a team of artists working together on a repertoire over a sustained period can achieve more than actors collaborating on a single project. In fact, a rolling ensemble allows the Company to retain its most successful repertoire from season to season, creating more time for training, research and development. This ensemble approach provides audiences with new levels of clarity in the work, deepening their experiences as artists push their own boundaries.

The principles of "Ensemble" filter through into all aspects of the RSC, increasingly playing a role in the Company's efforts to raise private support. The development office pursues a strategy that properly involves supporters and offers commercial organisations an experience that goes beyond the productions on the stage.

The development office could not make this happen without the commitment of the RSC's artists, who regularly engage with supporters post-performance or in workshops, with the understanding that they can provide first-hand feedback on how valuable their private support is and the difference it makes to the Company. Supporters tend to observe or participate in activities that have directly benefited from their patronage or sponsorship. Members of the RSC Actors' Circle (giving in excess of £10,000 per annum) receive invitations to events where they can witness or participate in a voice workshop, fight training or the creation of a stage costume. In turn, as new artists are introduced to the ensemble they become part of this "family", gaining an understanding of just how important funding is and the part they can play in ensuring the ongoing success of the RSC.

Photo: RSC/Ellie Kurttz

Richard Cordery, a member of the RSC acting company, demonstrates this:

"The RSC is one of the only organisations that offers artists, writers, actors and stage practitioners a dedicated and collective approach to theatre-making. This goes beyond the rehearsal room and stage. After many years of working in the Company I have often been involved with events, some open for the public and others dedicated to private supporters, to demonstrate that without an audience, individual donors and companies, we could not achieve what we are doing today and what we hope to accomplish in the future. It is fundamental that as a company, all working together on and off the stage, we engage, communicate with and thank the audiences which allow us to continue our work. It is also valuable and a privilege for the actors, like myself, to meet with supporters who provide instant feedback on our work and ask important questions about methodology and process. It can, in fact, have an impact on the way we see our role developing over the course of a run. Whether you are a veteran or newcomer, the principles of ensemble are the foundations of our success."

But there are still organisations which get it seriously wrong.

How not to do it

Mr Bridge had been a Friend of a performing arts organisation for 40 years, since the mid-1960s, and since their marriage in the mid-1970s he and his wife attended many performances every year, usually buying good if not the most expensive seats. They have also regularly attended performances at other venues in other cities putting on the same art form, and Mrs Bridge has been very involved in a volunteer capacity. They had also contributed at higher levels of donation to other companies, but not to this one. Mr and Mrs Bridge are not very wealthy but have good incomes, a nice house in the town and no children.

Recently, the venue put on a rarely performed piece, with an excellent cast and a leading director with a particular reputation in that repertoire. To ensure good seats on a day that suited them, Mr and Mrs Bridge booked best seats at £75 when the Friends booking opened, well in advance of the performance dates. About three weeks before the first night they received a letter from the marketing department offering them best seats at £50 each.

Mrs Bridge rang the marketing department and after persisting finally got through the phone system to a real person. She explained that they already had tickets for the show and asked if she could have a "credit" of £50 (£25 for each ticket) towards their next ticket purchase. The marketing person (Mark) explained that this would not be possible: she should regard it in the same light as if she had taken a charter flight to Tenerife. People often found that the person in the next seat had paid less than they had, especially if they bought their tickets through a bucket shop, and it was the luck of the draw for the different airline customers. Taken aback, Mrs Bridge asked again whether she could have a credit, pointing out that this response was a real disincentive to purchase tickets in advance in the future, that the venue had had their money for some months, and that they could and should have checked to see whether those on the mailing list had already bought tickets. This produced the response that *"I told them that they should de-duplicate the list, but they decided not to bother"*.

Embarrassed by this confession, since it revealed that someone in the organisation had actively decided that it didn't matter if some people were upset by the approach, Mark promised to see what he could do. Mrs Bridge was pleased to be called back the same day. The bad news was that there was no way that a credit could be given for tickets already bought. The good news was that it was within Mark's authority to offer them vouchers for a glass of champagne each in the interval. Recognising that Mark had probably done his best she accepted the suggestion. A voucher offering two glasses of champagne at any bar in the house arrived in the post the next day.

Mr and Mrs Bridge attended the performance, forbearing to ask what the people in the surrounding seats had paid for their tickets! They were seated on an aisle so at the interval reached the champagne bar near the head of the queue and presented their voucher. The bar staff refused to accept it. As the queue built up behind them the barman suggested they should try other bars in the building. Mr and Mrs Bridge stood their ground. Eventually with very ill grace, and only because the queue was getting restless, the barman served them the champagne. Various friends of the Bridges who also attended the venue regularly watched this extended transaction with amusement and amazement.

What went wrong?

- ○ The development office was not tracking loyal supporters who were very regular attenders, especially those whom wealth screening would show might be in a position to leave a legacy.
- ○ Even if they had, in this case the marketing department had no understanding of the ways in which long-term supporters see their relationship with the organisation, and why those people love the art form.
- ○ The voucher system had not been fully explained to the contract caterers, nor their part-time bar staff.

Data protection and major donors

By Lawrence Simanowitz, Bates, Wells and Braithwaite

As soon as a researcher starts to gather information about major donors they will almost certainly have to deal with data protection legislation, and in particular the Data Protection Act 1998 (the DPA). Any information about a living individual who can be identified must be handled in accordance with this legislation, with one helpful exception.

The exception for paper records
Before 2003, it was assumed that the DPA covered information held both on computer and in paper form. However, in December 2003 a court found that almost all manually held personal data is not covered by the Act. In other words, paper records do not need to comply with the DPA.

However, caution must still be exercised in the way paper records are used. A small sub-category of paper records do still have to comply with the DPA. This is where the paper is kept within a filing system that is "readily accessible" (i.e. highly organised). How well organised does it have to be?

The answer given by the Information Commissioner is that if someone who was not familiar with the filing system (for instance, a new temp) were to look for a specific piece of information, and could almost instantly locate it, then that information would be "readily accessible". In these circumstances, information, even if held on paper only, would have to be handled in compliance with the DPA.

Beware, too, that this court decision surprised many lawyers and it is possible that in a future case a court may rule differently. At that point, all of those paper records which had been outside of the DPA may again fall back within it.

The principles of data protection

The DPA sets out eight data protection principles and all information gathered on major donors should comply with these. The principles require that records are kept accurate and up-to-date and not held longer any than necessary. They also require that information is kept sufficiently secure – files should not be accessible without appropriate safeguards. These might include restrictions on who is entitled to access files, password access to computer records, and restrictions on the way in which information is disposed of or taken out of the workplace.

Providing fair information

Underlying the DPA is the intention that information about people should only be used in a way that is fair. The starting point is that individuals must be told at the time (or very soon after) information is obtained, the name and address of the organisation responsible for collecting the information and what it is being used for. These are known as the "Fair Information" requirements. They can be problematic for profile researchers who do not want to contact an individual until they have compiled sufficient information about them to make the right approach.

The Institute of Fundraising's (IoF) code of conduct on data protection suggests that individuals need only be supplied with this Fair Information at the time that they are first approached. In other words, they do not need to be contacted simply to tell them that their information is being held. The code does not say whether this view is strictly compliant with the law. It also rightly recommends a more cautious way of handling "sensitive" personal data (see below). An alternative to the IoF approach is to let major donors know, in general terms, the way in which information will be used. For instance, a potential major donor could be sent a charity's normal direct mail shot containing the charity's data protection statement. This statement should always supply recipients with the Fair Information. It is probably safe to assume that more specific details (and in particular that a profile is being developed) do not need to be given.

Consent....and a useful alternative

The Fair Information requirements under which an individual is informed about the use of data should not be confused with the separate obligation to obtain consent from that individual. Consent can be obtained in general terms. For instance, consent to provide information about an organisation's activities will usually be sufficient to gather information so that later an approach can be made giving details about an organisation's activities and asking for a donation. A key point, however, is that often, where data is not sensitive, consent is not necessary to use data (unless it is being used for direct marketing via email and other electronic media).

The DPA provides for a number of alternatives to obtaining consent for use of non-sensitive personal data. The most helpful alternative is that information can be used when it is in the legitimate interests of the user, provided the use does not lead to an unwarranted infringement of the individual's rights. Merely compiling a major donor profile and then using that to make an approach is unlikely to infringe that donor's rights. In such circumstances consent is, therefore, not required.

Sensitive personal data

The DPA contains extra restrictions in relation to "sensitive personal data". This is information about an individual's physical or mental health, political opinions and trade union affiliation, sex life, criminal record and allegations, religious beliefs and ethnic or racial origin. It can be helpful to note that financial information is not regarded as "sensitive".

With sensitive personal data, explicit consent to use the information must be obtained. There are not many useful alternatives to this. However, one option applies where the individual has already put the information in the public domain. This would include, for instance, accurate newspaper interviews. It would also include *Who's Who* entries as these are normally checked and approved by the individual. Another alternative applies to most charities where the information relates to an individual with whom the charity has an ongoing relationship, provided they do not share the information with a third party without consent.

Other key requirements

Charities should also beware of the following:

○ Consent must be obtained to transfer information to most countries outside the European Union unless there is an agreement in place with the recipient in a mandatory standard form.

○ Individuals have the right to request written particulars describing the information held on them, and are entitled to a copy of that information. There are a few limited exceptions to this. The main one applies in most, but not all, cases where the information requested also reveals information about another person who has been asked, and has refused, to approve of the disclosure. Of course, if the information is only held in a paper record then, as discussed above, it is less likely an individual will be entitled to exercise this right.

Cautionary tales from the world of data

By David Dixon

Cultural organisations, and particularly performing arts organisations, gather large amounts of data on their customers. This can be extraordinarily valuable for fundraising (see Chapter Seven for the value of databases), but only if managed effectively. The Phone Room (TPR) has come across many interesting, frustrating and downright comical examples of data hell. Amongst the best (or worst) are:

○ The regional organisation which engaged TPR to do 2,000 telephone contacts and when asked for the data supplied sticky labels.
○ The national organisation which could not work its own database and then found that the software supplier couldn't get the standard report to run either. After three months the entire database of 1.4 million records arrived with a request that we sort it out for them. We then discovered all but 200,000 were unusable (for any purpose) due to poor database management of various kinds.
○ The marketing department which refused to allow the fundraising team access to the organisation's ticketing database on the grounds that it was "marketing data".
○ The large touring venue which refused to allow a touring company access to data on people who had booked for the company's performances at the venue on the basis that the data "belongs" to the venue (it doesn't!).
○ Several organisations which (accidentally) included board members, the home addresses of local press contacts, very major donors, senior managers of sponsor companies and, in one case, members of the orchestra who had recently been made redundant.
○ And then there were the organisations which inadvertently supplied very interesting names indeed, such as Sven Goran Eriksson (he made a gift!), Helena Bonham Carter (she didn't) and Gerry Robinson when he was head of Arts Council England (he complained). Best of all was the large London organisation which supplied the data record of Her Majesty the Queen, Buckingham Palace, London, complete with phone number. We spotted that one before calling it!

Endowments

It is gradually but increasingly being recognised, by public and private sector alike, that the pressures of raising core costs, the volatility of earned income streams and the changing fashions in public funding do not favour long-term stability. When people look with envy at the US, they can sometimes forget the significant impact of the cushion provided by endowments. Although there has been a long tradition, particularly at older universities and conservatoires in the UK, of endowing teaching and research posts, and bursaries and scholarships, and while some hospitals benefit from long-standing endowment funds, the vast majority of institutions in the education, health and cultural sectors are significantly under-funded compared with their US counterparts.

This is because a significant level of US operating income is derived from endowment. In addition, restricted funding for research and scholarships entices leaders in their field and enables US teaching institutions to offer "needs-blind" places to promising students. There are several reasons for the levels of endowments in the US, many linked to different attitudes to the role of the state in funding such institutions, a different tax regime and attitudes of public funders.

Indeed, at one stage in the UK there was an apparent disincentive for publicly-funded cultural organisations to admit to having reserves of any kind; such prudent planning might be used as evidence that their need for public funding had diminished, often by the amount of income likely to be generated by the reserves! People were effectively penalised for thinking strategically, and adopted various devices, including establishing separate trusts, to disguise such foresight.

It is not only public funders who, seeing that an organisation has reserves, may divert resources elsewhere. Some private donors, trusts and foundations may also direct their donations away from institutions whose reserves show that they do not "need" the gift.

But ideas are developing. The Arts Council England appears to have had a change of heart. For example, at the turn of the millennium it recognised that the challenge for The Wordsworth Trust in raising its annual core funding revenue requirements from the private sector was disproportionate to its size and core mission, and that it would benefit significantly from an endowment which would provide a substantial contribution to its operating expenditure needs. In the context of a stabilisation review and investment in business planning and organisational capacity development, including in a professional development team, it made a commitment of £500,000 as a contribution to a planned £6 million endowment. This is believed to be the first "challenge" grant of this type. As we see from the case study at the end of this topic, the experience in raising the funds was mixed, for a number of reasons. Some were specific to the Wordsworth Trust but some undoubtedly are generic.

These essentially relate to the lack of experience in making the case for endowment, what are thought to be traditionally low rates of return reported by trustees of endowment funds, and fear that it will be harder to generate revenue on an annual basis.

Where an appeal for endowment might be incorporated into a capital campaign ("for every £1 you give, 30p will be put into a permanent fund to secure the future of this gallery/performing arts programme/conservation for this library"), it has been very difficult for consultants to make the case for developing a strategy on this basis. People fear that the campaign will take longer (it might), and cost more (it probably will, if the appeal target is significantly greater). Fundraising is hard enough without adding to the difficulties by trying to "educate" donors about endowment.

However, as we have noted, things are changing. It is probably fair to say that the way is being led, albeit slowly, by the higher education sector. The task force report on *Increasing Voluntary Giving to Higher Education*, published in May 2004 (see Bibliography on page 298), highlighted the need for changes in attitudes within the institutions themselves, and also for changes in the tax system, all of which were supported by the findings of *Why Rich People Give* and endorsed by this author.

In particular, the writers advocate the introduction into the UK of US-style planned giving vehicles, which are used to donate significant amounts to endowments in the US. They provide donors with tax relief and regular income in their lifetime whilst guaranteeing the institution capital on the death of the donor. With widespread ownership of assets among people coming up to retirement, and a historically low number of children to whom to leave this wealth, the time is right to develop such schemes in the UK. A growing coalition of charities, institutions, umbrella bodies and individual professional advisers is working to introduce "lifetime legacies"into the UK. It has not yet managed to persuade the Treasury of their desirability. More advocates would help! There is further information from the Charity Tax Reform Group (see website information) and a paper on lifetime legacies in Additional Information.

One tactic to consider is not to use the term "endowment" at all; terms such as "The Young Musicians' Bursary Fund" or "The Conservation Reserve" or "The Contemporary Art Exhibition Fund" could be used instead.

To supplement these comments here is the perspective of someone engaged in advising on fundraising for the cultural sector on both sides of the Atlantic.

A case for strategic endowment building in UK cultural institutions

By William J. Conner, managing director, Brakeley

The idea that cultural institutions should build meaningful endowments is not yet widely accepted in the UK. Endowment building is most often a board-led activity as it is about the long-term sustainability of an organisation's vision and mission. It is difficult enough to get boards to take responsibility for providing for cultural institutions' revenue funding needs, let alone to get them to enthuse about raising millions for long-term endowment growth. The American model of high-level board-driven fundraising is still uncomfortable and only a few organisations enjoy the benefit of community leaders taking responsibility for high-level giving and fundraising. To date in the UK, this is most often seen in the context of a few major and very successful capital projects.

The key benefit of endowments is to be able to sustain the work of a cultural institution over a long period through the ups and downs of their normal three streams of revenue:

- Commercial and earned revenues.
- Sponsorship, philanthropic gifts and annual giving.
- Public sector support.

The type of endowments that have been created in UK cultural institutions to date (either from founding benefactors or from legacies) have, for the most part, been for the fundamental purposes of the institution, for acquisitions, or for regular programme delivery.

Current circumstances in funding for cultural organisations clearly presents a strong need to undertake a more strategic form of endowment fundraising to:

- Insure against ever-costlier refurbishment programmes and consequent recurrent fundraising campaigns.
- Address the long-term decline in public sector funding.
- Address the decreasing competitiveness of UK museums in the acquisition marketplace.
- Supplement revenue shortfalls from earlier endowments.
- Create a stronger sense of long-term ownership of an institution by its trustees, donors and users.

The need to make the case for bigger endowments exists, and the lost opportunity cost if it is not done could have a long-term negative impact on the sector.

The American model

The Boston Symphony Orchestra is often cited as a model among American symphony orchestras for having built an endowment that produces about 20% of its operating budget (a $15 million contribution to the annual turnover). American cultural institutions have for some time been making the case for endowments.

○ Members of the top group of US symphony orchestras (25 orchestras as defined by the American Symphony Orchestra League) have built average endowments of over three times their operating budgets.
○ Members of the top group of opera companies (12 companies defined by Opera America) have average endowments a bit larger than their operating budgets.
○ Ten leading museums can claim an average endowment of over seven times their operating budgets.

Unlike their UK counterparts, most US-based cultural institutions do not enjoy much public sector support which makes the endowments all the more important. (In comparison, the best-endowed American private schools, universities and colleges broadly receive between 10% and 20% of operating revenues from endowments.)

How endowment funding works

Before beginning endowment fundraising, organisations should decide on a long-term endowment return rate. This rate, usually between 4% and 5%, is the amount that the organisation feels able to take from the endowment fund each year without diminishing its real value. Organisations also set endowment ambitions by reference to the size of the operating budget.

One way of quantifying an endowment ambition is to understand that every multiple of annual turnover in an endowment produces 5% of total revenues assuming a 5% pay-out on an endowment. For example, if you have an annual turnover of £5 million and you are operating on a breakeven basis, and you have a £5 million endowment paying you 5% of its value, then you have a £250,000 revenue stream coming from the endowment. This represents 5% of your turnover.

UK endowment return rates are generally less aggressive than in the US, because finance and investment committees tend to be more conservative. So the UK argument for endowments is harder to make, given that the immediate benefit of an endowment gift is relatively small. In the 1980s, Oxford University established a rate of return of 4.25%, whereas the university and cultural institution norm in the US is 5%. Some Oxbridge Colleges deliver only 3.25%

Frequently, donors and foundation trustees say they can invest their money more effectively and for much higher returns elsewhere, and so they would rather keep the capital and just give the money when it is needed to the institution. The response to such an objection should be that endowments are about providing organisations with an ability to plan for the long term with a secure income stream, and ensuring its independence from the influence of specific funders, whether public or private.

The way forward for the UK cultural sector

As the anticipated generational transfer of wealth from the baby-boom generation gains momentum, there will be many opportunities for cultural institutions to strengthen their case to receive some of this wealth, either through current giving or through legacies.

The pressures to be more innovative, to reach broader audiences live and through electronic media, to invest in new initiatives, and to supplement music and art programmes in primary and secondary educational institutions will grow.

Public funding in the UK is often said to be on the decline (although in some parts of the cultural sector this is not actually the case, at least not yet), so the urgency to replace secure public funding is likely to grow. Public funding has, to some degree, allowed British cultural institutions to take more programmatic risks than their American counterparts. Creating endowments may prove to be the alternative solution to risk management and programme innovation if public funding continues to decline as a proportion of overall funding.

The general wealth of the cultural sector is not to be found in its fund balances. It is in the pockets of its loyal patrons. In August 2006, *The Times* reported that the Edinburgh International Festival had received a significant and surprise legacy from a loyal patron which will endow its future activities. A job well done from the point of view of stewarding a good relationship with a loyal supporter. But we are left asking the question as to what might have been possible in terms of current annual giving, and current endowment building, if a more strategic relationship had been built with that donor during her lifetime. How many more patrons exist who could do something similar if they were only asked?

UK cultural sector organisations will be able to secure their global position as innovative leaders and programmatic risk-takers only so long as they grow the wealth needed to sustain their excellence and invest in talent and future audiences. Making the case for endowment, getting the sustained attention of boards of trustees to support this, and finding more champions to set examples are the tasks ahead. George Hume, the new president of San Francisco Opera, has publicly announced that during his presidency he intends to create an endowment that will generate 20% of the company's income, up from its current 5%. Who in the UK is likely to follow that example?

CASE STUDY

The Wordsworth Trust

- **Visual arts; academic study; contemporary poetry; heritage**
- **North West**
- **Total income: £1.6m**
- **Development income: £467,000**

By Michael McGregor, director of development

Background

The Wordsworth Trust was founded in 1891 as a living memorial to the life and poetry of William Wordsworth and his contemporaries. It is one of the world's leading centres for the study of Romanticism, an international cultural movement whose impact is still felt very much today. Its work embraces education, conservation, exhibitions, publications, conferences and contemporary arts.

In September 2000, the Wordsworth Trust was admitted to the stabilisation programme of Arts Council England, which recognised that it was a fundamentally sound organisation in need of support. What the Arts Council saw immediately was that the annual struggle to raise £250,000 to keep its programmes going was unsustainable in the long term, as it left the Trust vulnerable to environmental factors – a point proved by the foot and mouth epidemic of 2001. As a result of the stabilisation programme, the Trust undertook a corporate governance review and produced a five-year business and strategic development plan, with three clear objectives:

- O To rehouse the Trust's Designated Collection in a purpose-built centre – the Jerwood Centre – on its site in Town End, Grasmere.
- O To create an endowment – the Wordsworth Trust Development Fund – to secure the Trust's award-winning programmes.
- O To underwrite the Trust's core activities while it raised the endowment.

To complete these objectives, the Trust needed to raise over £11 million. Recognising that the director and trustees alone could not achieve such a challenging target, the Trust created a development office. The fundraising team (comprising four people) was supported by a fundraising consultant, who was instrumental in devising the endowment fundraising strategy and advised on the progress of the endowment campaign.

The Jerwood Centre

Since 2003 it has raised more than £8 million towards its target. This includes fully funding the Jerwood Centre and raising more than £2 million to underwrite its arts, education and conservation programmes. However, endowment fundraising has been less successful, with only a third of the target figure achieved to date.

Analysis of the endowment campaign

At this point, in the fifth year of the endowment campaign, it is possible to make a number of observations on the Trust's experience to date. Overall, with reference to the "seven stages of cultivation"[7] model, the Trust has been strong in the identification, research and planning stages, but weaker in the involvement and asking stages. The reasons for this are discussed later in this study.

The strategy was based on securing a small number of five, six and seven-figure gifts from high net worth individuals and grant-making trusts. In reality, more than 90% of gifts to date have been for less than £50,000, and on average the Trust has received less than 10% of its original gift estimate from each donor. Surprisingly, three-quarters of funds raised have come from the public sector. The Trust has received a disappointing response from grant-making trusts and from individuals, whose apparent reluctance to make endowment gifts could be attributed to a number of factors, including resistance to the principle of endowment (particularly from trusts and foundations), the prevailing economic climate (a decline in stock market values in the early stages of the campaign, coupled with low interest rates), and the lack of a clear return on investment (compared with capital projects).

However, perceived resistance to endowment does not tell the whole story. The profile and scale of operation of the Wordsworth Trust has also been a factor. It is likely that, for a number of donors, the Trust was not prominent

7. *A structured approach to donor cultivation developed by Henry Drucker and others, used by many campaigns. One approach is in Additional Information.*

enough in its thinking about charitable giving to the arts. Nor did they perceive it as a "large gift organisation", especially when compared to some of the major national institutions they already supported.

It is also true that it did not successfully close negotiations with enough of its key prospects within the timescale of the original fundraising strategy. There are a number of reasons for this:

○ The original cashflow was, on reflection, too optimistic, although it did anticipate the cultivation of prospects beginning earlier than was eventually the case. It may also have been that certain prospects were "talked up" to an unrealistic level of expectation before the cultivation process began.

○ The location of the Trust, in the heart of the Lake District, is its "unique selling point", but being 300 miles away from London has meant that few of its key prospects were willing to journey north.

○ The Trust tried to address this issue by hosting a number of cultivation events in London, but these failed to widen the potential donor base or attract enough "big hitters". This was partly due to the proliferation of events in the capital, but also reflected the Trust's difficulties in replenishing the prospect list and creating cultivation events that were sufficiently distinctive and exclusive.

○ Recognising that London-based prospects were not going to deliver at anywhere near the level it had originally anticipated, the Trust turned its attention to potential donors on its own doorstep. It has had some success here, but so far no-one has demonstrated the capacity to give substantial sums, although a number have joined the Patrons Scheme (£500 per annum).

○ There are, at any given moment, a number of competing fundraising campaigns in the arts and heritage sector, including those run by high-profile national organisations based in London. It is also true that there is a relatively small pool of "usual suspects" being chased for support by these organisations.

○ The original fundraising strategy stressed the need for a strong volunteer leadership, and for the Trust to maximise its existing network of contacts. At the outset of the campaign, the Trust established a core group of individuals to act as a fundraising steering group. Trustees and fellows were encouraged to take an active role in the fundraising process. The Trust also had a number of those among its "nearest and dearest" who could play an important advocacy role.

○ As the fundraising campaign progressed, it became clear that the steering group, while having some strength in both cultural and corporate sector contacts, did not have sufficient strength in depth to enable the prospect list to be replenished with new high net worth individuals as others fell away.

○ With regard to the senior management, the fundraising strategy envisaged that the then director of the Trust, Dr Robert Woof, would commit 50% of his time to fundraising for the endowment, based upon his outstanding network of contacts. Sadly, Dr Woof died in November 2005, after leading the Trust for more than 30 years.

Conclusion

The Trust has learned a number of important lessons from running an endowment fundraising campaign:

The importance of a strong volunteer leadership. A well-resourced development office is of limited use if you do not have volunteer leaders with access to those high net worth individuals with the capacity, propensity and interest in your work to make a major gift. Volunteer leaders should be willing and able to successfully close a negotiation, and prepared themselves to give (significantly), as well as to get. Above all, they should be willing to make you their fundraising priority. Periodic changes in the volunteer leadership may be necessary for longer campaigns, in order to refresh and expand the prospect list.

The need for persistence. The old fundraising adage – "no" means "not yet" – still holds true. Cultivation of high net worth individuals is a lengthy process, and some negotiations have foundered because the ask has been made too soon rather than too late. In this respect it is important for the fundraising team to maintain the long view when there is the inevitable pressure for instant results. However, it is also important to be realistic about your prospect list. Valuable time and energy can be wasted in the vain pursuit of prospects about whom an unrealistic level of expectation has been created.

Be focused, but be flexible. A major gift endowment campaign requires a high degree of focus from the whole organisation, not just the fundraising team. In the experience of the Wordsworth Trust, it is easy to be sidetracked by more immediate and tangible funding imperatives, which displace energy and dissipate momentum. However, flexibility is also important. A positive spin-off from some of its negotiations has been that, in lieu of endowment gifts, it has secured a number of one-off and recurring capital and revenue grants. Having a portfolio of funding needs means that you can respond to individual preferences and priorities.

Presentation is crucial. With hindsight, it would have been better at the outset to link the endowment to specific projects or programmes, rather than making a more general pitch based on organisational sustainability. Going forward, the Trust's plan is to refocus the endowment to link it to planned major capital developments. It is hoped that this integrated approach will make endowment a more attractive proposition to funders, particularly those that respond favourably to "bricks and mortar" appeals.

Events

The purpose of all events put on by cultural institutions should include some elements of thanking and cultivation. Cultivation may include encouraging current supporters to increase their level of giving, and inviting new donors to experience and learn something of the passion, creativity, innovation and development of artistic talent which underpins their mission.

Events are not only about fundraising
Many cultural organisations incorporate special events of one kind or another within their portfolio of development activities. Events present an opportunity to draw in people who might not otherwise come and allow board members and other volunteer leaders to invite potential donors. They may often have benefits related to the core mission, such as providing a showcase for young artists at the start of their careers or supplying a platform on which leading performers associated with the organisation may entertain. The Handel House, for example, believes that its development activities are about the development of the whole organisation, so that recitals for current and potential supporters are as much part of the overall mission of Handel House as other activities, because of the opportunities they provide to young artists focusing on the music of Handel and his contemporaries. Similarly, the readings of their own work by young poets are a core part of the mission of the Wordsworth Trust, but also provide an opportunity to cultivate and broaden local support.

Not all events are directed entirely or even mainly to fundraising: museums and art galleries usually have private views before special exhibitions open to the public. These provide an opportunity to give privileged access to existing donors but also to draw in influential potential supporters, the lenders of objects, politicians and civil servants, journalists and a wide network of opinion-formers and those with the capacity to be ambassadors for the institution.

Use your assets
Cultural organisations have a major asset not shared by those in other sectors: their core mission provides an opportunity to see the delivery of that mission at work. A performing arts organisation may set aside a block of tickets, and put together a package involving a pre-performance reception, complimentary programmes, interval

drinks, and a post-performance dinner attended by some of the artists. There may be a small raffle or auction. Hosted by the development office and ideally attended by at least one board member, such events piggy-back on the opera or play or concert or dance performance which is being put on.

The package may be offered at a premium price for existing supporters (for example the event at King Arthur for the US Friends of English National Opera (ENO), discussed later in this chapter). A similar arrangement may be structured to encourage board members and others to invite a group of potential supporters to enjoy a performance with additional privileges. The interval drinks or the post-performance supper provides an opportunity for the chair, another trustee or the artistic director to talk briefly about the exciting plans, the new season, the ways in which people may be involved.

For touring companies the challenges are more difficult, since they may have far less control over access to and the quality of the venue. But imaginative development directors can find a way to address this, for example, by persuading a local supporter to host an event. Welsh National Opera (WNO) has involved Jesus College for some years; it regularly provides the elegant venue and hospitality for drinks and supper surrounding WNO performances in Oxford[8].

Those not involved in the performing arts also have many opportunities to engage those who may have an interest in or even passion for their activity. A specialist lecture, a poetry reading, a private tour of an exhibition, a private visit with an expert guide to a beautiful house or garden, or an outstanding collection: all provide opportunities to enlarge the numbers of those who know about your work.

Crucial from the findings from *Why Rich People Give* is that people wish to be respected for the passion and knowledge which underpins their support, and this feeling is not only confined to the wealthy. People's thirst for knowledge and perhaps the desire for a glimpse behind the scenes are two strong motivators which can be satisfied by special events of various kinds.

And many events which draw in amateur practitioners can be the basis for developing new donors. Whether scratch Messiahs or marathon poetry readings, book festivals or film seasons, enthusiasts will emerge.

What makes them work?

Because the show, exhibition or performance may be happening anyway, trustees and others may think that something very special can be arranged at relatively little additional cost. Not counting staff time, this may be true – but nevertheless, all

8. See later in this chapter for a reference to the costing of tickets and hospitality for such events for touring companies.

require a significant amount of planning, attention to detail, impeccable organisation on the night, and prompt and focused follow-up. Many on the guest list will have lots of opportunities to be entertained, and will be used in their professional lives to highly competent administration. Things to bear in mind include:

○ Give people plenty of notice (several months ahead send a card asking people to keep the date).
○ Send the season's programme if you have one well in advance.
○ Always address people correctly and formally, and keep up the formality unless and until they ask you to adopt a more familiar form of address.
○ Note special dietary requirements so you do not have to ask them every time.
○ If there is a seating plan, double-check at the last minute to ensure that there are no gaps and key people are appropriately placed.
○ If there are badges, ensure that they are correct, and have spares available.
○ Ensure that all the "home team" is accurately briefed about the interests and support of all the current donors, and the concerns and planned "ask" for prospects.
○ If it is a fundraising event, have the basic follow-up packs already prepared to be sent within a week of the event and preferably sooner.
○ At a drinks event, where people move around, make sure that every donor and prospect is the responsibility of someone in the "home team".
○ If there is a timetable, make sure it is kept. People will have made arrangements on the basis on an event ending when it says so on the invitation.
○ The next day, debrief every member of the home team – whom did they talk to, what did they learn about their interest and concerns – and circulate this to the key people, along with any thank-you letters and other feedback.
○ Ensure that the covering letter to any follow-up proposal is personalised and appropriate for the donors and prospects, with a reference to their particular interests and opinions, and signed by their closest contact or the person looking after them on the night. This may not be the development director or head of individual giving.
○ Ensure those responsible for events understand why all this is important, have the authority and capacity to orchestrate the necessary internal collaboration, have excellent telephone manners, can write a clear letter explaining how things will work on the night, and have the necessary attention to detail.

The essential point about such activities is not only that they require investment to plan, organise and manage, but also to follow up. There have been too many events to which people came, had a wonderful time, wrote a pleasant thank-you letter and were never subsequently contacted. Board members and others congratulated themselves on a "successful" event but did not ask six months or a year later what the impact was. Among the various preparations there was no allocation of responsibilities among the "home team" for capturing the interests and preferences of prospects. No board member took responsibility for delivering a given number of new donors. There was no collection and collation of the key points of the various conversations. There was no request for a meeting, no letter offering a range of ways in which they might become involved, and certainly nothing as vulgar as asking for money. No strategy was developed on the basis of knowledge about specific individuals about how they might be drawn in further. Of course, people begin to think that there is such a thing as a free lunch – or free opera ticket or free private visit.

This is a particular risk with the visual arts, where pressure on numbers may not be so acute as, for example, in a theatre or concert hall. For regular events such as private views it is essential to review the guest list from time to time, and be confident that you know why every name on the list is there.

So far, we have been talking about events that in some way or another are an integral part of the mission of the organisation – an add-on to something that will be happening anyway, or an additional presentation of or access to an endeavour which is part of the standard portfolio of activities, such as a rehearsal, a special lecture, or a private recital. They may involve a small element of premium pricing, but can be managed within the resources of all but the smallest organisations.

There is also a very different type of event that requires far more investment and resources, is much higher risk, usually involves a large number of people to form a committee to sell tickets, and may produce very significant sums of money as well as raising the profile of the organisation concerned. It may be an opportunity to involve people from a social milieu beyond that usually reached by the organisation and may bring in six- and even seven-figure sums.

This is the gala ball, the glitzy first night, the annual summer party. For some organisations such events have become a regular part of their funding mix. The Almeida Theatre, for example, raised £120,000 in 2006 from its gala. Others may be embarking on such an activity for the first time. They would be well advised to take professional advice. We have drawn on the expertise of the leading company in this field, Act IV, for guidance.

Fundraising events – the dos and don'ts…

By Mary Morrison & Rebecca King Lassman, Act IV

Fundraising events are becoming an increasingly significant part of many arts organisations' development strategies. Events serve two main purposes:

○ To raise the profile of an arts organisation in order to facilitate other forms of fundraising, i.e. to make an organisation more attractive to funders.
○ To raise money and provide a vehicle through which to increase income from individual donors. (Fundraising events also allow access to different corporate budgets e.g. corporate/client entertaining.)

Making a name
A large scale or high profile event provides an ideal mechanism for raising awareness at a particular point in a fundraising campaign such as when a capital campaign is launched, or when the focus of a campaign shifts from "quiet" fundraising through traditional sources to aiming for large corporate donations, major gifts and individual giving schemes.

An event is an opportunity for the organisation to put across its message, both to those who attend and also to the wider public through word-of-mouth reporting of the event and press and media coverage.

It is often for this reason that arts organisations are so keen to attract a celebrity to such an event – two or three famous faces can attract photographers and newspapers (and, in many cases, television) to cover an event. Such coverage, while not necessarily supporting the artistic work of the organisation, raises its profile with the general public and potential supporters.

A relatively unknown arts organisation can be propelled into the limelight in this way and create a seemingly more stable platform for support. Think of the Serpentine Gallery, which pre-1993 was often referred to as "that little building in the middle of Hyde Park" and later became known as the Serpentine Gallery – where Princess Diana wore "that dress". One single photo opportunity created a lifetime of publicity and profile and made the task of fundraising across the board so much easier.

Raising money
It should be obvious that fundraisers need to budget properly to ensure the event really will make money. All costs need to be taken into account, including the hidden costs such as time spent by staff on an event, or – perhaps more importantly – money lost from other fundraising activity not taking place while staff time is diverted into the event (the "opportunity cost"). Fundraising events are very time-consuming and use valuable resources over a long period that might otherwise be employed in more certain ways of raising money, such as writing grant applications. Development departments are invariably overstretched and members sometimes do not have the skills or experience to run a successful event. Some arts organisations recognise this and bring in outside agencies to run fundraising events on their behalf.

Fundraising events should not be entered into lightly but, once decided upon, arts organisation should ensure that they are aware of the time it will take and clearly identify the aims and ambitions for undertaking the event.

Ticket prices should be decided so that ticket income yields real profit. VAT can only be recovered on fundraising events under certain circumstances, and then it must be charged (see Chapter Nine for a detailed explanation). Tickets must sell for more than the total cost of the event and not all may be sold. Fundraisers need to budget cautiously to ensure a profit and must include a contingency.

Ideally, a successful event will have at least a 3:1 income to cost ratio, although some events run at a lower ratio but can be more useful long-term and for donor cultivation.

It is essential to allow enough time to achieve all your ambitions and raise the projected income. We would advise no fewer than six months, and nine to 12 would be better. There are also certain "dead" months, namely July, August and December, where ticket sales are generally very slow.

Planning checklist
- What is the purpose of the event?
- How much is it trying to raise?
- What ticket price can the market bear?
- Is there an existing support base willing to pay the ticket price?
- If not, how can a group of people (committee) be brought together who will be able to reach the kind of guests who can pay?
- Can you get well-known performers to offer their services for free?
- What chance is there of raising sponsorship to cover the cost of the event – thereby making all ticket income net profit?
- Where will the event be held – at the organisation's own venue? Is it big enough and sufficiently well located?
- If it is not held at the arts organisation, how can the external venue be branded so that it represents the organisation and guests understand why they are there?
- Will there be a performance or just a party?
- How do you maximise PR from the event?
- Should there be additional fundraising activity over and above ticket sales, such as a raffle, auction, or games?
- What needs to be in place to make these activities successful?
- Is there sufficient time to organise a successful event and sell all the tickets?

Other important things to consider
How do you sell the idea of an event to your own team? Sometimes, staff in arts organisations do not like the idea of fundraising events as they are so

time-consuming and can impinge dramatically on the day-to-day running of the organisation. Some may consider them contrary to the overall ethos of an arts organisation as they can sometimes ignore issues of "access", education, innovation, creativity – the things many arts organisations are continually striving to embrace. By their nature, fundraising events are "exclusive" not inclusive, appealing to a very specific and tiny market who are often not the target market of the organisation.

Will staff be invited or will they have to work on the night? How will they be involved in the planning, lead-up, and at the event itself? Will their views be taken into consideration? The more they support the event, the more successful it is likely to be.

Events can be used as more than just a one-off night of fundraising by raising the public profile sufficiently to facilitate future fundraising efforts. A high profile makes it more attractive to a sponsor and encourages guests to become ongoing benefactors and supporters. It is also an argument to bring staff on board – the event will yield significant funds, not just on the night but on an ongoing, long-term basis.

The right kind of committee

The committee is perhaps the most important tool for a successful fundraising event. This group of people will work hard to ensure the event is a success and is very publicly associated with the event. The committee should help to secure sponsorship, auction/raffle items, in-kind support from suppliers and, perhaps most importantly, will sell the tickets.

For a committee to be successful there are two vital requirements: an inspiring and committed chair, and staff to service the committee efficiently, which can be at least one full-time job. Generally, the chair and members of a committee need a great deal of looking after, much "ego massaging" and hand-holding. A quick and efficient response to their requests is crucial. They may forget that there may be many other calls on employees' time and attention, and it is a good idea to appoint one person to liaise between the committee and the organisation.

It is also worth remembering that someone who joins an event committee might, in due course, become a high-level supporter of the organisation. This is a marvellous introduction to a potential new donor – they see how an organisation works and how their support is so vital.

Choosing the chair of a committee is perhaps the most important decision to be made. Choose someone who is prepared to work, and who is connected in some way to the organisation. They should be passionate about it and prepared to spread that passion around. Perhaps they should be a board member (who already has a sense of responsibility for the organisation) or a long-term supporter. The chair should be well connected and ideally well known (either publicly or at least within the field).

The other committee members should be equally committed to the organisation – though this is not always possible. Bringing in fresh people to a committee might provide new prospects for long-term supporters. Committee members should be aware of their role and a job description setting out exactly what is expected of them provides an excellent way of communicating that role. Some members will be invited to join for their name only (a high profile name on a committee will encourage people to buy tickets). Often these people will not be expected to work or sell tickets, and may not necessarily even buy a ticket for themselves. It should be made clear to committee members that they will be expected to buy their tickets (and this can be included in the job description) – complimentary tickets should be kept to a bare minimum. Each free ticket costs money and reduces the amount you can raise from sales.

Whether the committee should meet regularly or not often depends on how active the executive team is, or whether the committee is expected to do much of the work. It is generally beneficial to set up a manageable working group within the committee, so the full committee only meets perhaps at a launch of the committee and then at the event itself. The paradox is that whilst a committee is vital to the success of an event, it is also impossible to organise an event by committee. A careful balance therefore needs to be struck between giving these people the power to create a fantastic event and not having too many chefs.

Sponsorship
If the event can be sponsored, most ticket income will be profit and not just used to cover costs. This provides a certain security from the start and will ensure the event will be a success. Sponsorship is, however, notoriously difficult to obtain – and many events do go ahead without cash sponsorship (although many are clever with "in-kind" sponsors – wine, champagne, print and design). The process of finding a cash sponsor should begin at least one year in advance of an event.

Dare to be different
What makes one event different from any other? It pays to create a magnificent invitation: this is what will make people decide whether or not they want to buy tickets. What is on offer? Is it clear? Is it appealing? An event needs to have a USP – a Unique Sales Proposition. Many of the potential guests will get endless invitations through the post – what makes an event extra special?

Timing is all
Organisations are well advised to make sure the event does not clash with other major social, arts, charity or sporting events, or coincide with major religious festivals

or school holidays. The likelihood is that many of your potential guests will have school-age children.

Additional fundraising during the event

The decision to fundraise additionally on the night of an event should be considered very carefully. Often a great deal of time, effort and favours are used to put in place initiatives which may not yield significant income.

Ticket-buyers may feel they have made their donation to the charity by buying the tickets. However, many guests will have been invited by the host of their "table" and come to a gala expecting to spend money and support the arts organisation or charity. Various factors should be weighed up before beginning to work on additional income generation activities, in particular the appropriateness of the event, the make-up of the guests, or whether the fundraising activity will add to the enjoyment of the event.

Auctions

Auctions, for example, should always take place in a seated environment. An auctioneer can rarely gain sufficient attention from standing guests to conduct a successful auction. Only a small percentage of guests will actually bid, so if all are seated and quiet, those people will be seen and heard. Auction items should ideally be "experiences" or objects guests can't just go out and buy. Experiences for children tend to be particularly successful: work experience with a magazine, TV station, or a fashion designer; back-stage passes at concerts; a day in a recording studio with a producer; a visit to an artist's studio.

Art auctions are notoriously difficult. Artists are continually asked to donate works to auctions and really prefer not to do it. Charity auctions can have the reputation either for selling sub-standard works, or selling good works for a fraction of their market value. Perhaps the best way to conduct an art auction for charity is to ask dealers to reduce their commission, ensure artists receive a certain amount of money from the sale, and then collaborate with an auction house to provide its services free of charge.

Always make sure there are buyers in the room. It is best to try to pre-sell as many auction items as possible. The committee can help by calling friends and contacts prior to the event. The bidder does not even have to be there and can nominate a guest or the organiser to bid on their behalf.

Silent auctions

Silent auctions can be very effective given the right circumstances. New technology means guests can bid anonymously from their tables on handsets with smart cards (pre-programmed for each guest). The complete service is expensive, but guests seem to enjoy playing with the technology and the additional amount raised can more than cover the cost.

Raffles and prize draws
Activities where guests buy tickets, such as raffles and prize draws, give an opportunity for all guests to contribute additional funds on the night – even if they do not want, or can't afford, to bid in an auction.

Entertaining fundraising activities
There are all kinds of games and activities that can yield income and also warm up the atmosphere at the start of a fundraising event. Obviously, the activities need to be appropriate for the sort of guests attending.

Gift Aid
Gift Aid is a minefield in relation to events and is covered in detail in Chapter Nine.

Key points

Our experience highlights several important lessons:

- It is essential that the chair of the event committee has a knowledgeable interest in the organisation.
- Invitations to join a committee should be extended by the chair, but only after the executive team has, in agreement with the chair, decided how, when and whether invitations are issued.
- The nature of the event must be appropriate for the organisation.
- The ticket price must be appropriate for the nature of the supporter base.
- The details of any offer of "in-kind" support should be carefully checked before acceptance.
- Any arrangements and agreements must be confirmed in writing.
- There must be one ultimate point of responsibility which everyone understands and includes control over correspondence.

There may be pitfalls but there are also great benefits to be achieved if events are properly planned with sufficient investment. Events of this type are not suitable for everyone, and in particular there must be a really active well-networked committee and a captive market, usually drawn from the supporter base. Events do take a significant amount of time. Sometimes it may be possible to share an event (workload and proceeds) with another appropriate and complementary organisation.

For example, nearly 20 years ago this author, then employed by Save the Children (SCF), arranged a joint gala performance with English National Opera (ENO). Working closely with the then development director of ENO, the event was developed on the basis that:

○ ENO was about to launch a new production of Hansel and Gretel, with a very appropriate theme for Save the Children.
○ SCF had in-depth experience in event management and supporting high-level volunteer committees in London.
○ ENO had a built-in box office and ready-made event – a first night!
○ ENO had a database of ticket-buyers and supporters.
○ SCF had a number of high-level supporters in and around London, some of whom might like opera.

Arrangements were developed on the basis that the first night gala was attended by SCF's president HRH The Princess Royal, sponsored by Legal and General and supported by a ticket-selling committee drawn from ENO and SCF. The net proceeds were shared equally between the two organisations.

Friends or Donors?

By David Dixon

Many organisations choose to organise their individual giving programme in the form of a Friends scheme (or similar membership organisation). This can work well, since a Friends scheme usually has several levels, giving an obvious path for donation upgrades and such schemes are familiar to the public. In the case of organisations such as free-entry museums and galleries that do not capture customer data at the point of sale, an involvement scheme may be essential. But there are pitfalls.

Benefits
A Friends scheme implies giving benefits to the donors. Some schemes keep these to a bare minimum, such as newsletters, recognition in a donors' book, invitations to events. As soon as this basic level of benefit is exceeded, there are potential difficulties with Gift Aid and VAT since the membership fee is no longer a straight gift (which leads to some organisations splitting the fee into two parts, one part "buying" benefits and the other part a gift). Priority booking, invitations to exclusive events, complimentary tickets, specially produced mementos and some newsletters have all fallen foul of VAT inspectors (see Chapter Nine). Sometimes, many members of such schemes fail to use all, or sometimes any, of the benefits on offer, clearly implying that the benefits are not relevant for those members.

Joiners and non-joiners

A large performing arts company recently commissioned research amongst its regular bookers to find why more of them were not joining the Friends scheme. On the database their behaviour and personal profile (age, postcode, types of show attended etc.) looked very similar to the existing scheme members, so the company wanted to understand why they resisted concerted efforts to get them to join. The results of the research were clear – many people simply do not like the idea of 'joining' something and some said that Friends members would inevitably be staid and stuffy. The phrase "Friend of..." carries baggage.

Administration

A Friends scheme may require higher administrative costs than a donor programme, since it promises certain benefits to the member which must be delivered faithfully to keep the donors satisfied. Whilst a donor development programme (see Chapter Six) remains within the control of the organisation and can be managed flexibly, a Friends scheme is usually driven by commitments made in advance to the donors.

Marketing or fundraising?

A close examination of Friends schemes in the UK reveals that they are of several types, ranging from the purely philanthropic to the quasi-commercial. At one end of the spectrum are schemes where the word "Friend" is synonymous with "donor" – few or no benefits are offered – and at the other end are schemes where the "Friend" is simply buying ticket discounts or "free" entry. There is a world of difference between the two and the use of the same word "Friend" to describe both is quite misleading. An organisation running or starting a Friends scheme must be quite clear about its aims if it is to have any chance of achieving them. A good test of whether a Friends scheme is working for the organisation is to ask the head of fundraising or the head of marketing if they want the job of running the scheme – if neither does then there is clearly a problem!

External Friends organisations

There used to be a fashion for Friends schemes to be established as separate organisations in their own right, often with charitable status. This is strongly to be discouraged and, happily, has now generally fallen out of favour. The problem is that this approach creates a situation where some of the organisation's assets are legally controlled by volunteers who are not part of the organisation. The Friends Committee (or trustees) will raise and hold funds that rightfully belong to the organisation and often also control a database of members (donors) that cannot be accessed directly by the organisation. Although most Friends committees and their organisations work happily together, there are cases where the relationship has broken down, leaving the organisation's fundraising and marketing badly hampered.

Doing the sums on Friends schemes

Sadly, it is not unknown to find UK arts organisations that have loaded so many benefits into a scheme on which, after VAT is deducted, the organisation actually makes a loss! Yet these organisations still promote their Friends as a way of "supporting" the organisation. Perhaps more difficult to spot are schemes where the membership levels are set too low, or are too rigid, effectively encouraging people to give less than they might otherwise have done if asked for a straight donation.

The way to identify such a problem is to compare income per head of the Friends scheme with a straight donation scheme at a comparable organisation. Is the yield per member as much as the income per donor, after taking costs into account for both?

The bottom line

Organisations may have good reasons for running a Friends scheme, particularly if they offer free entry (see later in this chapter). However, from a strictly fundraising point of view the calculation is straightforward: will more people give more money as a result of the scheme than if the same people had been asked for a straightforward donation? Unless the answer is a clear yes, then the scheme has no fundraising merit.

Other schemes with audiences

Imaginative organisations have found other ways to involve audiences and draw them closer to the company. An example is Chickenshed which in 1990 set up its 100 Club scheme. The Clubs are essentially mechanisms, more often found in local churches and political parties, through which people pay cash in order to participate in a prize draw, in this case three times a year. Some winners make a gift of their prize and donate through other schemes. There are details of the Chickenshed scheme in Additional Information.

Gifts in kind and restricted gifts[9]

Are all gifts desirable?

For all non-profit organisations, not only in the cultural sector, sustainability means keeping the balance between mission, capacity, and capital. If one changes, the others must alter to maintain balance within the enterprise. Each gift to an organisation has an impact that exerts pressure on other parts, forcing the others to adjust to the impact of the first. Opposite is a familiar triangle where mission, capacity and capital exist in equilibrium.

9. Much of this section was inspired by an article by Clara Miller called Gift Horse or Trojan Horse in the US publication Non-Profit Quarterly of Spring 2004.

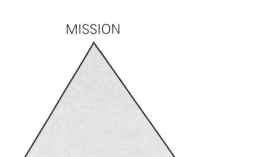

If any one side of the triangle changes, the other two must change. This takes place whether it is planned or not, whether the giver intends it or predicts it or not, and, above all, whether anyone wants it to happen or not. There are some perhaps self-evident implications.

○ The more restricted a gift, the lower the net positive financial impact, and therefore the higher the drain, most immediately on capacity and eventually on capital and mission.
○ The more illiquid a gift, the greater the call on the resources of the organisation.
○ The more liquid the gift of an asset, the more power senior management has to balance the points of the triangle while fulfilling the mission and also the wishes of the giver.
○ If a gift is both liquid and unrestricted (e.g. general operating support), it provides the greatest flexibility and presents the lowest risk and cost.

There follow fictional examples of how various gift types compare:

Restriction and liquidity

Gift type 1: Gift of a permanently restricted fixed asset[10]
The East Coast Trust is a small, locally-based, open-space preservation and campaigning organisation. It received a large bequest of coastal land. This will protect a key migratory bird habitat, and guide housing development away from valuable wetlands. For the East Coast Trust (ECT) this was a huge coup. The single full-time staff member immediately agreed to accept the very generous gift, embracing the donor in tears.

10. The National Trust has developed its own policy that addresses the need for an endowment to support the acquisition of land and buildings. Known as the Chorley Formula, after Lord Chorley who devised it, it calculates the costs of maintaining the property, estimates the likely income, calculates the funding gap and hence the level of endowment needed to secure the future of the estate. It is only in exceptional circumstances that the Trust agrees to take on a property without appropriate funding in perpetuity.

		CASH OR SECURITIES	RECEIVABLES	PROPERTY, PLANT, AND EQUIPMENT (PP&E)
Restriction Very high - - - - - - - - Low	PERMANENTLY RESTRICTED	**Gift type 2:** A gift, in perpetuity, of cash to endow a programme for elderly people at a regional museum		**Gift type 1:** A gift, in perpetuity, of coastal land for a bird sanctuary
	TEMPORARILY RESTRICTED		A five-year pledge to fund a new dance programme annually	A gift of a building for the purpose of housing interns and students on short courses
	UNRESTRICTED	**Gift type 3:** General operating support		A telephone system
		Liquidity: High		Low

The donor's conditions provide that the land must remain untouched, and may not be sold or developed. In other words, it is a permanently restricted fixed asset. It can't be sold or used for any typical money-raising purpose. Moreover, it will almost certainly require funds to care for and protect it.

Despite the positive impact of the gift, the trend is for expenses to increase faster than revenue. As the Trust is small, it saw no reason to build management capacity. After a time, despite the fact that a second full-timer had been hired (or possibly because of it), the increase in expenses outpaced the increase in grant revenue. As growth – in the form of increases in gross revenue – is proceeding, net revenue is declining, or not keeping pace with the size of the whole enterprise. The sharp increases in expenses are because the new land needed to be insured, and there were legal bills. Birdwatchers who were ECT's long-time supporters wanted access, but had nowhere to park, and there were no marked trails or disability access. The donor's heirs were unhappy and threatened a legal challenge which was a distraction and a cost.

Although ECT is looking for ways to develop earned revenue, and diversify fundraising, each new activity requires its own investment. It has neither a pool of wealthy prospects, nor a development department (to raise the money), nor experience operating a "social enterprise" business.

One unintended effect is that the gift induced ECT to take on a completely new business without any working capital, staffing, or for that matter, consciousness of a major change! While this alone would have been a colossal challenge, the effect on the existing environmental campaigning activity is daunting as well. Who would keep all that going?

The trustees were shocked by the tangible change in the balance sheet. With the gift of land, Property, Plant and Equipment (PP&E) grew from 20% to 99.9% of the balance sheet: the market value of the land was about £3 million.

Previously ECT had been essentially a campaigning and education organisation with one employee. By taking the gift, ECT became dominated by its property management business. And nobody – not the donor, nor the Director of ECT, nor the board – appeared to realise that the gift would require a major change (addition) to the core business of education and advocacy. Accordingly, neither the donors nor the recipient had prepared for the business implications of the huge change.

Scoring
Mission: A+ This is such a fantastic gift; its "mission impact" outweighs practical considerations at the outset.
Capacity: D- With this gift, the donor has placed his faith in an excellent, community-based organisation that has a dedicated, charismatic leader with no track record in management (beyond managing campaigning volunteers) and no formal knowledge of land management. The risk is that the gift will over-extend an excellent leader of a small organisation, and lose the very values and style that originally attracted the donor.
Capital: D- With this gift, ECT has experienced a major change of business with no provision for the working capital or a source of revenue for that business.

Gift type 2: A gift of permanently restricted cash (endowment) for a prescribed programme purpose (temporarily restricted)
The new education and project manager of the East Yorkshire Museum and Regional Archive was passionate about the importance of engaging local people in and around the town and encouraging them, particularly the growing number of retired people, to participate in the various activities and share their own experiences of local history. She was a skilled internal advocate and designed a local fundraising campaign with a focus on businesses, professional firms and wealthier individuals.

In spite of the difficulties she managed to persuade a local insurance company to put up a challenge grant, and in due course raised a £2 million education fund. The interest was to be used to develop education and outreach programmes for the active retired, including the provision of transport for those from local outlying areas.

The first year of the programme was very successful. The museum expanded its staff, trained them and volunteers, set up a newsletter and, in response to demand, developed a computer and internet training programme for inexperienced older users to facilitate participation and exchange of ideas. Demand took off. The museum developed an internet café for its programme participants in an underused space in the building. One of the new staff was very inspirational; word spread, and more time and more computers were needed to develop and support activities to maintain communications with the growing group of users who formed an informal club. People from all over the region were now part of the museum's "extended family" and popped into the internet café on a regular basis. But what was taking place on the balance sheet? What capitalisation questions were arising?

While certainly suited to the mission, the programme's popularity had exceeded all expectations. But to the disappointment of all, a bitter lesson proved once again to be true: runaway mission-related success for a non-profit organisation is almost always a qualified financial success, if not an outright disaster. In this case, the success was confined to one project area among many, and served a geographical area that extended far beyond the envisaged local boundaries. The museum needed to institute planning time and investment to catch up with this innovative programme.

In fact, the growth of the project, the demands of the continuing capital, capacity building, and programme needs pushed the museum to the limit. By 2009, the programme will have exhausted its own self-generated working capital and will be making disproportionate demands on the capacity of the organisation. Now there is intense competition for planning, fundraising and general leadership between this programme and the core activities, and other outreach projects such as those with young people. The director, who had seen herself as an intuitive entrepreneur and leader, now longs for a structured planning process.

Scoring
Mission: C+ This is a very positive project, but somewhat distorting for the museum because it focuses so strongly on only one part of its constituency (older people) and takes them from beyond the original geographic boundaries. The director is very supportive, and understands the potential of the project. After all, there will be a growing market of older users. But she can also see that this very successful scheme is very draining.

Capacity: C+ The museum has sound management, but it is very stretched, and focused on a traditional museum model. It has chosen to use cash to fund a complex fixed asset (computers), which depreciates rapidly, requires extensive management and training, and needs to be integrated into the rest of the operation via intensive and repetitive training, hiring of additional personnel, and more. Essentially, this fund incurs a substantial increase in core operating costs without any matching increase in income, support from the local authority or other sources of funding. It's probably well worth it, but the hardware itself is probably one-fourth to one-third of the total cost of the change in operations.

Capital: C If there is an overall scarcity of resources (especially cash) when an organisation makes a decision to use cash to purchase a fixed asset, it will reduce operating and financial flexibility to the extent it invests in that asset. The asset – in this case, rapidly depreciating technology – places the organisation into a cycle of replenishment (PCs need replacement every three years), training, and technology infrastructure, that goes far beyond anyone's plans. While it may be a wonderful move in project terms, to do it well involves a change to the capital structure, and its maintenance, that is completely new for the institution.

Gift type 3: Unrestricted cash

The Capability Brown Centre (CBC) is an organisation for teenage drug-users and drop-outs. It helps them to come off drugs and provides training in garden maintenance and design. It has a network of alliances with outstanding gardens that provide practical experience, and a very successful track record of teaching a skill and self-esteem, and encouraging a healthy lifestyle. Many go on to become creative and successful gardeners, while others return to the formal education system.

The CBC phone system used for referrals from drugs counsellors and contacts with the host gardens was increasingly unfit for purpose. It occurred to the director that one of the former alumni, although only 33, was now well established as a City trader, so the director called him to ask if he knew anyone who might be able to donate a phone system. The trader was a little puzzled that a charity with eight extensions would want an out-of-date phone system from a City trading company with 65 traders. Would they be able to make it work? Wouldn't it cost money to adapt? Why did the charity not buy the most appropriate current system and ask him for the money?

But the director of CBC was determined. He explained that CBC's trustees and funders did not want to see any overhead expenses in the accounts. If the system itself was donated, even if old-fashioned, it could be buried somewhere in the books. However, the office manager/head of operations was very irritated when she heard this, pointing out that it would have been much better to ask for cash – as the trader had suggested. It would be madness to have an outdated over-sized system that would have to be adapted (at a cost that might come to more than the cost of a new system), rather than buy a new one which fits the specification. The telephone system and ability to respond very quickly to calls for help is part of the core business. The director was persuaded and with some trepidation called the trader again.

Swallowing his pride he explained that he had made a mistake, that after all they would prefer the cash for a new system. The trader responded instantly and positively. He knew how important the phone system was, and the impact the organisation had had on his life. He asked how much the new system would cost and offered to bring in others to help fund it. This knowledgeable and potentially generous patron did not want to give a gift that created unnecessary cost. It is most commonly poor communication and lack of understanding on both sides of the transaction that leads to gifts that distort capital structure, change business focus, spur inappropriate growth and sap operating strength as growth occurs.

Scoring
Mission: A This equipment is aligned with the core business and mission. The centre knew what it needed and (eventually) clearly stated it.
Capacity: B+ A gift to purchase phone equipment probably merits some conversation about what kind is needed, the provision for training, the size, and other planning aspects. The office manager was clearly equal to the task of researching for the right fit.
Capital: A CBC identified an investor-donor with business brains who wanted to do the right thing for the organisation. And, with the input of the office manager who would actually be operating the system, the director pulled back from the destructive course. Further encouraged and nurtured, the generous trader may give cash in excess of the exact purchase price, which will get the state of the art, right-sized system in place and the staff trained.

What does this tell us?
Non-profit organisations exist to take on causes that for one reason or another are not commercially viable – their missions are the reason they stay in a commercially non-viable business.

The more restricted a gift, the easier, generally speaking, it is to raise. This includes legacies, as we see from the legacy programme of the National Trust, which very successfully focuses on restricted bequests. More experienced and confident recipients may negotiate with donors to invest sensibly. More experienced donors – like knowledgeable investors – may find people and projects they care about and have faith in, review the plans to see if they are reasonable and will have a real impact, and then back them with unrestricted cash, trusting management to pull it off.

The challenge is to plan for success. Too often, when they do succeed – and need to embrace the business realities of growth, replication, and change – many non-profit institutions fail to understand the degree of adaptation needed to make things work at a new level.

Programme growth often means business vulnerability, at least in the shorter term. Unfortunately, grant-makers and directors alike often anticipate that programme success – more coverage, more clients, etc – will mean financial success. It's almost always the opposite, and more grants are required before stability is achieved.

It's about being alert to new opportunities, but not thinking that the organisation necessarily has to run them. While the East Yorkshire Museum example describes an organisation with computer skills and market awareness, the reality of actually running a computer-based training and networking operation is completely new. The Education Fund created an opportunity to start such an activity, but the larger question is, what is the best way to embark on a new business activity? The museum may be in a good position to contract for, rather than immediately enter, the business. Outsourcing for non-core operational functions is a real possibility for many such business shifts until core capacity can be built internally (or forever). The key is to focus investment on nurturing the core competency of the organisation, not scaling a business that is dependent on technology where draws on capital will continue and not diminish with scale.

It is about looking very carefully at gifts, particularly gifts in-kind. What will it cost to make use of the gift, whether land, a collection or a phone system? Of course, it is understood that from a mission point of view there will be some opportunities that, however daunting the business consequences seem, should be grabbed nonetheless and sorted out later. And the corollary of this for donors is to encourage them to think that for an organisation with a strong track record, great leadership, reasonable financial statements, a compelling case statement that aligns with their own philanthropic intentions, mission, and growth objectives, the best possible backing is unrestricted operating support.

Investment to income ratios

A key element in success is the level of investment. In development this is directly linked to staff levels, not only in the development office. For example, a chief executive allocating time for major donors may need to delegate additional tasks. Every activity is expensive – implementation of a coherent communications strategy, donor development, excellent servicing, research, liaison between departments, attention to detail. But is it too expensive? What is the "right" level of investment?

Because of the need for first-class research and excellent support, and because it may take well over a year and sometimes more to engage with potential donors, investment in donor development is likely to be high. In some cases cost ratios reach 25% or more. In a 2003 Fundratios report (initiated by the Centre for Interfirm Comparison) there were 41 participants, including heritage organisations, with 15 in the major donor category. In 2003 major donor income per £1 invested was £3.55, a cost ratio of about 28%. This compares with income of £5.29 per £1 invested for all fundraising, or about 19%, and £4.89 in 2002, or about 20%.

A more recently published analysis[11] over three years shows a 300% increase in major donor fundraising over the past three years, although it still represents barely 2% of overall voluntary income. Legacy income accounts for over 40% of income, and committed giving (usually in the form of regular monthly contributions) provides 29% of non-legacy income. The report also shows that for every £1 invested in fundraising, the sector makes an average of £4.86. Another way of looking at it is to say that the cost to income ratio is about 20%. But this is for all forms of fundraising. As we know, legacy fundraising is very inexpensive (see article on legacies following this topic). Even if we assume that the cost to income ratio is as much as 5%, and remove 40% of the income and the associated costs from the total, we find that the cost of raising funds other than legacies is about 33%.

Too often, people, particularly trustees, express concern about levels of investment. But there is no evidence that levels up to 30% or more are resisted or resented by donors, and indeed, since so few cultural organisations publish their accounts for donors in the same way as charities engaged in social welfare provision, few people have any idea about the levels of fundraising investment for cultural organisations.

Let us consider some hypothetical cases.

Examples of cost ratios and net income for the organisation at different levels of investment					
Money raised £:	1,000,000	2,000,000	3,000,000	4,000,000	5,000,000
Costs £:	100,000	300,000	600,000	1,000,000	1,500,000
Ratio:	10%	15%	20%	25%	30%
Net revenue £:	900,000	1,700,000	2,400,000	3,000,000	3,500,000

11. Fundratios report, *commissioned by the Institute of Fundraising, published July 2006.*

This raises some questions:
- ○ Which organisation is serving its users best?
- ○ What is the best indicator of effectiveness?
- ○ Assuming the market is there, what investment level would most benefit the institution and its users?
- ○ How important is the net revenue result?
- ○ How important is the ratio of cost to income? To whom? Why? Evidence?

And, in casting an eye at what others are doing, are we comparing like with like? Some organisations may need to invest 30% to make £900,000 net because of the nature of their cause, the specific marketplace, their remote location, limited appeal and so on.

The stage of maturity of the development function varies from organisation to organisation. The Royal Academy of Arts, for example, has always had to depend on private sector funding and has a long-established development office. Others are relatively recent, or have relatively recently raised the level of investment in development. Because it takes time to build up the relationships that are at the heart of a development function, and because recruitment of donors is more expensive than retention, as we see in Chapter Seven, those who are now investing in, for example, higher-level giving schemes spend more than those who are maintaining them in a steady state.

And crucially, the more high-level volunteer peer-to-peer fundraising, the more this is based on a donor-get-donor approach, the more likely it is to bring substantial major gifts. This will in the longer term have a double positive impact on the ratio: a few very large gifts will add significantly to the income side of the equation, and while volunteer leaders need support, they are not paid staff.

In addition, organisations categorise income, and costs, in different ways. Some organisations report overall income for a different financial year to that of the development office. Some organisations have separate Friends operations, usually within the marketing department. Some report development income net into the overall accounts. Some put certain categories of income into one or more separate trusts or foundations, but the costs of raising that income may be part of the development office budget. Some organisations net off (some) event costs, and there are various ways in which the cost of entertaining donors and prospects is charged to the development office, particularly in the performing arts. This can range from full cost recovery to an allocation of complimentary tickets and programmes, and a discount on catering and other costs. Some development offices bear their own communications costs while others take no charge for corporate communications and PR.. .. and so on.

An organisation in a successful growth period may be investing significantly in a future income flow. Should we make a distinction between investing for the future and paying the cleaners or the phone bill? Different types of income are raised with a shorter or longer return on investment (from rattling a tin to developing long-term relationships that culminate in a legacy).

Some organisations raise money from the private sector outside the development budget, for example, for education or other special projects.

Well-established charities have a wide portfolio of income types, and the more "expensive" is balanced by other sources. For example, as we have noted, the cost-to-income ratio for legacies is low once a regular legacy income stream has been established. A cost ratio as low as 3% would not be unusual for a large national charity. If that element is taken out of major high-profile national organisations, voluntary income cost ratios can reach over 60%. For individuals it should be emphasised that most charities build a major donor scheme on the back of a significant level of awareness on the part of the donor, and through personal relationships.

It should also be noted that it is harder to raise un-earmarked income or core costs – and even more so for an organisation that is relatively unknown and receives little or no unsolicited income. This issue has been at the forefront of concern within the charity sector for some time. For many charities the main sources of unrestricted income has been interest on reserves and tax recovery on covenants and, now, Gift Aid. We looked at the question of endowments earlier in this chapter. Because of the desirability of this type of income, trustees may wish to consider approving a higher ratio of cost to income for sources of income that are unrestricted in their use.

And as we have seen, development is not something that only the development office does. Support for the chief executive spending time nurturing donors, or the cost of an effective communications strategy are seldom taken into account when assessing appropriate levels of investment.

And looking at the question in terms of income per development office employee brings the same constraints on comparing like with like: differences in art form, reputation, trustee involvement, database systems and income mix all have a significant impact.

What can be said is that the organisation in the left-hand column of the table on page 212, whose trustees may proudly boast that they are "only" spending 10% on their fundraising, could almost certainly do better in the long term for their institution and its users by investing more in development.

But apart from questions of cash flow, why does this investment ratio matter? Many charities use investment ratios in two ways:

a) **As a management tool.** Investment ratios are seen as a main indicator of effectiveness, against which issues of quality often have to fight hard. Sometimes it becomes a control mechanism of the board. Some organisations may insist that it serves the board well. But there are other ways in which issues relating to mission, strategy and quality could be brought into the picture, as well as taking account of the external environment. It is good practice to assess cost-effectiveness and control overheads, and, of course, improvement over the years in any one area (with no increased investment) should certainly be monitored. (Managing and monitoring the investment in fundraising is reviewed in detail in Chapter Seven.)

All fundraising and indeed other activities such as education and outreach interact with and complement each other. There may well be long-term fundraising opportunities arising out of the awareness and reputation of the education work. Such benefits are, in the short term at least, indirect and non-quantifiable.

b) **As a marketing tool**. Investment ratios are an indicator of effectiveness and efficiency, and said to be one of paramount importance to donors. But there is in fact little evidence of this (unless of course the situation is scandalous), and it certainly doesn't appear to be an issue for arts, heritage and education organisations.

In this context we see that in May 2006 it was reported that the Charity Commission censured the Diabetes Research & Wellness Foundation for spending 83% of its income on fundraising and was pleased to see it now halved at 43%. It noted:

a) The costs of fundraising are a legitimate matter of public interest. Trustees should ensure that these costs are shown properly in the accounts. They include publicity costs associated with fundraising or raising the profile of the charity. They do not include costs of purely educational material produced by the charity as a way of achieving its purposes.

b) The choice of fundraising methods is a matter for trustees to decide. However, charities need to be alert and sensitive to public opinion and criticism. Fundraising methods that meet with disapproval can damage the charity and reduce public confidence in the sector as a whole. It is therefore essential to spend time before undertaking any fundraising exercise to develop a strategy: some forms of fundraising can be costly and it is important to be sure that the costs will be justified in terms of a realistic return. The strategy will need to cover the following points:
  ○ The need for funds – are funds required for a special project or part of the charity's rolling programme of work? How much is needed? Would it be

> possible to collaborate with other charities operating in the same field to
> meet the need?
> ❍ *Possible sources of funding – for example, grants from local or central
>   government, grant-making charities or companies.*
> ❍ *The resources available to support fundraising – fundraising costs
>   money. Costs can range from producing appeal literature to employing a
>   professional fundraiser and organising fundraising events.*
> ❍ *The proportion of gross receipts that will be left after fundraising costs
>   have been met. We strongly recommend that trustees agree, in advance,
>   the likely proportion of the gross receipts that will be spent on the costs
>   of fund-raising. "*

Actual performance needs to be monitored against that target and the trustees
should satisfy themselves that the expenditure is justified.

So it is the responsibility of the board to set standards for and oversee the
investment in fundraising. But those standards and expectations should be based
on an informed assessment of the marketplace and what is appropriate for the
particular organisation at the current stage of its development activities. We have
seen that in the culture sector benchmarking is especially difficult, the more so
because there is so little information-sharing. Those who have contributed to this
study have helped significantly with this.

It is not unreasonable to expect a return of £400 for every £100 invested in individual
giving (and corporate support) after, say, a three-year period (or an investment ratio
of 25%), as a first attempt at planning for this element in an organisation's budget.
But each one must be prepared to review this regularly in the light of experience,
and to consider with which organisations it would be most appropriate to try to
exchange benchmarking information.

Legacy fundraising and the arts and heritage sector

By Richard Radcliffe, legacy fundraising consultant, Smee and Ford

Despite the fact that only a tiny percentage of people leave legacies to charities in
their Will, legacies still represent a huge source of income for charities. However, only
a small proportion go to arts and cultural organisations. In a typical year charities will
receive £1.6 billion from legacies. This is given by just 29,000 people – only 5.4% of
those who die, who each leave on average three legacies to charities in their Wills.
But out of these 85,000 legacies each year, only 600 are for the arts and heritage
sector (excluding The National Trust which gets over £40 million a year from legacies).

There are three reasons for this:
○ The arts sector often concentrates more on corporate sponsorship, grants from trusts and gifts from major donors. This support is often for specific short-term projects rather than long-term development and security.
○ Trustees hold back from investing in legacies because they do not know the possible return on investment (ROI) in terms of cash or when they will receive it.
○ Legacy fundraising is sometimes seen to be ambulance-chasing and focused on death.

These are not good excuses. Arts and cultural organisations should adjust their emphasis on the traditional sources of funding and include more focus on encouraging legacies. The financial argument for this is based on the return on investment (ROI). A long-term study carried out by the Centre for Interfirm Comparison, shows that typically every £1 invested in legacies will have a return of £48. Legacies almost always provide the best return on investment for any form of fundraising. It is less easy to say when that return on investment will come. People die on average 4.1 years after making their last Will, so in theory the ROI should really begin to show within three to four years; and it usually does.

Nor are legacies focused on death. Legacy giving is life-driven and only death-activated. For most people it is the only time they can afford to give a large sum. The gift is motivated by their desire to make a huge difference to the museum, gallery, or arts venue they love, but it costs them absolutely nothing.

However, it is true that most people leave legacies to "life-saving causes" – in other words charities such as Cancer Research UK, which received £128 million from legacies in 2005. Life-enhancing charities – such as museums, galleries, the performing arts etc – are often not seen as important in a Will. So the "case for support" or vision for the future has to be strong, tangible and inspirational. But there is one other interesting dimension.

The public, even loyal and generous Friends of arts organisations, do not think of arts organisations as charities, even though virtually all of them have charitable status. Generally, people leave legacies to charities; they do not think of leaving a legacy to an organisation from which they gain personal pleasure. They might if the branding environment reminded them that their favourite venue was a charity.

To gain a greater insight into attitudes to legacies for arts and cultural organisations, Arts Council England South East and Smee & Ford sponsored focus groups with trustees, volunteers and supporters of five arts organisations. The findings are similar to those of other focus groups carried out for leading national arts organisations.

Focus group outcomes

There were far more male supporters than in most focus groups for charities. Normally 65% of charity supporters are female. This is an important difference because almost 70% of legacies are from women, mainly because they live longer. If arts organisations have more men than women as members, they should be trying to meet their spouse or partner as well. A legacy is a private way of giving and the partner/spouse is very often consulted and the legacy often only comes to fruition after the second death. (This recommendation echoes the findings from *Why Rich People Give*, in which it was clear that most major giving decisions involve partners.)

Two other very noticeable differences applied to arts supporters:

○ Only 2% of those who attended had left legacies to the host organisations – this figure would normally be nearer 10% (or even higher) depending on who was on the focus group. And yet the average number of legators to charities in these groups was 34%, typical of mainstream charity focus groups. So they are legacy givers – just not to the arts.

○ The overall feelings were that arts organisations are "entertaining" rather than charitable. Typical quotes included:

"It never occurred to me that it was a charity" (the most common response by around 40% of all those attending the groups).

"It is an entertainment and therefore nobody worries about how it is funded."

"We pay to be entertained; it is as simple as that."

"I pay enough for the tickets. I don't want to be asked for more."

"I didn't realise it did anything charitable."

This begs the question, in terms of all fundraising activities, why does each arts organisation not promote itself more as "a charity relying on voluntary donations to develop our entertainment"?

Not a single trustee or staff member expresses an inspirational vision that legacies in the future would enable that organisation to develop. Contrast this with cancer research charities which have a clear vision: to rid the world of cancer, thereby saving lives of future generations of your family.

If arts organisations are not seen to be charities they will not gain support from the public – or if they do it will be a "token thank-you/repayment" rather than wanting "to make a real difference".

Brand strengths/weaknesses of focus group members

Regional arts festival The festival has a stunning reputation but is seen as a "local arts celebration" rather than a charity with ambitious plans for the future.

This is not surprising as the festival is an annual event and therefore not constantly in the minds of local residents. This is of great relevance in terms of a campaign encouraging legacies which needs to be regular throughout the year to be uppermost in people's minds when they are updating their Will. A typical festival also has multiple locations that may not build a tangible, loyal, relationship with a single venue.

Touring performing arts body in local communities This focus group member is an arts company that is very active with local elderly people and attracts considerable funds, including legacies, from individuals because they benefit from the work directly – it makes their lives better. Indeed, such an organisation may hold the greatest potential for legacies of the five organisations interviewed because its activities are so tangible and in such small communities. It also has local contacts to spread the word before and after each event. There might well be huge empathy for "people like me" (i.e. older and less mobile/independent) to benefit.

This kind of organisation typically also carries out educational activities that make it a popular cause with large fundraising potential, including legacies. Well-known city theatre supporters are truly passionate about the theatre which has had successful capital appeals in the past and members/Friends are used to being asked for money.

It has a very strong relationship development/fundraising programme and the director has been in place for many years and is viewed as a strong and good leader with excellent plans for the future. This theatre therefore has a strong fundraising culture where a "legacy ask" is totally natural. Indeed, it already has a number of legacy pledgers.

Modern art gallery This is a leading contemporary gallery and again passion ran high on its quality. But it is "newer" to individual fundraising and is still seen as a place where people love to go rather than as a charity. Somewhat surprisingly, annual visitors number around 100,000 and yet there is little investment made in cultivating these people into supporters. There is huge potential to develop individual fundraising, including legacies, with the first step being to register these visitors on a mailing list and ask them for money.

Theatre and music venue Once again, this focus group member reported a great deal of enthusiasm for the venue with some people coming to virtually every concert or show –annual attendance is over 150,000 from a mailing list of around 50,000. But there was only a "sketchy" knowledge of its charitable activities – in spite of the excellent information on the website and in programmes. Those attending the groups assumed that their tickets pay for everything. With more "needs" expressed it may be fairly easy to convert that enthusiasm into money. This might not necessarily be legacies as it is unlikely that the relatives of the current audiences will visit the venue (they live elsewhere) and therefore there is no generational continuity. The biggest opportunity for this venue is to promote the community education programme for young people and disabled people – an ideal activity for a legacy.

Communications – opportunities for fundraising generally
None of the organisations interviewed publish newsletters telling supporters "more than the programme". Supporters have no information on:
- The fact that the organisation is a charity.
- Community/education programmes.
- Ambitions for the future.
- A case for support, or case studies, that explain the difference made by voluntary donations.
- A vision for the future, the cost to fulfil that vision and how a legacy could help these dreams become reality.
- "Thank-yous" to individual donors
- Testimonials praising the activities of any of the organisations.

This is a huge missed opportunity.

Will-making and legacy outcomes from the focus groups
Around 73% of the individuals taking part had Wills – a typical/average response level. The number of people who had left legacies to charities was typical/average at 34%), although only one supporter had included a legacy to one of the five arts bodies.

When asked if a local "special offer" (i.e. £25 donation to the participating organisation from local solicitors) would make a difference, their reactions were mixed, ranging from suspicion to saying they would do it. Many were uncomfortable with the idea, even though some knew of the special deals offered through Cancer Research UK and a scheme called Will Aid.

It seemed that such an offer might only be acceptable if/when organisations have a strong fundraising culture. To offer Will writing deals, and possibly make people aware of the need for legacies, when supporters have never considered giving money, may at best seem surprising and at worst antagonise supporters.

The potential for increasing legacy income in the arts world
The overall outcome from the focus groups was very straightforward. You can only ask for a legacy if/when there is a fundraising culture.

Supporters need the following before considering becoming legacy prospects:
- An awareness of the fact that the organisation is charitable.
- An awareness of the need for funds and what those funds will achieve.

○ Knowledge of the future ambitions of the organisation.
○ A shopping list of ways they can give, including legacies.
○ Assurance that admin/support costs are "prudent".
○ Finally, it is worth alerting people to Inheritance Tax savings.

Legacies can be integrated into a general awareness campaign of the need for charitable funds. A legacy brochure is probably not needed, and might even be counter-productive if a strong fundraising culture has not yet been established.

The way forward
○ Promote legacy messages, focusing on future ambitions, in any existing communications but without being pushy. The tax benefits (Gift Aid and Inheritance Tax) are worth explaining regularly and could be done immediately.
○ Have posters in venues alerting audiences to the fact that the venue is run by a charity and that voluntary donations can help develop more projects/ programmes/ educational and community activities. They can also publicise how a gift in a Will can help to secure the future of the venue for future generations.
○ For organisations with an established fundraising culture, an annual review looking back at achievements and forward to future plans would be a good communication tool for legacy messages. In effect this replaces a legacy brochure that might be too direct.
○ For performing arts, an announcement made before and/or after each performance along the lines of: *"This venue is run by a charitable organisation and voluntary donations/membership etc will help us to expand our education/ community work as well as to secure our future and develop new programmes/ commission new work"*. The annual review could even be put on each seat. (Annual reviews are discussed and advocated as a medium of feedback and information generally in Chapter Four.)
○ Legacy messages, or perhaps initially, messages about the need for funds, could be integrated into all communications including stationery, tickets, receipts or even small cards at each purchase point in cafés, box offices etc.

Only organisations with a really strong fundraising culture (such as the well-known city theatre above) could or should even consider a direct mailshot asking for legacies. All direct mail can integrate an awareness of the need for legacies but a legacy letter should only come after years of supporter development.

Defining the legacy message
As legacies are particularly sensitive, any brochure or article on legacies should have an identified author telling a story in order to develop a trusting relationship with supporters. The most suitable candidates according to the focus groups are:
○ The chair (but might be seen to be able to afford to leave a legacy themselves).

○ An enthusiastic supporter of the organisation.
○ An enthusiastic volunteer.
○ An artist/performer.

Interestingly, none wanted a director of development or marketing person to make the ask. This is important and it is possible that the performers/artists or person fulfilling the charitable aims and objectives are the most credible and trustworthy.

The legacy story is straightforward and is usually summed up in what is called a legacy vision which needs to:
○ Detail the inspiring plans for the long-term future.
○ Explain the thinking behind the plans.
○ Show the funds are to be well spent and not wasted.
○ Relate it to future generations of the local community.

In cases where an arts body receives no legacies, stories showing how they benefit mainstream charities can be very useful. Arts bodies who receive only a few legacies should publicise case studies showing how they made a difference. A funny story always attracts attention. Charities have been left a stuffed parrot, stuffed cats, cars, pubs etc. One favourite legacy was from the man who said: *"I leave my testicles to my bank manager because he has no balls of his own".*

The arts and heritage sector – what does the future hold for legacy income?
The potential is good – very good, albeit building on such a small base. The key for all arts and cultural organisations is to promote themselves as charities and to publicise their charitable services, which usually focus on education and community services. People give more to a good cause than a nice place of entertainment. Potential also depends on the development of loyal, tangible, trusting relationships while informing supporters of the organisation's long-term visions and the benefits they will bring[12].

Charities conducting legacy fundraising receive around 34% of voluntary income from legacies. There is no reason why cultural organisations cannot raise at least 10% of voluntary income from legacies once a fundraising culture is established[13].

---

12. *It was reported in August 2006 that Lean Scully, who had been attending concerts at the Edinburgh International Festival for 30 years, giving £45 a year, had left property worth over £3.5m to the Festival. Although she had enigmatically promised the organisers that she would "see you right when I am gone" they had no idea of her wealth. The money has been invested in a trust which will generate £150,000 a year to be spent on bringing young artists to the Usher Hall, her favourite venue.*
13. *And, it could be added, linking this to a permanent education or conservation fund – i.e. an endowment in all but name – see the Endowments topics earlier in this chapter.*

Changing demographics

○ The population is growing older and these changing demographics offer an enormous legacy fundraising opportunity.

○ The number of people over 65 will double from 9.8 million to 16 million in the next few decades.

○ At the moment a huge army of older people (6+ million) are asset-rich but relatively liquid-poor. In addition, they are worried about living so long that they will not have enough money to see themselves through.

○ This army of traditionally philanthropic people are giving up lifetime memberships of local and national art galleries, theatres, museums and other bodies. They love a day out with friends to an exhibition but are cutting back and cannot continue to have multiple memberships. A legacy is ideal for this age group. They can give generously after their death but at no cost to themselves.

The downside to this is that as we all live longer we will have less to leave. The average legacy to a charity is currently £20,000 – that might drop; but few supporters give that each year when they are alive. Almost all could give at least £1,000 when they die, and many could easily give £20,000. At the end of the day, a legacy is one way of giving and everyone should be given the option.

Recruitment

By Moyra Doyle, managing director, Richmond Associates UK

The development of fundraising as a career and profession in the UK is still in its infancy yet the demand for effective fundraisers has increased sharply over the past 10 years. The need for effective fundraisers is set to grow further, with charities looking to diversify their funding sources, universities challenged to increase their fundraising capabilities and new initiatives developing in the health sector. In order to attract scarce talent the test for arts and heritage organisations is whether their recruitment strategies can differentiate the opportunity, attract eligible candidates, provide fair and efficient recruitment processes and select for suitability.

Before embarking on a recruitment drive, trustees and chief executives must be able to articulate clearly the organisation's mission, have been involved in the creation of a long-term plan and be committed to its delivery. They must also be clear about their contribution to and role in the fundraising effort.

An experienced fundraising professional knows that success in a new role depends heavily on the organisation's leadership team, the quality of their long-term planning, their interest and engagement in the fundraising effort and the personal chemistry of the relationship between the fundraiser and the director or chief executive, and, for major donor development, the chair.

The clarity of the mission, the coherence of the long-term plan, clearly defined fundraising objectives and an understanding of trustees' contributions are essential to facilitate the creation of a relevant job description and realistic person specification from which an appropriate recruitment strategy can be developed.

The most appropriate recruitment strategy will depend on the organisation's reputation and profile, potential career opportunities, the remuneration package versus market rates and the degree to which the role is critical to the success of the organisation. Arts organisations that differentiate through their vision can often attract exceptional candidates that empathise with their work.

Having decided on how the role should be positioned, the scope of the opportunity and remuneration on offer, the next decision is how it should be marketed to maximise a quality response, how that response should be dealt with and who should manage the process. Typically, for the less critical positions, larger organisations who have the capability will manage the process themselves, sourcing candidates by marketing through advertising for maximum response, occasionally looking to recruitment agencies for additional candidates. Again for less critical positions, small to medium size organisations may look to recruitment agencies to advertise on their behalf, sift CV's and arrange interviews.

For a position that is critical to the success of a fundraising initiative and where talent is scarce, use of a specialist recruitment consultancy should be considered. This is a consideration for larger organisations, in particular, as the rigour of the recruitment process plays a large part in determining the success of the assignment. A specialist consultancy should bring in-depth knowledge of the sector and candidate market, assist in the development of job description and person specification, advise on advertising and candidate sourcing, have access to a wide network of candidates, and work closely with clients and candidates throughout the process.

The key points and elements to consider in recruiting a fundraiser for a critical position are explored in detail in Additional Information. They apply particularly to smaller arts organisations creating a new fundraising operation.

A successful recruitment strategy must be approached in the same way as a marketing strategy, and should be as well planned. A strong commitment of resources by all involved to develop excellent lines of internal and external communication, predetermined guidelines for all participants, and established time and review parameters, bring an added value to the organisation through a cost-effective hiring and retention process. The better the recruitment and selection process the more likely the successful candidate is to stay with the organisation for the longer term.

Trustees and senior managers have a duty of care to their organisations and also to their staff to ensure the fundraisers that they employ are competent, trained and professionally developed.

When recruiting a fundraiser, you will obviously be used to looking at their CV for suitable experience, but you also might look for specific details which demonstrate their commitment and competence. These might include membership of the Institute of Fundraising, the professional organisation for all those working in any aspect of development or income generation. Membership demonstrates that a fundraiser has signed up to the Institute's Codes of Fundraising Practice, the best-practice guidelines which also provide the backbone to the Fundraising Standards Board. The Institute also runs the professional qualification in fundraising – the Certificate in Fundraising Management. The letters MInstF (Cert) indicate that this has been awarded.

When considering either the recruitment of staff or the development of your employees, you also might want to consider their record of CPD (Continuous Professional Development). There are many training courses and events in the sector. The Institute of Fundraising's National Convention – in London each July – is the largest gathering of fundraisers outside the US, last year attracting 2,500 delegates in over 150 sessions. The Institute also runs one-day conferences in technique-specific fundraising as well as training courses, jointly managed through the Directory for Social Change (DSC). For organisations operating outside London, regional training and events are operated though the National, Regional and Special Interest Groups.

Arts & Business also runs courses and seminars around the country and the active Development Forum is a very useful network for professional development staff responsible for individual donor development.

Research

The importance of a first-class, well maintained, research and donor information system cannot be stressed too strongly. It makes the difference between success and failure, particularly for major appeals.

The success of fundraising is 90% prospect identification, research cultivation and preparation, and 10% in the asking. For any prospect, organisations need to know:

○ Who has the capability and interest, current or potential, to warrant an approach?
○ What are their assets, income, history of philanthropy?
○ Who is the right person to approach in a family or partnership? Who controls the giving?
○ Who is the right person in the organisation to lead on and develop the relationship? And undertake the asking? Who commands the respect of the prospect?
○ What activity of the organisation would the prospect be most interested in supporting?
○ How much should the organisation ask for?
○ Is the prospect ready? What cultivation is appropriate before asking?
○ When, where and how should the prospect be solicited?

For major gift prospects you also need to ask:

○ What relationship does, or might, the person have with the organisation?
○ What is their profession or business interest? Does the organisation know others from that profession?
○ What are their interests? Religion? Club? Sports?
○ What are their giving habits? What other causes do they support?
○ What family do they have? Who are their close friends?
○ What personality traits does the prospect have which might influence the manner of asking? What values are important? As far as you can tell, do they have any interest in any type of recognition or benefit? How have their other beneficiaries responded?

The sources for this kind of understanding are a mixture of hard data, often published, and soft information. Hard data may come from a huge range of directories and registers – *Who's Who*, *The Sunday Times Rich list*, *Debrett's*, *People of Today*, *Britain's Top Privately Owned Companies*, company reports, the Corporate Register for shareholdings and salaries, directors of quoted companies, yearbooks for several professions... and that's not all. Information must be constantly updated. There are several monthly or quarterly publications such as *WealthWatch*, the

Funding Digest and *Donor Digest* which report (in a more or less serious manner) on the wealthy and influential. A lot of this information is now online. (See the topic on data protection earlier in this chapter for points to watch.)

There are also regular publications such as *Professional Fundraising, Arts Professional, The Art Newspaper* and *Third Sector* which report on major donations and also cover developments in the legal and tax framework for giving to charities.

And there is softer information – feedback from meetings, feature articles about the prospect, news items in the financial press, feedback from other organisations with which the prospect is involved, and simple gossip.

Anything and everything should be scanned, from *The Times* to *Tatler*, from the *Financial Times* to *Hello*, from annual reports of other arts organisations and charities in your sector to the sections on donors in opera and amateur football programmes.

It is the job of the development office to undertake or commission this research, but it is important that everyone in the organisation understands why research is important, and that useful nuggets of information and feedback from a conversation during the interval or at a private view should be fed back to the development office.

Other tasks also include the establishment of a research library and the regular review of specific specialist journals.

It is also essential to keep an eye on what others who are raising money are promoting and experiencing. This is not only about being sure that your organisation is an exemplar of best practice. It is important to recognise that most prospects will see a range of proposals from the same sector, if they are known to be interested in your art form or heritage activity: it is very much a buyers' market. You can always learn from others.

So organisations should build and maintain detailed competitor information files, updated regularly with new materials and press cuttings. At the very least, they should gather and maintain an up-to-date collection of all promotional materials, newsletters, "ladders of giving", donor lists (with level of gift if possible) and donor benefits of comparable institutions. Some consideration should be given as to which organisations these might be.

Additional Information gives a fictional digest of John Doe showing the kind of profile which can be developed. This was provided by Factary, one of the leading practitioners in this field. It has also provided the professional advice below, and a briefing note in Additional Information.

Research for donor development

By Christopher Carnie and Elizabeth Dixon, Factary

Research for donor development – or "prospect research" – is a growing, challenging profession throughout the non-profit sector. Amongst arts organisations there are more and more people taking on the role – full- or part-time – of researcher supporting a development team. But in too many organisations there is just not the time.

In a busy arts organisation there are a million things to do, most of them by yesterday. There are events to plan, the launch of the new gallery, that catalogue to complete and don't forget to invite Mrs Schlickenbacker to the design lecture…

> "Mrs Schlickenbacker? THE Mrs Schlickenbacker?"
> "Yes, you know, the one that Daphne met last year on the Paris trip."
> "But isn't she the heiress, the one who talked about how much she loved our porcelain collection last year…?"

…And all of a sudden, you are doing research.

Because research is like this. It's a combination of the dry dusty facts (Mrs Schlickenbacker's address, her biography) with the personal background and connections of your colleagues. Good research is good knowledge management.

Knowledge is a combination of information, skills and experience[14]. The key is that knowledge means more than just information; knowledge allows us to use information to take decisions.

Cultural organisations are packed with knowledge, and much of it is directly relevant to research for fundraising and donor development:
Your director has people in their email address book who can lead you directly to a potential donor.
Your expert on porcelain, or modern dance or whatever is your area of work: their expertise, at the heart of your organisation, is of enormous interest to potential supporters. They know who your competitors are, and may know how they function. You can use that expertise to find out who funds them (and thus who might fund you).

---

14. A formal definition is: "The combination of explicit data and information to which is added tacit expert opinion, skills and experience to result in a valuable asset which can be used to make key decisions. The essential factor is adding meaning to information." Competing with Knowledge, *Abell and Oxbrow, tfpl, London 2001.*

Your finance department has a list of the companies that supply your organisation. Amongst them could be potential donors.

Your filing system Down in the archives are the lists of people who attended and supported the gallery opening 10 years ago. Invite them back for the Tenth Anniversary, and sift out the potential donors.

Your box office, visitors' book or enquiries desk Lists the people who visit you regularly. These people are keen on your organisation. Amongst them are people with the potential to make a gift. See Chapter Six for more on database screening.

The strategic management role of anyone taking on fundraising research is to start to manage all of this knowledge, to draw from it the contacts and the information needed to approach strategic funders[15]. Often this means breaking down barriers.

Breaking down barriers

We worked with one museum which had a substantial fundraising need, but the fundraising team was on one side of a green baize door, and the rest of the museum on the other. The door was rarely open. The researcher and the fundraising team took simple, practical steps to break down the barriers. First, they appointed a team within the fundraising office to look at how knowledge was gathered and where it was held in the museum. They invited museum staff in to the fundraising office, one evening a month, for a glass of wine and a chat. They arranged workplace exchanges with people in other departments. And they ensured that one member of the fundraising team spent at least part of their time moving around the museum, learning about key departments and informing them about activity in the fundraising department.

The workplace exchanges resulted in a number of substantial gifts, and the improved relationships between staff ensured that the green baize door opened frequently, helping fundraisers to learn from their colleagues, and curators to learn from fundraisers.

Your database is a key part (but not the only part) of good knowledge management in prospect research. A well-designed database will allow you and your colleagues to enter, share and update information about prospects. It will also allow you to build lists of prospects based on specific characteristics, and to define relationships between people – people who went to university together, people who meet across the table of a company boardroom, friends, neighbours, family members... These relationships, and the ability to map them, are at the heart of good fundraising.

15. Strategic funders are substantial investors in your organisation – they are likely to include trusts and foundations, companies, people and statutory funders.

Research is hard, research is easy

Finding the facts about a potential donor is straightforward, if you are organised. To start, draw up a table showing what you want to know (on the left) and with plenty of space for your notes (on the right.)

Prospect profile

Name
Address
Email
Phone
Company directorships
Brief company profiles
Trust and foundation involvement
Trust/foundation profiles
Connection to our organisation
Interest in culture, arts etc.

Each organisation has its own special requirements. If your organisation specialises in radical re-staging of ancient Chinese poetic drama, then you probably need to find donors who have expressed at least some interest in China, poetry or the theatre. Your blank prospect profile should reflect that.

Then start filling up the right hand side of your profile. Organise your search, starting with internal sources (your database, filing system, colleagues) and going on to published directories (biographic directories such as *Who's Who* or *People of Today*, as well as company information from **http://uk.finance.yahoo.com/**, **www.hoovers. com**, or **www.dnb.com** for example). Only once you have the details from these sources should you venture to the wider web for news research (**www.factiva.com** or **www.lexisnexis.com**) or search engines such as Google.

There are many sources of specific help to cultural organisations and these include specialist periodicals such as *The Art Newspaper* and *Art Review*. Looking at the donor boards and annual reports of other cultural organisations is also very helpful when trying to identify the key players who give to galleries, museums and the performing arts.

The hard part in research is making sense of the facts: turning data about a person's business interests and shareholdings into information that will help you to estimate their capacity to give; analysing the relationship between your organisation and the donor in order to develop an approach strategy that works; considering motivations and interests based on what you can find out about past giving.

These are all specialist areas and it is worth considering training for a member of your team, or employing a professional prospect researcher for the job. Professional researchers are members of the Institute of Fundraising "Researchers in Fundraising" special interest group (**www.institute-of-fundraising.org.uk**).

Research does not stop at the creation of a prospect profile. It's a continual process, made much easier today by ability to track, electronically, news and other data on prospects (noting always the requirements of the Data Protection Act). Plan and manage it as a process, not a one-off event.

Research costs

Research costs, but not researching costs more. Cultural non-profits, like companies, produce goods and services that are "sold" (in a broad sense) to the public. Cultural organisations investing in research – audience, artistic and prospect research – can expect to out-perform other organisations in their sector.

A proposed budget of 4%[16] of turnover is a good starting point for a debate in your organisation on "how much should we spend on research?". For the largest arts organisations in the UK – there are two with an income over £65 million – that would mean a research spend of around £2.5 million per annum, enough to finance very thorough work on audience, art and major donors. But a much more modest budget will cover research supplies and time. For example, a budget of £40,000 would provide a well-equipped research office.

Researcher – in-house or agency	£25,000
Publications, data, subscriptions	£12,000
Training and staff development	£2,000
Filing and archiving	£1,000
TOTAL	**£40,000**

A sensible ratio is one full-time equivalent researcher per four fundraisers. This allows the researcher to do a thorough job but not drown in demands for information. Make time for organised, managed research in your organisation. You, or your colleagues, are probably already doing it, so now it's time to manage the process, set the objectives and the budget, and clear the time for research on donors. It will pay off – even if it only persuades Mrs Schlickenbacker to give one more enormous gift.

16. *Promoting research and development in the UK, the Department of Trade and Industry defines* "R&D-intensive" companies as those that invest at least 4% of sales on research and development, and demonstrates that companies investing in R&D out-perform their rivals *(see www.innovation.gov.uk/rd_scoreboard/index.asp).*

Transnational giving in Europe

Some organisations may be in a position to attract donors from other European countries. However, it is well known that most EU countries do not provide incentives for donors wanting to support a foreign beneficiary. Income tax deductibility is not granted for donations made by individuals and corporate donors to foreign beneficiaries, while cross-border donations and legacies are often taxed at the highest applicable gift and inheritance tax rates. The launch of the **www. givingineurope.org** website and the promotion and extension of the Transnational Giving Europe (TGE) network are two important initiatives from the King Baudouin Foundation to improve the environment of cross-border philanthropy in Europe. This brief article by **Jim Myers** focuses on TGE.

The Transnational Giving Europe network (TGE) is currently the only practical and secure solution for tax-effective cross-border cash donations. The network is a partnership between the Charities Aid Foundation (UK), King Baudouin Foundation (Belgium), Fondation de France, Oranje Fonds (Netherlands), Maecenata International (Germany) and the Foundation for Poland. TGE's function is to enable donors – both corporations and individuals – resident in one of the participating countries, to give financial support to non-profit organisations in other member states, while benefiting directly from the tax advantages provided for in the legislation of their country of residence. A donor resident in one of the participating countries wishing to make a gift to a public interest organisation in another member state can contact the foundation in the country where they live. The home foundation establishes contact with the foundation in the recipient country for an assessment of the beneficiary (which must be another non-profit organisation). If the evaluation is positive, the donor makes the gift to their home-country foundation which then provides the donor with a tax receipt. There is a longer article on this subject in Additional Information.

The European Association for Planned Giving (EAPG), a UK-based association of charities and professional advisers, is working closely with the King Baudouin Foundation to raise awareness of the TGE network and to find new partner foundations in European countries not yet represented in the network. At the time of writing several new foundations are in the process of joining the network. For more information on TGE or EAPG visit **www.plannedgiving.org.uk**.

US – fundraising from across the Atlantic

Many organisations look wistfully across the Atlantic and, sometimes at the behest of their trustees, ask whether they might be able to raise significant sums in the United States. The question to ask is, why would American individuals support you?

Individuals who are most likely to support you will have the same range of motivations as UK donors: a passionate interest in some aspect of your work and a belief that their gift will make a difference. They will also enjoy strong relationships with one or more of the categories of senior staff and experts, the volunteer leadership and other donors. They may possibly have family ties to the region where you are based. But, except for the last factor, they will usually have ample opportunity to identify an organisation that matches their interests close to home.

So where to start? How do you identify prospects? The constant advice, including that from David Wickert of Chapel and York, the leading UK expert in raising money in the US, has been that US visitors to your organisation are among the most likely potential sources of support. Capturing their contact details, and if possible their particular focus of interest, should be a priority. As in the UK, prospect research is essential. Examples of categories suggested for systematic research have included those with post-graduate qualifications in relevant subjects, those who have supported comparable institutions with overlapping aims, and those featuring in various directories with origins in your region. In an increasingly global marketplace, collectors have international interests.

In parallel with this, identification of American expatriates as a potential source of volunteers and donations is a strongly recommended tactic by those with expertise and experience in this field. It is possible that some individuals may be attracted by an invitation to a prestigious event in the US, but that is not usually sufficient to ensure fundraising success. We will return to this.

It should be remembered that volunteer activities, particularly board membership, is of major importance for giving among the wealthy in the US. As Francie Ostrower reported in her seminal work, *Why the Wealthy Give* (1996), 75% of her interviewees served on a non-profit board. With striking frequency the largest gifts went to organisations with which the donor had a relationship other than as a giver. Board membership, being a user of the services and having a close relationship with someone linked to the organisation were key factors. This was true for over 90% of all gifts in the culture sector. Nearly 45% of the largest gifts to cultural organisations went to those where the donor was a board member.

Some organisations have reported some success with US fundraising, including the following examples.

Tate
With a staffed office (two people) in New York established in 2002 and excellent volunteer leadership support, Tate is raising $8 million a year from the US, in the form of gifts and pledges of money and works of art (both have tax benefits not

available in the UK). The focus of the support is almost entirely linked to acquisitions of American art. Most donors are regular visitors to London, where they receive special treatment – private views, visits to artists' studios, visits to private houses and collections, and special dinners at the Tate, with opportunities to meet other high-level donors, collectors and artists. Recognition for a gift of a given value (say $100,000) is more lavish than that for a gift of the same value to, say, the Museum of Modern Art (MoMA). Donors may be members of the prestigious International Council and there is regular engagement with Tate director Sir Nicholas Serota, including during his US visits. This initiative developed out of a very successful and high profile capital campaign and is itself based on significant and continuing investment in prospect research.

The American Association of the Royal Academy Trust
After some 20 years of having a New York office (two staff), over $35 million has been raised for the Royal Academy Trust. The focus of the current effort and support is a very glitzy annual dinner which now raises of the order of $700,000, with a further $300,000 coming from donations and memberships. The dinner is organised by the very prestigious committee which forms the board of the American Association. HRH the Prince of Wales has hosted dinners, cocktail parties and receptions in London and Highgrove. However, the director of the office has said that she does not feel able to ask supporters for significant donations, above a relatively low-level membership (in US terms) and the cost of the dinner because the UK board is not engaged in US-style planned giving. (Indeed, the former chair of the UK Royal Academy Trust is a leading player in the coalition to introduce "lifetime legacies", based on a Charity Remainder Trust model, into the UK.) US supporters ask why should they give significantly when the UK trustees are not giving.

As with the Tate, those involved are regular visitors to London and benefits include private views and visits, dinners, and opportunities to meet like-minded people who become friends over the years. It is like a private club.

But it is not only the major institutions that are having some success. The Handel House Trust is just one organisation that has garnered significant support.

CASE STUDY

Handel House Trust

- Visual arts; performing arts; heritage
- London
- Total income: £446,000
- Development income: £300,000

By Theresa Lloyd

Handel House has become such a part of the London music and tourist scene that it is hard to remember that it only opened in 2001. Handel lived at 25 Brook Street, London W1, from 1723 until his death in 1759. The museum celebrates the life of the composer and promotes knowledge of his contribution to British and international cultural life. It occupies Handel's former home and part of the adjacent house, and allows display and interpretation of objects relating to his life. Rooms are used for musical rehearsals, bringing to life the house where masterpieces such as *Messiah*, the *Coronation Anthems* and *Music for the Royal Fireworks* were originally composed.

Photo: Matthew Hollow

This is the first museum devoted to a composer in London and offers access to beautifully restored Georgian interiors. For most of the 20th century, the house was an antiques shop, and it required visionary leadership and determination to undertake the project of acquiring the lease, restoring the house, building a collection and raising the resources to do all this.

A key element in the funding portfolio for both the capital and the ongoing revenue funding has been the creation of strategic alliances with leading classical music organisations based in the US, most importantly, the Handel and Haydn Society in Boston, Massachusetts. Founded as a choral society in 1815 by a group of Boston merchants, the Society is among the oldest continuously performing arts organisations in the US.

What is noteworthy is that there are mutual links on both organisations' websites. The Handel and Haydn Society site encourages visits to Handel House, and mentions specifically the support of its executive director Mary

Deissler who has been actively engaged in encouraging her members to support the Handel House campaign for both capital and revenue funding.

The Handel House US campaign was started in Boston and has now spread to New York and Minneapolis/St Paul, where the museum has relationships with the St. Luke's Chamber Orchestra of New York and the St. Paul's Chamber Orchestra, as well as other American cities.

Why has the Society done this? Because it wants to make its own donors feel special and when they come to London the Handel House Trust ensures that they do, organising private visits to Handel House and other special events. A typical major donor might give $10,000 a year to their US organisation and $1,000 a year to Handel House. A few may give more.

Collaboration with other organisations is a characteristic of Handel House. In summer 2006 a visiting group of Handel and Haydn Society supporters was entertained at a reception at the residence of the US Ambassador in London to mark the opening at English National Opera (ENO) of the Society's joint production of *Orfeo*. As well as the US visitors, among the guests at the event were major UK donors of both ENO and Handel House. Indeed, some Handel House supporters contributed to the *Orfeo* production at ENO.

This kind of engagement has resulted in significant revenue funding, building up from the capital campaign, and over the years about $1.5 million for capital and revenue has been raised from US donors. This is a very significant element of the £6 million raised for capital and revenue since 1998; indeed, it virtually matches the 20% of visitors who are from the US.

In addition to the 4,000 or so American visitors each year (by far the largest national group after the British), a large proportion of the volunteer force of 80 is American. These are usually young people gaining work experience for a career in arts administration.

How did this significant support from the US happen?
The broad-minded approach and active commitment of the executive directors of the three US organisations mentioned when persuading their own supporters to donate to the Handel House has been a significant factor. The main impetus has come from two people.

Chair of the Handel House Trust, Christopher Purvis, has spent two or three weeks each year in the US, plus time to prepare and follow-up – an annual allocation of three to six weeks each year (in addition to Handel House responsibilities in the UK) for several years.

This has been matched by the involvement of an equally committed person based in the US who has been willing to spend time, effort and money to make things happen between visits and who has helped to galvanise other American volunteer leadership support. The current volunteer driver in the US is the (paid) head of the Handel and Haydn Society. Mary Deissler is passionate about Handel and recognises the benefits for her own board members (and other donors) of the link to a London-based organisation with a complementary mission and the capacity and willingness to host visitors to London and arrange a bespoke programme, which also provides the opportunity to meet like-minded people and make new friends.

Another smaller organisation is The Royal Academy of Music (RAM). Normally a conservatoire would be an unlikely focus of US funding, but the RAM was able to hold a very successful one-off concert in New York. The $1 million proceeds were spilt 50:50 with the Juilliard School which provided most of the orchestra, the administration and the audience; the RAM provided one of its distinguished alumni – Elton John!

There are several other membership organisations such as the Royal Opera House, Glyndebourne and the Royal Oak (National Trust) that, over many years, have built up a loyal following of American supporters who are regular visitors to the UK, particularly but not only to London, and visit the organisations in question. Indeed, crucially for these and most of the organisations discussed in more detail, the visits pre-dated the formation of a US structure, and it was the impetus and enthusiasm of such visitors and audience members that led to the creation of a legal entity which could be the focus of US donations.

Of course, many US citizens do not only visit London, but come to live there. The English National Opera is an example of an organisation that has been successful at encouraging such people to become enthusiastic supporters.

CASE STUDY

English National Opera – American Friends based in London

- Opera
- London
- Total income: £33m
- Development income: £3.5m

Photo: Talula Sheppard

Year 2 pupils perform Lionhunt: an ENO Baylis project at the London Coliseum.

By Theresa Lloyd

English National Opera (ENO) has had the basis of an American Friends organisation for about 10 years. The organisation had a 501(c)(3) status so US citizens can donate tax-effectively (see below). It had operated with limited success until 2003, when Wanda Kim, an American banker based in London, arrived on the scene.

Wanda became president and began to recruit people who were prepared to make a real commitment and be actively involved. Under her leadership, with enthusiastic support from the development office, and encouragement and recognition from the board, they started to plan events.

ENO has built up a very active network of US citizens living in London. The organisation is events-led. It has its own board of seven people that meets monthly. It operates as a separate entity, and for the last year has been supported by a part-time (2.5 days a week) coordinator who is paid for by the American Friends. This person is based in the development office. Her role is to focus on American Friends, handle donations and membership renewals, organise mailings, follow up after events, gather presents for "goody bags" handed out after events, and generally provide all the support required to an active group of committed and very busy people. They are reported to be hard taskmasters, and keep the coordinator on her toes.

This approach achieves results – ENO has developed a reputation for throwing the best parties! As well as events, including recitals and auctions, income comes from memberships, the cost of which ranges from £150 a year to £5,000. There are about four at the top level. Membership is payable in pounds sterling. There are currently almost 50 members.

The American Friends gave significant support to the ENO's Capital Campaign, a contribution recognised by the naming of the American Bar. They make a gift to ENO at the end of each financial year. The 2005/06 donation was £75,000; the amount the previous year was £60,000.

The most recent event (at the time of writing) was a "weekend gala" consisting of a number of activities surrounding the opening of a new production of *King Arthur* at the end of June 2006, for which tickets cost £300. About 100 people turned up.

Why does this work?
○ A very committed volunteer leader with the capacity to encourage others.
○ Recognition of the need for dedicated administrative support, and the means of financing it.
○ A hardworking committee that wants to organise its own events.
○ Active support from the development office at ENO and the whole company, involving singers and musicians for events such as private recitals.
○ Recognition by the company in the form of letters of appreciation from the chair, executive director and so on. (These are usually initiated and prepared in the development office.)

These examples are outweighed, however, by the many cultural organisations that have failed to raise significant sums, although on the face of it they might have been expected to attract support. They have launched appeals with prestigious events, but did not have the infrastructure in place to research prospects, follow up, cultivate and nurture those who attended events on a systematic and sustained basis, or make a sufficiently strong case for people to support organisations outside the US when there is demonstrable need, and more opportunity for engagement, within the country itself.

The lessons are clear. Success factors have included:

○ Willingness to make a long-term investment in prospect research and relationship management.

○ An investment in involving London-based expatriate US citizens.

○ A US office or organisation funded or prepared to handle the research, administration and follow-up.

○ Expertise in US mechanisms for tax-efficient giving such as Charity Remainder Trusts and gifts of works of art.

○ Significant commitment from the highest level in the UK (director or chair).

○ A committed volunteer leader and leadership structure in the US.

In the successful cases described we also see:

○ A London base and venue, convenient for visitors from the US.

○ A focus on opera, music or the visual arts – interests more likely to be shared beyond national boundaries.

○ Prestigious, enjoyable and bespoke events and entertainment during London visits.

○ Opportunities to widen the circle of like-minded London friends.

The RAM experience was an opportunistic exploitation of a combination of circumstances, clearly not replicable!

Reference was made to events. It must be emphasised that however prestigious the host or honorary guest, one-off events are not sufficient, any more than they are in the UK, to release significant gifts. People give large sums because they have a passionate belief in the cause, and because they think they can make a difference. Belonging to a circle of like-minded donors may be an additional attraction, but if that is the main driver it does not require a major gift – as in the UK, membership of a major donor circle may cost no more than $1,000 or $2,000. (Compare with the Beaumont Group at the National Gallery – £2,000.)

Organising major events that are not an integral part of the activities or the organisation can be a huge distraction. Even when they are – first nights of operas, private views of exhibitions, privileged out-of-hours access – they are very labour-intensive, as we have seen earlier in this chapter.

Foundations

Although the main focus of this book is about individuals, it is perhaps worth referring briefly to foundations in the context of US fundraising.

There are several American foundations that include support of cultural organisations outside the UK among their giving interests. The sums allocated have reduced significantly since 9/11. Values of endowments have dropped and there is a massively increased demand from US-based organisations.

Some foundations make grants based on the founder's interests. As in the UK, fundraising from trusts with founders still alive and active means fundraising from the founder. The comments relating to individuals apply.

Most of the larger foundations, including those that support overseas arts organisations, have established grant-making interests which are available in guidelines, in directories and online. Similarly, application forms can be downloaded. There is no point wasting effort in applications to foundations whose requirements cannot be matched, or in not following the application procedures exactly.

Replicable projects are of interest as they allow a foundation to invest in something that could be used elsewhere. Projects that have attracted other funding are often favoured. Most foundations will ask for details of what has been raised, from what sources, and what it is planned to raise, with supporting evidence. The Kresge Foundation has supported several Lottery-funded capital projects in the UK. The gift chart it requires to be completed is on its website. Like individuals, most US foundations want to see that private donors in the UK, including trustees, are doing their bit. Foundations will also seek information on the background of trustees, looking at diversity and expertise.

What are the implications of all this? You should consider very carefully why you are looking to the US. Be wary of trustees who have no understanding of the issues and have made an insignificant investment in fundraising in the UK.

An essential preparatory step is to establish a 501(c)(3) organisation – a tax-exempt entity. American individuals, foundations and companies get a tax deduction (only) when they give to 501(c)(3) organisations. This is not as difficult as it sounds, and there a various ways of managing this, as David Wickert explains in his article at the end of this section.

As well as the success factors listed above you also need:
- The allocation of a major part of the time of the director.
- Identification, creation and sustained maintenance of appropriate strategic alliances.
- Planned programme of activities.
- Participation of buzzy people.
- Involvement, possibly as trustees or other "Council" members, of one or two

younger very well-networked people who are active in the world of culture and the arts, including US citizens based in London.
O Significant private sector support in the UK.

As in the commercial sector, entering a new marketplace is a high-risk strategy. The more one can prepare the better.

As well as drawing on the experience of organisations in the cultural sector we asked David Wickert, a leading adviser in this field, to contribute his advice.

Raising money from US sources

By David Wickert, director, Chapel and York

If you love the work of your organisation, then take the US seriously as a source of funding. Americans are enthusiastic optimists, and if your organisation is brilliant and you care about it, there is a great chance they will too. Americans give serious money to what they care about.

Resources
First consider the resources you need to make US fundraising effective. To maximise the income you will need to consider staff (or volunteers), time and money. You may have to purchase information and probably consultancy. It is prudent to establish challenging but achievable targets. And the project will have an impact on your whole organisation and some priorities may need to be adjusted.

It is a mistake to imagine that US fundraising is a quick and painless way of hitting your fundraising target. It is hard work and may be costly. But the rewards can be tremendous. It is made more complicated by the fact that the Brits and Americans seem so similar (seduced by our similar languages) but, in fact, both are foreign countries to the other – almost everything is different, including attitudes, history and culture.

Tax and legal framework
US tax and legal issues regarding philanthropy are completely different from charity law in the UK, too. There's no Gift Aid. In the US a tax deduction can save a US donor as much as 40% to 50% of the cost of a gift. But the problem is that a tax deduction is only available when the donation is made to a US non-profit organisation – technically called a 501(c)(3). So a charitable organisation outside the US either needs to set up a 501(c)(3) to support it, or identify a 501(c)(3) that is willing accept donations so that donors can take a tax deduction.

Americans are very comfortable with tax deductions because they get them for every dime they give. Although an American may make a modest donation to a charity outside the US without a tax deduction, when it comes to giving a substantial sum, a tax deduction is an absolute requirement.

Fortunately, there are US non-profits that as a part of their mission accept donations from US taxpayers and support non-US organisations. Examples of US organisations that accept donations and support charitable organisations outside America include the British American Arts Association (US) Inc c/o Centre for Creative Communities (**www.creativecommunities.org.uk**) and The American Fund for Charities Inc (**www.chapel-york.com/services/usfund.htm**). There are also many firms in the US and the UK, attorneys, accountants and consultants, who will advise regarding the establishment of a 501(c)(3), and Chapel & York Limited in the UK **www.chapel-york.com** also does this.

Make giving easy

When you have sorted out a 501(c)(3), put the details on your website and on all your literature. Make sure that Americans know that they can get a tax deduction for a gift to your organisation and use terminology that sounds familiar to them. For example say:

> "Gifts to this organisation are tax deductible to the extent allowed by law."

This is the American equivalent of quoting your registered charity number in the UK. In America there is no number to quote.

Your aim is to ensure that the process of making a donation to your organisation is, for an American, as similar as possible to making a donation to an American organisation. Obviously, this must include a tax deduction. Then your donor's focus can be on the work of your organisation and not on the mechanics of giving, because the mechanics are familiar.

Where do you find Americans?

This isn't as stupid a question as it appears. Americans are all over the world as well as in America. There are thousands of US citizens living and working in the UK. There are American tourists. There are young Americans who may visit many times during their lives. And there are Brits who work in the US and can use a US tax deduction because they pay US tax.

The presence of US citizens in the UK is vital for fundraising because the vast majority of all American funding comes as the result of personal contact. And Americans know other Americans, and you want them to spread the word about the work of your organisation. So individual Americans are your first fundraising priority, starting with those who already know your work.

When you receive a donation, it may not arrive as a personal cheque but as a cheque from a foundation or company. This is because many wealthy Americans set up foundations to handle their giving during their lifetime and often after their death.For example, The Ford Foundation, **www.fordfound.org** – which wasn't set up by the Ford Motor Company but by its founder Henry Ford and his son Edsel – continues its tradition of funding non-profits throughout the world.

Unless the work of your organisation has specific American ingredients, or is outstandingly innovative and replicable in the US, it is unlikely to be of interest to a US foundation. Unless you are lucky enough to have an admirer inside the foundation!

All this points to the crucial importance of cultivating creative relationships with individual Americans.

Developing creative relationships
The first steps are to develop imaginative and unobtrusive ways of identifying everyone associated with your project in any way – visitors, audience, clients, guests, suppliers, volunteers, with their consent. Exactly what these methods are will depend on your organisation.

Amongst those you identify, some will be American. How many depends, of course, on your organisation and where it's located. So, for example, email makes it easy to be in regular contact with very large numbers of people in return for an email address that can be keyed directly into a database either where you are or on your website. You only need their address initially. The more information you ask for, the fewer will respond. And you will want to ask for more information when a dialogue has been established. Virtually every American who visits the UK has an email address. So every effort should be made to collect email addresses, even attracting small discounts on admission perhaps! Developing contacts into relationships is that valuable.

Use the email addresses to send information designed for a wide cross-section of people of all ages – the kind of material they will look forward to receiving regularly and that reminds them of the great experience they had with you.

Then most organisations have various areas, all of which will be of interest to different people, for example: creative, educational, technical, professional, historical, pictorial, managerial and financial. Individuals can be invited to subscribe free to the email information that interests them, and from time to time they can all be updated on financial needs and opportunities and their financial assistance can be requested. This needs to be a two-way process, so invite response, consider using email discussion groups and blogs.

For an example of cultivating creative relationships, look at the website of the Royal Academy of Arts **www.royalacademy.org.uk**. Go to "Support – As an Individual" and look at Benjamin West Group and American Associates. You will see that the Royal Academy specifically caters for Americans in the UK and Americans in the US. Last time I looked there was a dinner in the Rainbow Rooms in New York and a reception at the British Embassy in Washington for patrons.

Unsurprisingly, Americans respond well to projects that relate in some positive way to America. For example, an American season, an American in Residence, an exhibition with an American theme; these and many others are ways of encouraging American participation and funding.

Naming opportunities are familiar to Americans, so offer to name a room, or a building, always display the names of those who have contributed, send beautifully designed thank-you letters signed by an appropriate "A" list celebrity which can be framed, include information in your annual report (and send them a copy), and on your website. And indicate in advance that you will do all this when you ask for a donation.

Many Americans are in the UK as the spouse or family of someone working here, and they have time to volunteer. They know the American way of volunteering, which is, broadly speaking, enthusiastic and organised. Listen to their advice, ask them to do something remarkable, and when it's over thank them, thank them, and thank them again. Only Brits find it embarrassing to be thanked! Volunteers bring friends along. You need someone who really knows your organisation to support the volunteers.

Touring your work in America
Finally, if you can, when you can, take your very best work to America. This is the Holy Grail of American fundraising, and is only open to a relatively small number of organisations who have something to show, usually a performance or an exhibition. This is the way to develop a vibrant worldwide American Friends organisation and a significant ongoing funding stream. Sadly, some organisations fail to capitalise on the fundraising potential of a US visit because of a lack of informed planning, inadequate resources and a failure to follow up.

Everything worthwhile and reasonably sophisticated takes time, usually more than you estimate. The advice in this chapter, if put into operation with modest resources including a dedicated and trained person in the lead, is at least a five-year programme for a medium-sized organisation. But the effect is like planting a seed; and seeds that are cultivated grow and flourish.

Visitor and audience fundraising without ticketing data

By David Dixon

Some organisations do not routinely capture ticketing data. In some cases the organisation could capture such data but does not yet do so, in which case the remedy is to install appropriate software and change ticket-office procedures – the benefit for both marketing and fundraising income should justify the initial investment. However, there are two types of organisation that cannot capture ticketing data, making database-driven fundraising more difficult, although not impossible.

Museums and galleries with free entry
Most publicly-funded museums and galleries have free entry and do not record details of visitors. Of course, this does not mean that their visitors do not appreciate them and would not give donations, but approaching them by mail and/or telephone is not possible without data. Several organisations have got round this problem by creating schemes that encourage visitors to volunteer their contact details. Examples include:
○ A Friends scheme offering benefits.
○ A mailing list offering additional information.
○ Staff with clipboards simply asking visitors for their address details (or the equivalent online).
○ A competition (prize perhaps donated by a corporate supporter).
○ A "points" programme offering discounts in café and gift shop for multiple attenders but where the visit must be logged (a swipe card achieves this).

All of these methods have been used by UK museums and galleries and in some cases have led to the creation of databases of tens of thousands of supporters. All are amenable to web as well as physical capture on entry, and all have other uses for the organisation as well as providing a base for fundraising (see National Portrait Gallery and National Galleries of Scotland case studies in Chapters Four and Six).

Touring organisations
Organisations that produce work for touring usually do not collect their own ticketing data; rather it is captured by the venue where they are performing. Some venues are amenable to passing on the data, whereas others refuse to pass the data over, often incorrectly citing the Data Protection Act (see earlier in this chapter). It is a moot point as to whether a customer has come to the theatre (or concert hall etc) specifically to see that company, or simply because they always go out to the theatre on Friday evenings, but it can be assumed that a proportion of ticket-buyers deliberately chose to buy tickets to see that company. For high-profile touring companies this will certainly be the case, and acquiring attender data for marketing should be a priority.

The sharing of data can be a tricky political issue since the venue may want to keep "its" customers for its own marketing and fundraising purposes. For this reason it can be quite difficult for the fundraiser working alone to access this data and the transfer of data, within the restrictions of the Data Protection Act, should form part of the contract between the visiting company and the venue. Since the data has a clear value to both parties, it should be covered in the contract in the same way as other commercially important matters.

Once the data is available to the fundraiser of the touring company it can be treated in the same way as described in Chapter Six i.e. segmentation, testing and rollout by phone and/or mail.

Volunteers

Nearly all arts and heritage organisations depend to a greater or lesser extent on volunteers. At the very minimum they have a volunteer trustee board, whose members give time, expertise and, sometimes, money. Many organisations draw in help on an ad hoc basis, for a specific project. Many prevail upon supporters with a particular expertise to provide advice as a gift-in-kind to the organisation. Several engage dedicated supporters for tasks such as the management of a Friends organisation. We see in the story of the Southbank Sinfonia in Chapter Three the importance of an experienced volunteer working in the office almost full-time to ensure first-class donor servicing.

There are some organisations, not only the smallest, who could not survive without volunteer commitment. The Handel House is one, as we see in the case study earlier in this chapter. "No volunteers, no National Trust" is the emphatic conclusion of new research carried out to uncover the scale, diversity and impact of volunteering in the National Trust. The Trust relies on 43,000 volunteers contributing 2.6 million hours through 180 different ways of helping. People may volunteer in houses, gardens and parks, countryside and coastline, shops, restaurants or offices. They may be room stewards, gardeners, wardens, education assistants, speakers, working holiday leaders, fundraisers, building conservators. Details about the wide range of volunteer opportunities can be found on the national trust website **www. nationaltrust.org.uk**. The National Trust, like many conservation and social welfare charities, invests significantly in volunteer recruitment and management and in endeavouring to ensure that their voice is represented and respected.

Of course, not all volunteers are an unmixed blessing. Many organisations in the culture sector report board members who behave as though they do not take the commitment seriously. They do not turn up at meetings, or if they do have not read the papers; they do not act as ambassadors, do not understand the non-executive role, attempt to influence artistic decision-making inappropriately, use an allocation of tickets to entertain their friends who have no intention of becoming donors, and do not give themselves. There is a section on board development earlier in this chapter; essentially these problems arise from a lack of leadership and a serious commitment to corporate governance, lack of a clear job description and terms of reference for board members, and lack of regular board assessment and the implementation of appropriate sanctions for those whose contribution is minimal.

Many board members are, however, highly dedicated and effective, and appreciated as such. But too often in the arts there are stories of volunteers feeling unappreciated. This is particularly the case when people do not have a formal role, such as board or committee membership, which provides a channel of communication, or where there is no formal structure for volunteer or intern engagement. But even board members may feel unappreciated if they take on a task beyond their trustee role, or assist on an ad hoc basis. In the course of discussions for this book people reported helping with recruitment by sitting on a selection panel, undertaking an options analysis for a new office move, introducing a number of prospects, providing pro bono professional advice in a range of expertise. In each case they felt that they were not kept informed of progress, often hearing nothing until there was a public announcement, had no idea whether their efforts were really welcomed, and had no communication from any board member. They felt taken for granted and not respected.

Yet the value of this support in-kind is enormous. It is both good manners and enlightened self-interest to recognise this commitment. After all, volunteers have friends and colleagues. They may be able to leave a legacy.

The challenge for the organisation is that too often the formal arrangements with the volunteer are fuzzy. The volunteer may do what they are interested in, and not what is needed. They may make a commitment to produce a report or attend a meeting and then have other priorities. They may not be competent. Internal politics and sensitivies may intervene. It is hard to ask someone who became involved as a favour to a friend on the board to leave. As with board and committee members, it is advisable to have very clear processes of recruitment, terms of reference and guidelines, to set out in an engagement letter that covers matters like attendance, working facilities and any training opportunities (for example, on the database system). There should be opportunities for regular performance review and for senior volunteers to contribute formally to the development of the organisation, for example, by attending department meetings as appropriate. Volunteers may undertake tasks for which they are over-qualified, and their intellectual capacities and potential to contribute should be understood.

In calculating partnership funding for major Lottery-funded capital projects, the value of volunteer time was often estimated and "counted" as part of the total. It is a useful discipline. It is essential to understand how the volunteer sees the relationship. Someone working four days a week in a role that, if paid, would command a salary of £25,000 a year, may see themselves as donating the equivalent of £20,000 a year. Someone who undertakes a study or provides advice that would have cost the organisation £5,000 may feel that they have given that as a gift in-kind. Someone who gives a significant discount on their fees feels that they have donated the difference to the organisation. The fact that the organisation could never have employed someone in that position, nor paid fully or at all for the expertise, or values their help at less, is irrelevant to them. In other words, they may see themselves as major donors, particularly if they have been engaged through a relatively formal process. Does the beneficiary organisation treat them as such?

It is impossible to remove all the sensitivities of managing a volunteer relationship. But many of the problems are avoidable, or can be significantly reduced, by careful management and by valuing the huge potential asset represented by volunteers.

Checklist
- Do you allocate responsibility for volunteer relationships to a member of the senior management team?
- Do you ensure that the board is aware of all volunteer support and its value to the organisation?
- Does the chair write to every volunteer at least once a year to thank them?
- Do you ensure that those who give professional support on a pro bono basis are engaged and managed as though there were a financial arrangement, including agreed outcomes and processes of communication?
- Do those who give time instead of money feel that they are truly appreciated?
- Do you have systems in place for reviewing volunteer performance and asking those whose contribution is unsatisfactory to leave?
- Are volunteers who contribute significantly included in events involving major donors?
- Do you report on the contributions of volunteers in your published materials?

Wealth screening

There have been several references to wealth screening. Essentially this is about matching information on visitors and supporters – Friends, donors, ticket-buyers, members, shop customers and so on, past as well as present – against publicly-available information on wealthy people. Such matching gives the development office a basis for identifying potential major donors and prioritising its work.

Techniques for wealth screening have become increasingly sophisticated and we asked one of the leaders in the field to describe their work with ENO.

Wealth preview at the English National Opera

By William J. Conner, managing director, Brakeley

The objective at the beginning of the wealth screening project at English National Opera (ENO) was to create a new annual revenue stream of at least £1 million to sustain its ongoing operations. It is also expected that the number of lower-level givers will double during the course of the three-year project. Work began in January 2006.

The need to renew and expand the company's donor base was considered paramount to any future successes in fundraising. The ENO has had considerable success over the last two years with the acquisition of new donors and the stewardship and upgrading of existing donors to higher levels of giving. This needs to be the core activity in any professional development office, and by the end of 2005 the ENO had achieved the highest levels of giving from the highest number of donor households in its history. As with many not-for-profit organisations whose need for private support has grown significantly in recent years, the hunt for new wealth among ENO's constituency had become ever more urgent.

Wealth screening products of various kinds have been available in the US and UK for some time and are designed to uncover unknown sources of wealth in an organisation's database. These products have evolved over the years and with the advent of the new technologies over the last decade, more information on people's affairs and resources have become readily available than ever before.

The primary benefit of wealth screening is that it helps to prioritise the work of the development office. It is not a substitute for prospect research, but it helps to establish priorities in deploying staff resources. The larger the organisation's database, the more important this process is. A major gift officer can only manage about 150 prospects at a time. If you have one million names or even only 10,000 names, where do you start?

In January 2006, the Brakeley Wealth Preview did its second beta test (a product testing process) at the ENO. Some 468,000 records covering 15 years of ticket-buyer and donor records were screened. There were 147,000 matches or 31% of the database, meaning that information was found in at least one datasource about 31% of the names submitted. The ENO has three full-time equivalent major gift officers spread over five people.

The work to be done was segmented according to the following chart.

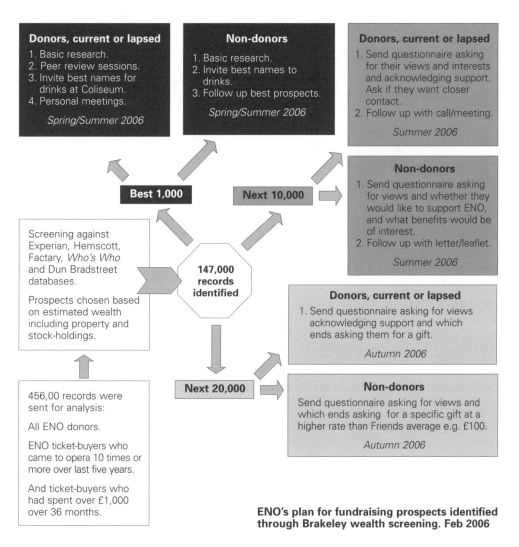

Donors, current or lapsed
1. Basic research.
2. Peer review sessions.
3. Invite best names for drinks at Coliseum.
4. Personal meetings.

Spring/Summer 2006

Non-donors
1. Basic research.
2. Invite best names to drinks.
3. Follow up best prospects.

Spring/Summer 2006

Donors, current or lapsed
1. Send questionnaire asking for their views and interests and acknowledging support. Ask if they want closer contact.
2. Follow up with call/meeting.

Summer 2006

Best 1,000

Next 10,000

Non-donors
1. Send questionnaire asking for views and whether they would like to support ENO, and what benefits would be of interest.
2. Follow up with letter/leaflet.

Summer 2006

Screening against Experian, Hemscott, Factary, *Who's Who* and Dun Bradstreet databases.

Prospects chosen based on estimated wealth including property and stock-holdings.

147,000 records identified

Donors, current or lapsed
1. Send questionnaire asking for views acknowledging support and which ends asking them for a gift.

Autumn 2006

456,00 records were sent for analysis:

All ENO donors.

ENO ticket-buyers who came to opera 10 times or more over last five years.

And ticket-buyers who had spent over £1,000 over 36 months.

Next 20,000

Non-donors
Send questionnaire asking for views and which ends asking for a specific gift at a higher rate than Friends average e.g. £100.

Autumn 2006

ENO's plan for fundraising prospects identified through Brakeley wealth screening. Feb 2006

The first work to be done was to assign the unknown names of the top 1,000 to portfolio managers for immediate attention. Working through the new names would take some time, but within the first four weeks of starting the project, five new donors were successfully solicited for annual gifts of £1,000 or more. Prospect research has been commissioned on selected names and over the course of 12 months, a good list of new qualified prospects will emerge. The second and third tiers (next two blocks of 10,000) require further market research. In each tier the 10,000 most promising-looking names will be selected. This is primarily dictated by their level of ticket-buying activity and previous donor history. The expectation in the market research activity is that a certain percentage of the people receiving the questionnaire will respond and provide the information requested.

The market research began in May 2006 with a test mailing to 1,000 people in the second tier. The questionnaire included 30 items covering their spending habits, incomes, support of other organisations and their views on the ENO. A surprising 20% of the test households responded, freely giving answers to all the questions asked. Of the 20%, 65 households specifically asked for information on supporting ENO. Prospect research will be done on the 65 households to see which ones might be capable of giving a major gift and the balance will be asked for general support.

The work at ENO is still in the early stages. The strategy on how to use the wealth screening output is clear and the development office team is working through the process as quickly as staff resources allow. It is too early to declare success, but early signs are good. It will take all of the projected three years to take full advantage of the wealth screening output. In the meantime, it has given direction and focus to the individual giving team as it strives to support the ever-growing financial needs of the organisation.

Working on commission

Many people, especially from the commercial sector, suggest that fundraisers should work on a commission basis, particularly in start-up situations. They make an analogy with selling, with the implication that professional consultants and freelance fundraisers somehow work harder if incentivised in this way. They also forget, or are unaware, that the main reasons why people support a particular arts organisation are completely outside the control or even influence of the development office, let alone an independent consultant. This is reviewed in more detail in Chapter Ten.

There are several reasons why engaging freelance fundraisers on a commission basis is inappropriate. One is that this approach reflects a profound misunderstanding of the nature of successful fundraising, which is not about engagement with an individual fundraiser but the development of long-term relationships between donors and those who deliver the mission. People will not usually support a specific institution or activity or project just because they know the fundraiser (except perhaps at a very low level); they will support it because they are convinced of the need and have complete confidence in those who are delivering the mission – the artists, specialists, management team and trustees.

It is also important to distinguish between the role of the consultant and that of the freelance fundraiser. The role of a consultant is to advise on the creation and implementation of a strategy, including prospect identification, and the presentation of a case that will maximise the potential of those links and a passionate commitment to the cause, and the best way to alert prospects to the opportunities to support this crucial institution. A consultant may advise on board development, or on the use of particular techniques, staff development or the development of strategies for one or more donor constituencies. A freelance fundraiser could help with the implementation of this strategy and essentially act as a temporary development manager or director. Success will depend on many things, not least resources allocated and time allowed. If the organisation employs an in-house person or team, part of what the consultant should do is to transfer their expertise so that it becomes institutionalised.

If people are engaged on a commission basis, there are a number of difficulties, including understandable resentment from those who may commit significant time but receive no additional fee. Research shows, not surprisingly, that payment of fundraisers on commission is the area most disliked by donors. Indeed, the requirement of the 1992 Charities Act – that if the consultant or independent fundraiser who solicits support is paid on this basis then the prospect must be told of the remuneration arrangements – can be a disincentive. Prospects don't like this, and the requirement is often forgotten or ignored.

This is also the area where there have been abuses, as undue pressure may be placed on potential donors, leading to short-term revenue but very low donor retention. Indeed, one of the main arguments against commission payments is that it replaces a risk of a small loss with the near certainty of paying the fundraiser too much! It is a direct incentive for the fundraiser to pick the low hanging fruit, take a lot of cash for work that is relatively easy, and then not bother with the more challenging prospects.

There are also practical difficulties – over what period of money coming in is the commission to be calculated? Suppose someone makes a multi-year commitment? Is the figure gross or net of tax reclaimed?

And in some cases the commission may be disproportionately high or low: a consultant may have to work extremely hard to generate £1 million for cause A; a colleague may work equally hard to generate £100,000 for cause B. This approach does not recognise the nature of the cause, commitment or time spent. For many fundraisers this is a key issue. Payment on a fee basis recognises, respects and rewards them for professional services and commitment. A non-contractual bonus that recognises exceptional effort is, of course, always welcome, to employee and freelancer alike, but this is quite different from a pre-determined format written into an agreement.

And it is unlikely that a reputable professional fundraiser would agree to such a contract: the code of conduct of the Institute of Fundraising, of which anyone engaged should be a member, advises strongly against such arrangements. (The Institute position on this matter is being reviewed at the time of writing, and the current position is set out on its website **www.institute-of-fundraising.org.uk**.)

It is recognised that many trustees consider this route, particularly in start-up situations, not only because they misunderstand the nature of fundraising but because of lack of resources. But there are other ways of dealing with this.

One way to protect the organisation is to negotiate break-points in contracts. Another, for an established consultant[17], is to propose deferral of some proportion of the fee, on a basis that recognises the impact of the cashflow delay and higher risk for the consultant.

However, it is usually the case that the initial fundraising investment, including the strategy development, is a small fraction of the amount to be raised, especially for a major project or capital campaign. If the trustees cannot find, from themselves or their own networks, sufficient funds to invest in the project as founder supporters, you might ask about their commitment to and confidence in the project. Indeed, the request for someone to operate on a commission basis can be seen as an attempt to transfer risk from the trustees, who should know more about the organisation or project than anyone, to an outside expert. An alternative to investment is underwriting a bank loan, or indeed to approach an organisation such as the Charity Bank (**www.charitybank.org**) with a well-structured proposal for an investment in fundraising. Some charitable trusts have been known to support investment in the development of a fundraising strategy.

However it is done, the important point is that the fundraising costs, including those of consultants and freelance advisers, must be planned as an integral element in a project development budget.

17. *An established consultant is suggested, as they are more likely to be able to manage the impact of the deferred income.*

Chapter Nine

Understanding tax legislation

By Graham Elliott

Tax regulation and legislation might not be the most scintillating aspect of a fundraiser's work, but it is an important one, and one that is not always well understood, even by HM Revenue & Customs (HMRC) which administers it. That is not to say that taxation cannot in itself be a motivator. That point is clearly demonstrated by the tax rebate system in the United States.

However, UK fundraisers often find it a thorny issue and commonly remark upon the disparity of treatment meted out by different officers of HMRC as regards a Gift Aid or VAT issue, to charities in identical positions.

The problem lies in that there is no one set of consistent rules. So much in this area is grey, open to interpretation, or insufficiently litigated to be sure of a final answer, that decisions can come down to a matter of weighing up the odds and using common sense. This book cannot remove that element of a gamble, but points to areas that need to be handled with particular care.

Common areas for arts fundraising

This chapter deals with the key areas of concern for arts and cultural fundraisers as they relate to individual giving (not corporate), namely:
○ Seeking exceptional one-off funding from individuals (e.g. in a capital campaign).
○ Seeking recurrent committed giving from individuals (usually in some kind of membership scheme).
○ Generating profits through fundraising events.
○ Seeking grants from charitable foundations, local authorities, and other grant-giving bodies such as the Arts Council.

Individual giving

Giving by individuals is usually divided into two categories – requests for one-off donations (particularly in relation to capital campaigns) and the encouragement of ongoing periodic giving. The tax and VAT rules relating to both usually overlap significantly.

Two key ingredients govern the taxation mix for these activities. First, the Gift Aid scheme allows a UK taxpayer to make a declaration to the effect that the charity is able to treat the donation as having been made net of income tax at the basic rate. Upon a claim to HMRC, this tax is paid over to the charity, enhancing the value of the donation. At the time of writing, the value of this claim was 28p in every £1 actually given by the donor. In addition, where donors are higher rate taxpayers, they are able to make a tax deduction in their own tax return for the difference between the basic rate and the higher rate, subsidising their own donation from a reduction in their taxation. Fundraisers in arts and cultural organisations will generally be targeting these higher rate taxpayers, so any error in respect of Gift Aid could result in a severe loss of value both to the charity and to the donor. This chapter concentrates on the areas that can give rise to specific pitfalls for arts organisations.

The key concept in this area is that, for Gift Aid to apply at all, the payment made must be a bona fide gift and not payment for services, although it is possible to provide token signs of appreciation and acknowledgement of donations without negating the potential claim of Gift Aid. Thus, a payment can be seen to be a donation even if something is given in return, as long as the value of what is given is within certain prescribed limits (see Additional Information), and, generally speaking, is essentially tokenistic. The starting point for Gift Aid is therefore to assume that the payment is made for entirely altruistic purposes, and the law allows situations where there is some degree of reciprocity from the organisation.

This mindset for Gift Aid contrasts starkly with that for VAT. In the world of VAT, the word "donation" has its more strict meaning. A donation is a payment given with the expectation of nothing specific in return. Nothing is to be "done for" the payment received. In any situation where something is done in return, then VAT case law says that the payment cannot have been a donation in the first place. This is one of the most confusing paradoxes in fundraising, namely that a payment that can be treated as a donation for Gift Aid purposes (as long as it falls within the permitted benefit limits) may be treated as consideration for a supply in the world of VAT. Where a perfectly valid Gift Aid claim can be made in respect of a payment, that payment may yet be subject to VAT at the standard-rate (currently 17.5%) as though it was not a donation at all. Whether it will actually be subject to VAT rather depends on exactly what is provided in return. There are zero-rates for VAT, and exemptions from VAT, which may have the effect of removing a good deal of the actual VAT from the payment.

Some readers may question this stark distinction, and particularly the analysis concerning VAT, because they will have obtained from their HMRC officer an agreement to treat a payment which gives rise to benefits as partly a donation and partly payment for the services. They may believe that VAT is only due on the cost value of those services, or the market value. This arrangement has often been agreed with officers of HMRC. Particularly some 10 years or more ago, prior to the notorious Tron Theatre case, the general perception of VAT inspectors was that tax should only apply to the market value of any benefits given. But the Tron decision established a different analysis, which was that all of the payment given would be treated as payment for the services or goods supplied (however tokenistic those might be compared to the payment received), as long as the only means of obtaining those benefits was to pay the entire donation in question. The decision made by the Court of Session in Scotland is considered a notorious one, because it defies all common sense. It creates problems and complexities of which the following are perhaps only a sample.

First, if (admittedly in an unlikely event) all of the components of the benefit offered in acknowledgement of the donation are genuinely available to all comers at a standard open-market value, then it would be entirely wrong to tax the entire donation because the donor could have obtained their benefits for lower fixed prices elsewhere. In that situation, HMRC agrees (as it has to) that only the true value applies. The difficulty with this concept is that there are usually aspects to the benefits package which do not have open currency and open availability.

Second, it is not always the case that, where a donation is made, a suggested value is placed upon a donation, such as will secure the relevant benefits, but rather that benefits are provided without reference to a particular level of donation that would give rise to them. This begs the question as to exactly what value can possibly be attached to the benefits, since no specific value has been put forward by the charity as necessary to secure the benefits on offer. In this situation, if the arts organisation can demonstrate that, below a given figure, the benefits in question were not available, then HMRC will usually accept that the price of the benefit is the given figure alone. Any donation element above that figure can be treated as pure donation.

Third, the Tron rule is apt to cause HMRC officers to assert that a payment cannot be a donation at all if the donor is asked to make a suggested level of payment in support of the fundraisers' campaign. For example, if they are asked to tick a box saying they will give £150 per year, this is sometimes erroneously looked upon by HMRC officers as indicating something other than a donation which has been voluntarily given without any prospect of anything in return, simply because a specific number has been suggested and accepted.

Fourth, there are certain situations where the benefits given in return are so valueless by comparison to the amounts being offered by way of donation, that even HMRC regards the Tron principle as being stretched beyond all credulity, and they should be prepared to enter into negotiations to discuss a more reasonable value that could be attributed to those benefits in order that the VAT burden more closely reflects the value of the supplies made. But it should be noted that this is much more likely to be negotiable in situations where the gap between the value of the benefits and the value of the payment received is significant. It may also be regarded as unlikely to apply to corporate giving, and so is an aspect that is likely to apply only to individual giving. Unlike Gift Aid, which has set benefit limits, there is nothing in the VAT legislation which prescribes this, so the fallback position is that the entire "donation" is viewed as consideration for the benefits received unless the position is negotiated upfront with HMRC. In this situation, therefore, it pays to enter negotiations at the beginning of a fundraising campaign, and not to seek to apply a rule along these lines without negotiating.

There are two further areas in which the Gift Aid rules depart materially from the VAT rules and can cause confusion.

The first of these is as regards to what we can call "cause and effect". For VAT purposes, a transaction does not arise unless both parties enter into it willingly, and in reasonable knowledge of what they will get out of it. For this reason, if a donor makes a payment, without any knowledge or expectation of receiving a benefit, then, strictly speaking, no VAT will apply, since the benefit will itself be a pure gift to the donor. However, there may be some difficulty in demonstrating where an unsolicited benefit has been given, because it is possible for an arrangement to be made orally (that is without paperwork), and still be a binding contract for VAT purposes. The natural assumption of HMRC will be that there was an agreement to give a benefit unless there is some form of proof otherwise. Furthermore, even if a benefit is not promised, but is habitually given to people who make donations above a certain limit, then the repetitive expectation will form some kind of agreement, although at what point in time that kind of expectation crystallises is a difficult point.

It is, however, true that, on the back of this particular approach, organisations have not paid VAT where they indicate that a benefit may or may not be forthcoming. The idea here is that, if you tell a donor that there is some prospect of a benefit, but they are not guaranteed it, then you cannot be entering into a transaction, since you do not guarantee to provide the benefit. This seems an attractive argument, but the difficulty is that the possibility even of being selected to receive a benefit is governed entirely by having made the donation in the first place, and that in itself creates some kind of benefit. So organisations which put the point in this way to their donors should be aware of the legitimate expectation aspect of the arrangement. If they do provide the benefit they said they might provide, then it is difficult to argue that they only might have provided it, rather than they were offering it as a more or less certain benefit. Because there is so much fluidity in the treatment of VAT and donations/benefits, this kind of approach can work, but is certainly not without its risks.

But, to return to the basic principle that governs VAT, there is no VATable supply without a bargain struck between the payer and the recipient of the benefits. This must be contrasted very carefully with the position under Gift Aid, where it is sufficient for a benefit to arise "as a consequence of" the making of a donation in order for the benefit to be counted against the minimum benefit limits within the Gift Aid rules. This is a very different kind of "cause and effect". In this instance, the donor may have no desire for any benefit, and may be completely unaware that they will receive one. Nonetheless, the benefit is counted because they received it as a consequence of having given a donation. Thus, a benefit which could escape VAT because it was not bargained for, will not escape the benefit limits for Gift Aid on that footing. This means that unsolicited and unwanted benefits are a major danger in the Gift Aid regime. If a major donor is to be thanked in a material way, outside any agreements as to benefits that can be rendered, this can play havoc with the Gift Aid position on their donation. It is vital to avoid any uncontrolled and unsolicited acknowledgements that could be construed to be such benefits because they will then exist outside your control, and could cause significant difficulties.

The second fundamental difference arises in the nature of what actions are to be perceived as benefits, and which are not. The following analysis is based partly on published guidance produced by HMRC as regards both VAT and Gift Aid, and partly on what appears to be tradition. The table below gives examples of "acknowledgements" which can be ignored (though not always for both aspects) as being something other than a benefit. "Yes" designates that a benefit does arise and "No" that it does not.

Response	VAT	Gift Aid
Thank you letter (private)	No	No
Bare acknowledgement	No	No
Naming of room or building	No (potentially)	No (potentially)
Newsletter about charity's activities	Yes	No
Priority booking rights	Yes	No
Admission to view property, plants, animals, etc	Yes	No (potentially)

The term "bare acknowledgement" is intended to refer to the listing of the donor's name in a list of such names, the intention of which is merely to provide the most basic acknowledgement. That list can appear on a board in a building, or some similar display, in a yearbook, or in the programme for an event. A key point is that the donor's name should appear in ordinary type without any comment about the donor whatsoever. There does not appear to be a problem in mentioning a donor more than once in two different fora, but it is preferable to limit the number of acknowledgements to as few fora as possible. Repeated acknowledgement could be regarded as creating a form of publicity for the donor which might be seen as some kind of benefit. There appears not to be a problem over ranking donors by the amount they have given in such a list, rather than in alphabetical or random order. However, it would be very unwise to give one donor a larger type size than another. The newsletter which is disregarded for Gift Aid has to be one which deals with the activities of the charity, rather than being a newsletter about, say, a particular subject. Therefore care should be taken as to the scope and range of the newsletter contents.

Note, in the world of arts, Gift Aid appears to be blind to the issue of priority booking. This has always been a bone of contention with regards to VAT treatment because the principal benefit arising from priority booking appears to be for the charity rather than the supporter – the charity receives the ticket sales money earlier that it otherwise would. But it cannot be denied that in certain situations priority booking allows a person to receive access to better seats than they might have got through general booking, so it is helpful that Gift Aid seems to ignore such an arrangement, despite the fact that VAT does not. However, agreement should be obtained from the Gift Aid office for anything that goes beyond simple priority booking, such as absolute guaranteed booking, or intervention by staff of the charity concerned to ensure that a booking is made on behalf of a major donor.

Gift Aid benefit valuation

In administering Gift Aid, the next step is relatively simple as regards any interaction between a donor and the benefits received. Having determined which features are not regarded as benefits at all, the fundraiser needs to list the remaining features to determine whether their value stays within the minimum benefit limits given in the appendix to this chapter (see Additional Information). In order to do this, they have to follow the following broad valuation principles:

● If there is a specific open-market value (that is a price in the shops, so to speak) that a benefit attracts, then that will be the value to be placed upon that benefit.
● Failing this, if there is a similar product that has a value, that value is adopted.
● If neither of the above apply, look at the cost of the product or service. The cost may include components that are not direct costs to the charity, perhaps because an altruistic organisation is willing to bear the cost. The Gift Aid rules do

not ignore costs borne by organisations outside the charity. Thus, for example, if you throw a drinks party which is entirely sponsored by a local company, the cost to the local company would be regarded as the cost base of the benefits in question. This can cause problems, because the company may not wish to divulge that cost to you.

When using the cost-based approach, you also have the difficulty of working out a unit cost per donor. This may be straightforward in situations where a single costed product is being produced, but usually this category is inhabited by such things as educational talks, backstage tours, drinks receptions and similar. These will generate definable costs, but those costs are shared between many donors. An approach which can be sanctioned by HMRC is to divide the overall cost into the number of donors that took up the benefit. (Note that this is not the same as dividing the cost into the number of donors who had access to the benefit). Thus, if a party is organised with a capacity of 50 attendees, and 200 people could attend (but in practice a maximum of 25% are going to accept), then the cost of the party is not necessarily divided by 200 but rather potentially by 50. This in itself assumes that 50 people do actually attend the party. If in the end, it is attended by only 35 people, the cost is divided between 35. This can create difficulty in predicting the value that would apply to any such benefit, because the number by which the cost is to be divided may not be known in advance. This can give rise to Gift Aid being unavailable for the donors who did attend the entertainment, even though it might be preserved, in theory at least, for those who did not.

Such a situation is obviously perilous and steps should be taken therefore to agree with HMRC (in advance) of a more practical way of dealing with this cost. This writer has, despite the above comments, noted that HMRC has agreed in certain circumstances to allow the cost to be pro rated across the entire donor base (but this should not be taken for granted). It may, however, be possible to agree that the benefit should be restricted to a prearranged budget of expenditure per attending member. Taking the above illustration, that budget would assume attendance of 50 and therefore there would not be a penalising effect for the fact that only 35 had actually attended.

In general, where benefits are offered which may have a variable cost, and where the only way of defining the Gift Aid value is by reference to cost, there are significant traps which ought to be addressed at the stage of determining what the benefits ought to be.

- Where a benefit does not generate any extra cost whatever, either to the charity or any external organisation on its behalf, then there is no benefit for Gift Aid as long as there is no ascertainable market value. This can classically arise in regard to offering such things as a meeting with the chief executive or the artistic director. Those individuals may give time, but that does not create a specific cost to the organisation, and no other costs are incurred in putting on the activity. Therefore, despite the fact that such an activity could be seen as the most invaluable acknowledgement of a donation, it is, paradoxically, likely to generate the least problem for the Gift Aid status of the donation.

Two comments from fundraisers often arise out of the above analysis. The first is what to do about external organisations that have agreed to give benefits to your members, but where there is no cost for a function or a product as such. A classic example is where donors may be given special status or treatment at a hotel near an arts venue in recognition of having supported it. The hotel is providing a potential benefit either in enhanced service or reduced prices, but does so largely for a commercial reason – to attract a generous and probably wealthy individual into their premises. There is a risk, however, if the arrangement is packaged in such a way as to provide obvious financial benefits, that HMRC may treat it as a benefit for Gift Aid purposes. In such a case, it is obviously preferable for the assumed benefit to the donor to be as vague as possible, and to remove the prescriptive nature of any such offering. This can be very difficult where the donor arrangement is structured as a "membership" but it is worth trying to soften the impression of benefits being derived from a donation, as distinct from the arrangement being to the commercial benefit of the hotel as well as the donor.

The second thorny issue is drinks receptions used for development purposes. It is often remarked that inviting a donor to such an event is really an invitation for them to make a further donation. They are not receiving their invitation because they have made a previous donation, but in expectation of some new donation. The difficulty with this concept is that, despite all of the above points, the donor may have been invited as a consequence of giving the previous donation, simply because it is a well known fact that a previous donor is more likely to be a future donor. Thus, the cause of the invitation is rooted in having made the donation in the first place. Equally, the Gift Aid legislation does not specify that the benefit has to come *after* the receipt of any donation that triggered it. It may be that a benefit precedes the donation. Therefore a specific invitation to an event that can engender a donation could be regarded as a benefit that is consequent upon that donation. That said, most commentators would currently accept that this would only be likely to apply in unusual circumstances, such as where a promise of a later donation was made, though the point is not particularly clear.

As a consequence, in order to help disassociate such an event from a benefit consequent upon a donation, and particularly where there is a track record of donations being made by the invitee, it is safest to arrange matters so that the event is intended to showcase some aspect of the organisation's development or activity for general interest to potential donors and non-donors alike. Although one purpose behind the event would be to engender further donations, the event could be open to those who are unlikely to make them, such as journalists, members of the government or related civil service organisations, employees of other arts organisations, suppliers to the charity, and so on. This will make it easier to say that the donor's invitation to the event was simply coincidental with their actual donations, and that the event had a wider purpose.

VAT valuation

The situation with VAT is entirely different. The first thing you have to determine is whether any of the features you offer constitute a benefit, by reference, for example, to the preceding table. If there are no benefits as such, then the entire payment is by way of donation, which is outside the scope of VAT (there is no supply). But if there is a supply, then the next thing to determine is whether there might be an argument that part of the value of the payment relates to a donation rather than to that supply. This is only likely to arise if the donation is substantial by comparison to the value of the benefits, and is a situation that needs to be negotiated with HMRC in advance rather than assumed. The initial assumption should be that any payment which gives rise to benefits is solely made in relation to those benefits, however counter-intuitive that may seem.

If it can be agreed with HMRC that only part of the payment is for benefits, it must also be agreed how to value those components. This will usually be done either by reference to some kind of open-market value or to the cost of any component. It could involve a mixture of both. However, there are going to be examples where there is no open-market value, nor is there a cost. A classic example in the world of arts is priority booking. Unlike with the case of Gift Aid, where, if there is no open-market value and no cost, there is no issue, VAT officers insist that a value of some sort has to be ascribed. More often than not, this involves plucking a figure out of thin air. But even such a baseless valuation has to be given some form of rationale, and that can sometimes be applied by reference to a percentage of the value of tickets which a typical customer might buy. For example, priority booking may be worth 10% of the value of the likely purchase of the tickets in question. But, this is an area where there is no prescribed rule at all.

In the event that the donation or membership subscription is not sufficiently large to justify departure from the general rule (that the entire payment is consideration for services), then the entire amount of money has to be apportioned against individual components of the benefits package. As mentioned above, this is overridden automatically where all of the components of the package are ones that are widely available at an open-market price. In that situation, it is obvious that the open-market value of each benefit is the one to be ascribed to it. However, even if only one element is not available for an open-market value on readily available terms, then a more sophisticated valuation system has to be entered into. This can be a bespoke approach, which means that any rational suggestion could be put to HMRC as part of a negotiated settlement. The starting point, however, is to look at the cost components of each element to determine the percentage that each benefit makes up of the whole. To give a very simple example, if there are four distinct benefits, and the cost of providing each of them is (conveniently) exactly the same, then 25% of the payment made by the donor will be attributed in VAT terms to each of the benefits in turn.

It may be possible, in certain circumstances, to argue that certain elements that have an open-market value should be attributed to that value, with only the remainder being divided by reference to a cost ratio exercise. But, again, as there is a risk that this is not an arithmetically sound basis upon which to carry out the apportionment (because cost and market value are dissimilar comparators), the issue ought to be discussed in detail with HMRC at the outset.

The reason for identifying a value (or proportionate value) attributable to each kind of benefit is that not all benefits will be subject to VAT at 17.5%. Alternative VAT treatments are the zero-rate (0%) and exempt services. On the surface of it, these might appear to be the same, but they are different for reasons to do with your cost base. In simple terms, whereas VAT can be reclaimed on costs which relate to making taxable or zero-rated supplies, the VAT on costs of an exempt supply is largely irrecoverable in your VAT returns. The impact of making exempt supplies (if any arise) needs to be discussed carefully with the finance director.

In general, a benefit will be standard-rated unless there is a specific zero-rate or exemption that applies to it. It is worth looking at these exceptions.

Classifying benefits for VAT

The zero-rated benefits are almost entirely likely to arise in respect of the provision of a printed newsletter, programmes for performances or events, a yearbook, or set of annual accounts. As long as these are physically printed and sent out in hard copy to your members, then subject to certain detailed rules (which need to be investigated), they should be zero-rated. Note, however, that if the newsletter is sent by electronic means, or issued in CD or similar formats, then the supply will be standard-rated. In many cases, the only component which departs from the usual standard-rated liability is this printed material. However, the following activities could be exempt from VAT.

If you provide an insurance benefit (which is not unheard of where a membership scheme is concerned) then that is likely to be exempt. The provision of certain educational activities is also potentially exempt, although the rules surrounding these are likewise complex and perilous. It does, however, open an opportunity for you to consider whether, if one of your benefits is essentially educational (for example, invitations to talks on the development of a certain kind of theatrical practice), it might count as exempt education.

The key potential exemption, however, is in relation to the provision of tickets to allow entrance to your cultural offering. Certain organisations are able to exempt their activities under a "cultural exemption" in the VAT legislation which allows the admissions charged to customers to be exempt from VAT rather than taxable. The finance director of each organisation should be well aware of whether or not this applies to them. If it does, then any inclusion of admission rights of this nature in the membership package, or in response to the donation, should be exempt from VAT. There are very good reasons why certain cultural organisations do not qualify for this exemption, and no assumptions ought to be made.

Where cultural exemption does apply, there is a somewhat grey area concerning kinds of activity that could be regarded as falling within that remit. Where, for example, should we classify the ability to attend a rehearsal? The likely view is that this qualifies as part of the exemption because it is admission to a kind of performance. It should not matter that it is not strictly a public performance. However, the point has not been tested in the courts, so is not absolutely certain. And what about priority booking, and reserving seats in other guises, all of which of course are integral to the tickets that are being reserved or booked? There is nothing in the legislation that says that the supply of the right to have a priority on a waiting list is the same as the supply to which the waiting list finally refers. Therefore, the likely interpretation is that priority booking and similar derivatives will be taxable, even if your organisation is culturally exempt. However, even that point has not been aired in the courts.

We cannot leave the question of potential exemption of payments without nodding in the direction of an exemption for subscriptions to philanthropic bodies. This is a very narrow exemption which is supposed to relate solely to membership arrangements (so it will not apply to one-off donations). It only allows membership subscriptions to be wholly exempt if the services in question are referable to a philanthropic objective of the organisation. On the whole, philanthropic arrangements are regarded as ones which are aimed at relieving human distress or improving the living conditions of humans in general. A somewhat bizarre VAT tribunal decision has held that a nature conservation trust did so by preserving wild fowl, and therefore it is not beyond the bounds of belief that an arts organisation could be looked upon as being philanthropic in this narrow sense. But even then, the fairly obvious purpose of the legislation is that those benefits should be made widely available, and the member will be paying a small amount for a very heavily subsidised charitable access to a range of sustaining benefits. It does seem unlikely that a cultural or arts organisation would be able to argue that this exemption applies. Nonetheless, certain HMRC officers may have agreed that it does, and any organisation in that happy position will be able to exempt the entire subscription, as long as the benefits are seen to fall within the purposes of the philanthropic body. Before leaving this topic, it should be noted that invitations to drinks parties are hardly likely to be included in that definition.

Therefore, it is possible that a donation or membership subscription can be split between elements which are standard-rated, zero-rated, and exempt from VAT, and that this can lead directly to a modified effective rate of VAT being applicable to the payment received. And since it is at least conceivable that a package of benefits will fall within the Gift Aid donor benefit limit, the VAT treatment described above may go hand in hand with the treatment of the payment as a donation for Gift Aid purposes, whereupon the charity will be able to reclaim around 28p in every £1 given from HMRC. There has never been any suggestion that the VAT treatment covers any part of this tax rebate, and it should only apply to the amount that is actually paid by the donor.

Tiers of membership
A particular issue could arise on VAT with membership schemes involving tiers (basic, bronze, silver, gold, etc). A classic format of this arrangement is for the basic level to be built upon, such that the next level up includes all of the benefits of the basic level, but with certain additional benefits. In each case, there is at least a possibility that the enhancement in benefits is very minor, such as an extra degree of priority booking, or simply a more detailed newsletter.

Sometimes, however, the base level of benefits are not improved upon at every level, and the only enhancement the member receives is in being able to regard themselves as a bigger supporter (an essentially philanthropic motive). Their name may appear high on an acknowledgement list, to show that they have generosity beyond the mere material benefits achieved from the donation. In this case, there will be a defined level at which all the benefits are given, and any payment above that is a donation. For example, if the base membership level delivers all the benefits that are available at any level, then the price of base membership is the limit of the value of the benefits in question, and no higher price need be used.

However, there is usually some enhancement of benefit available at the higher levels. Naturally, the degree to which the benefits are enhanced tends to reduce the higher one goes up the chain. Nonetheless, unless HMRC can be induced to agree that high levels of the chain largely involve the making of a donation, any enhancement of the benefits, however trivial, will create a potential extra VAT liability based on the value added in the membership segment in question.

To illustrate this, say the base membership value is £50 per year, and all of this value is attributed to benefits, of which one is priority booking, and the bronze member pays £150 a year and receives an extra week of priority booking over their base level counterpart then, unless otherwise negotiated with HMRC, the £100 difference paid by the bronze member is all attributed to priority booking, and therefore all technically subject to VAT. If the silver member, paying £300 per year, only receives the same benefit as the bronze member, then the valuation of their package can only be based on £150, and not the full £300. However, if they also receive, say, an invitation to a drinks party in addition to the bronze member's allocation of benefits, then the extra £150 they pay over and above their bronze counterpart will be attributed to attendance at the drinks party. Again, there may be room for negotiating with HMRC a lower value which can be attributed to that incremental drinks party, by reference to a value of £150 per head being absolutely excessive.

As we know, many of the more generous donors are seeking a sense of involvement and feedback rather than any additional benefits. It may be possible to agree with HMRC that a distinction between a bronze and silver level would be simply the agreement that the donor will be contacted by telephone once a year to describe how their extra payment, over and above the bronze level, has been allocated within the mix of the activities of the charity. HMRC may be willing to see this as no more than feedback on the use of the donation, and not a benefit as such. The less any such activity could be interpreted as a form of entertainment for the donor, the more likely it is to achieve success in this aim.

In very general terms, the more that responses to a donation or membership are geared to feeding the genuinely altruistic and philanthropic motivations of the benefactor, the less the VAT liability is likely to be.

Phantom benefits
An extremely common issue both for VAT and Gift Aid treatment of donor benefit schemes is the tendency for the fundraiser to exaggerate the things that the donor will receive in return, even going as far as offering benefits which are not specific to the membership. This can arise in two basic ways.

First, the member may be told that they will be able to do something, or have some kind of benefit, without being told that in fact they do not need to be a member in order to qualify for it. These are activities that anybody can have free, albeit they may not be aware of that, and they may not be told about it in structured terms otherwise than through being a member. For example, if they are promised to be invited to a model showing once per year, this will only count as a benefit of their membership for both VAT and Gift Aid purposes if the general public cannot attend. But, if the model showing is open to all comers (without preferential terms of access being made to the member), then the model showing cannot be a benefit of membership, because membership is not required to enjoy it. Hence, a donor has been told of a benefit which does not actually exist.

The second way that it can happen is that a scheme of potential benefits is put together by enthusiastic fundraisers who offer things which it transpires are not valued by the donor. These offerings are never taken up. For example, if it is an event such as a social gathering, for one reason or another, the gathering never takes place.

The difficulty, particularly in the area of VAT, is that such benefits remain apparently a contractual term of the relationship which gave rise to the payment by the donor. The mere fact that something has not happened, does not mean that it has not been "made available".

In both of the above kinds of instances it can be very difficult to dissuade an HMRC officer from taking the view that a tangible benefit does exist. In the case of the benefit which is genuinely open to everyone, and not to the membership alone, it can often be difficult to prove that this is the case. An arts organisation cannot assume that an HMRC officer understands how the arts world works. If you promise that members will be able to go backstage and talk to any actor or musician who happens to be willing to talk to them, then the mere fact that this is, of course, equally open to any enthusiastic member of the audience, will count for very little with the average HMRC officer who would not imagine that this was true.

Even if the matter went as far as a tribunal hearing, it might be necessary to describe why it was not the case that the member had some form of enhanced opportunity to meet with actors and musicians. In the case of the second example, where the benefit is promised but nothing occurs, the difficulty is that VAT legislation makes it reasonably clear that it is the opportunity to access a benefit which is the benefit, rather than the reality of whether the benefit ever takes place. Thus, if a member could have insisted under the terms of their contract to be invited to a social gathering, then they have effectively bought that right, and the benefit is there whether they take it up or not. That benefit can be taxed accordingly.

The general lesson from this is to avoid a phantom benefit. No doubt that is also a good lesson to be learned from a purely marketing point of view.

Very major donors

The issues affecting very major donors are similar to those given above, but the emphasis can sometimes be different. In this case, whilst it is possible that certain of the responses that a cultural body will give to their major donor will be set out in writing, others will just be offered intuitively. In particular, where a major donor likes to be recognised by the staff of the organisation and treated in a particularly friendly way (as though they were indeed a personal friend), the mere fact of giving the donor that kind of kindness and respect should not constitute some form of benefit that they have purchased by their donation either for the purposes of VAT or Gift Aid. But the major donor who believes that their donation is so substantial that they can simply drop in and be included on lectures, shows, exhibitions, etc. without paying a ticket price can cause severe problems.

In particular, it pays to bear in mind that Gift Aid works on the basis that benefits are valued even where these have not been promised, but where they are engendered by the giving of the donation. This means that a demanding major donor might invalidate a Gift Aid claim, and their own higher rate taxpayer Gift Aid claim, by seeking to be included in casual attendances of this nature without making payment. The value to that donor of a warm feeling that they can simply drop in any time they like and not pay their way is immaterial compared to the enormous value of the tax issue both to the donor and to the cultural body. Every step must be taken to warn such a donor of the consequences (entirely unavoidable from the fundraiser's standpoint) of that kind of behaviour. Equally, where the degree of friendship that the organisation feels for the donor induces it to wish to provide the donor with hospitality by way of parties or a meal from time to time, these fairly specific benefits can cause great difficulty with Gift Aid. As shown in the Additional Information, the maximum Gift Aid limit is so extremely low that even one wayward step in this area can cause tremendous problems.

These difficulties can be extended to VAT, even though there was no particular agreement for such benefits to be provided at the outset of giving a donation. The difficulty here is that HMRC might argue that VAT applies to all benefits irrespective of the fact that they were not bargained for at the outset if there was a general assumption on the part of the donor that their donation had purchased this kind of free and easy access.

Naming rights

Very major donors are often acknowledged not merely by name in a yearbook or programme, but by a permanent or semi-permanent allocation of the name to a part of the cultural organisation's infrastructure, commonly a room, a wing, or indeed an entire building in certain cases. An acknowledgement of a very major donation in this way is not fundamentally different from a bare acknowledgement given in a yearbook, but given the sums involved, great care ought to taken, including obtaining, if at all possible, written clearance from HMRC that the non-VATable and Gift Aid-friendly treatment of the donation will be respected by them. A greater area of risk is where the name happens to have some resonance in any local or national market from a commercial standpoint, though this arises more often with donations from substantial trusts, which go beyond the scope of this chapter.

The VAT manuals issued by HMRC also instance the naming of a university chair, and state fairly unequivocally that such a naming will not be regarded as a benefit. By analogy there is every reason to assume that the naming of a particular position, such as an orchestral place, the position of a director of a theatre, or some form of curatorial role in a museum, should be regarded as not giving rise to a benefit, always assuming that the naming has no advertising benefit for the donor.

Such namings do not appear to have to be permanent in order to attract this tolerance. In certain cases, the naming is given on the basis of a donor's pledge which is not always fulfilled. In such instances, the naming may be removed where the donor does not keep up the donations, or after the donor has ceased making agreed donations. To date there has been no indication that HMRC has equated the temporary nature of a naming with the actual flow of funds to suggest that there is a reciprocity that gives rise to a transaction. That said, it could decide to launch such an attack in the future, so care has to be exercised in the whole area of naming rights.

Charitable foundations

The above mentioned Gift Aid rules do not apply when the donation has been received from a charitable foundation. That is, Gift Aid cannot be claimed on the receipt of a payment from a charitable foundation, since the charitable foundation itself does not pay either income tax or capital gains tax. Gift Aid simply does not arise. That is not strictly true of VAT, where any benefits offered in return for the charitable foundation's payment will be dealt with in the same way as above. There may, however, be certain minor differences in the VAT treatment where the mere fact that the supply is not being made to an individual could have a bearing, but these would be rarities.

Certain of these charitable foundations are of course known highly colloquially as "private charities". No such thing exists in law, but they can sometimes appear to be so. This is a situation where a wealthy individual makes a donation to their charity for the charity to distribute in various ways. No doubt that charity will claim the appropriate Gift Aid relief. The difficulty comes when that charity distributes money to another charity, which provides tokenistic benefits in return. The Gift Aid that the family charity has reclaimed is based on no benefits having been passed back to the original donor. If benefits arise from the next charity down in the chain of giving, this creates a dilemma, because the benefits provided by that charity, added to other benefits as may pass back to that individual, could breach the minimum benefit limits, and appear not to be carried on in a control environment. But, as the receiving charity will not be reclaiming Gift Aid, this is more a problem at the level of the charity which is making its donation. Nonetheless, given that one of fundraisers' key aims is to be sensitive to all aspects of their donor's position, they should at least be aware of the potential conflict. Many arts organisations will not accept that a donation from a charity carries any benefits, even of a tokenistic kind, for the originator of the wealth for this very reason.

Indeed, it is because of this kind of issue that the Finance Bill 2006 has introduced rules intended to stop "major donors" from extracting substantial value from a charity in return for their "donation", whilst still benefiting from tax-related donation reliefs. Although this legislation was framed almost entirely with family or "private" charities in mind, the fact that it is not possible to define a charity along those lines (private charities do not exist as such), has meant that the rules relate to all charities. The rules appear only to "punish" situations where a form of tax relief has been enjoyed by the donor, and some or all of the value on which that relief has been enjoyed is extracted out of the charity once again. It remains to be seen whether, in practical application, seemingly innocent scenarios are caught by this legislation as certain commentators believe is possible. The detail of these new rules is in Additional Information.

Splitting benefits from donations

The straitjacket represented by the Gift Aid benefit rules in particular, and VAT to a slightly lesser extent, has given rise to a practice which it seems HMRC readily accepts as long as it is properly executed. This is to create two different payments, one for the benefits that arise, and one which is a pure donation. Again, this is a somewhat counter-intuitive measure, because the benefits are, in the minds of both the donor and the fundraiser, an acknowledgement for the donation. Nonetheless, if it is made clear in the agreement with the donor that one payment goes towards the benefits (valued broadly in line with the above guidance) and that a separate payment is a pure donation, then the benefits are not counted in the Gift Aid claim, which is limited solely to the donation. The benefits, however, also do not count towards the donor benefit limits for Gift Aid purposes. Clearly, it must be obvious to the donor that it is sufficient for them to make the payment for the benefits alone in order to enjoy those benefits. The donation has to be freely given with no expectation of the benefits in return. Most major donors will understand the rationale for this and will accept the arrangement without trying to take advantage of it. The possibility that advantage might be taken does, however, need to be taken into account.

If any donor in this category seeks to "take advantage" in the way described above, then the organisation has no choice but to allow them to do so. If it resists, by depriving the donor of the benefits, or failing to agree that the payment purely for the benefits will be sufficient to secure them, then it casts significant doubt on the entire structure, and could cause the invalidation of the Gift Aid claim on all of the donation elements within the same category. HMRC recommends that two separate payments be given for these two separate activities.

On the whole, however, a single payment may be given, as long as a declaration is signed by the donor which includes the split of the payment for the benefits on the one hand and the Gift Aid donation on the other. It would be wise to obtain professional advice on the way in which this split is to be described, in order for it to be valid. Given that the split in value between the benefits and the donation may differ year on year, donors may need to be persuaded to make the declaration repeatedly. This may cause resistance in donors who believe that a Gift Aid declaration only has to be signed once in order to cover all subsequent gifts, but in the case of this kind of split donation, where the percentages relating to the gift and to the benefits are not necessarily fixed, the process has to be repetitive.

In this instance, and as long as the same point applies whereby the donor does not need to make the donation in order to receive the benefits, VAT will be automatically limited to the price for the benefits, and will not apply to any part of the donation. Again, if a VAT officer takes the view that in reality and practice the full amount would have to be paid in order to access the benefits, this will override the split arrangement, and the whole payment (or both payments) will fall subject to VAT.

Direct tax consequences of gifts of shares and real property

It is also worth mentioning that, if a potential donor holds quoted securities or real property, substantial tax savings of up to 80% of the value of the gift can be made if these are gifted to a charity. Admittedly, the savings are unlikely in practice to reach the theoretical maximum and they would accrue to the donor rather than to the charity, but, in the right circumstances, this could still be a very attractive option for all concerned.

In the event of a gift or sale at undervalue of a qualifying investment or interest in land to a charity, no capital gains tax will arise on the disposal. The actual tax savings will depend upon the circumstances, but in the event that an asset with no base cost is gifted by an individual who is subject to tax at the higher rate and that no taper relief or annual exemption is available, the maximum of 40% could be achieved. This compares with a maximum saving of 32.75% for a company paying tax at the marginal rate.

In addition, the difference between the market value of the asset (plus any associated costs of making the gift) and the aggregate proceeds (including the value of any benefits received by the donor as a consequence of making the gift) qualifies for relief as a deduction from the income of an individual and as a charge on income for a company, resulting in a maximum further tax saving of 40% and 32.75% respectively. Note the contrast between the lack of a limit to donor benefits, which merely act to increase the deemed proceeds, with the treatment under Gift Aid, where tax relief can be denied on the whole of a substantial gift because the value of donor benefits exceeds the minimum value, currently £250 (see Additional Information).

If you compare the position where an asset is sold (with a chargeable gain arising for the donor) and an equivalent amount of cash donated under Gift Aid (where, in the case of an individual, only 18% of the tax benefit accrues directly to the donor), it is clear that a donor can sometimes pass significant real benefit to a charity for a comparatively low real cost to themselves. This is particularly relevant for individual donors and the charity must seek to impress this upon them.

Fundraising events

Certain of the above rules are overridden by others which are specific to "one-off fundraising events". Unhelpfully, the definition of "one-off fundraising events" shows that the events need not be "one-off" at all. These are events which are special in some way, and arise from time to time, but are not continuous. They are only where a primary purpose of the event is to raise funds for the charity and where the event is "held out" or advertised as primarily for that purpose. These conditions themselves present problems considered shortly. However, it is important to understand how such an activity is treated in any case.

Where an activity can be treated as a one-off fundraising event, all of the receipts from the activity are exempt from VAT. Also, by reference to an extra-statutory concession C4, these activities are not subject to corporation or income tax when organised by the charity. On the surface of it, this gives what might have been a VATable and taxable activity a very convenient exemption.

It should be noted, however, that an exempt service for VAT purposes denies recovery of VAT on the relevant expenditure, so there is the distinct possibility in certain cases that the benefit derived from the exemption is marginal and in rare cases it can have a negative impact.

The exemption covers such things as ticket sales for the event, merchandise sold on the day, or shortly before, business sponsorship associated with the event, and any other receipts such as intellectual property rights and broadcasting receipts. It does not, however, apply to sales that would otherwise be zero-rated, such as sales of printed programmes or the auctioning of donated goods.

For VAT purposes, there is no choice as to whether an event be treated as taxable or exempt. If it is exempt under the criteria of the one-off event rules, then it must be exempt even if that is disadvantageous. This is not the case with the corporation tax relief for charities, since that is no more than a concession, although it is very doubtful if there is any situation where it would be beneficial not to take up that concession.

But for VAT there may well be a benefit. This could arise in a situation where the majority of the income arising from a one-off fundraising event comes from organisations which would be able to reclaim VAT charged to them. The kinds of events that subsist heavily on broadcasting money, where the television companies are able to reclaim any VAT charged, are disadvantaged by being treated as a one-off fundraising event. As there is no choice in whether to apply the exemption or not, it can only be avoided by making changes that disqualify the activity from being a one-off fundraising event. Clearly, professional advice ought to be obtained on this issue.

The exemption for one-off events applies to the charity that is to be the beneficiary, a group of two or more charities that are to share the benefits, or the wholly owned subsidiary of a charity (presumably the beneficiary) where the profits of that subsidiary are paid out to the charity, whether those profits are derived from the event, or from any other activity. Hence, the exemption for a one-off event can be broken by carrying out the activity through a company which is not a wholly owned subsidiary of the charity. Conversely, where two charities come together to organise a one-off fundraising event, and they wish the exemption to apply, they should avoid using a shared company to do it, since that will invalidate the exemption.

It is also possible to invalidate the exemption from a one-off fundraising event by deliberately not holding it out as such. If, for example, an event also marks an anniversary or other significant date, it can be held out purely as a celebration of that fact. Great care must be taken, when trying to invalidate the VAT exemption on this footing, to ensure that there is nothing in the literature which could be construed as a fundraising message which may cause the exemption to apply nonetheless. It should also be borne in mind that if a charity invalidates the VAT exemption, it will also invalidate the direct tax extra statutory concession which allows it to carry on the activity without paying tax on any profit. However, if it can justify the activity as being within its primary purposes, it would not pay tax in the first place, so that disapplication is not necessarily disadvantageous.

The extra-statutory concession for direct tax only applies when the activity is carried out in a charity, since when the activity is carried out in a wholly owned subsidiary, the corporation tax would be removed through the Gift Aided profit distribution.

For charities in general, the biggest trap in all of this is a failure to hold the activity out specifically as an event for raising funds, or in aid of, the charity. The legislation is unhelpful in saying that this must be specifically undertaken, and it often happens that an event which is so famous for raising funds, and which could hardly be regarded as having any other purpose, nonetheless is not specifically "held out" as a fundraising event. HMRC may be willing to exercise leniency where it is simply impossible to conceive that the event was anything else than this, though strictly speaking the legislation would allow it to disallow the exemption. Accordingly, irksome as it may seem, any event which would otherwise qualify for the exemption ought also to be held out specifically as one for fundraising, even though the general public may be very well aware that this is the only purpose it could possibly serve.

There is also the question of whether any of a charity's normal activities can be hived away from the general run of things in order to form a one-off fundraising event. As cultural bodies frequently become involved in activities which have a similar nature to fundraising events (such as special viewings, concerts, etc), it is tempting to think that a certain number of these day-to-day activities can be earmarked as a fundraising event, publicised accordingly, and treated as falling within the exemption rules. This is a risky approach, unless the event has a very distinct character from the general run of activities. This is because the underlying rationale of the legislation is that only ad hoc activities can be treated as exempt, and anything that is part of an ongoing continuing series appears not to qualify. Merely nominating one of the run of performances or exhibitions, for example, as your fundraising event, will probably not be sufficient to give it an exemption. Fortunately, many organisations are exempt under the cultural VAT exemption mentioned above in any case. Nonetheless, it is fairly obvious where an event has a very different character to the usual run of activities, and is clearly a "fundraising event". There should be relatively little difficulty in persuading HMRC where such clear-cut differences lie and where the exemption can therefore apply under the one-off fundraising rules.

One of the key criteria for treating an activity as a one-off fundraising event is that it must fall within the "15 events" definition. This confusing rule allows that up to 15 events can be carried out within the 12-month accounting period of the charity, without disqualifying the "one-off" nature of this exempt activity. In addition, only events of an essentially similar nature at the same location are counted towards the 15 events. This means that events of a dissimilar nature going on at different locations could amount to many more than 15 per year without the exemption being invalidated. Overriding this, however, is a presumption that in doing so the charity will not create unfair competition with commercial concerns, and therefore it needs to be aware of that potential sensitivity. If HMRC receives a complaint from a local commercial competitor, it may invalidate the exemption.

This 15 event rule can cause very serious difficulties where charities act in common with other charities for such events. If one charity has exceeded its 15 event allocation, then both charities are unable to treat the joint event as exempt from VAT. This, of course, has the same knock-on effect therefore to the direct tax extra-statutory rule. Furthermore, should a charity venture beyond the 15 events allocation in the given period, it will lose exemption for all such events during the year (along with the tax exemption), not merely those that exceed the 15. In response to this, the general rule followed by charities is to stay well within the 15 event limit, which has to be viewed as an absolute outside limit rather than an allocation that should automatically be fully taken up where possible.

There can be difficulties in defining exactly what an "event" is. It appears on the surface to be very wide, including even "virtual events" which can take place over the internet. Nonetheless, it is often the case that a charity will seek to create a fundraising event within an existing event. An example might be a theatrical performance where the hall will take 2,000 people in the audience, and in which a charity purchases, say, 1,000 tickets for its fundraising event. Half of the audience is made up of those who are seeking to benefit the target charity for fundraising purposes, and half are normal punters who have paid the usual price for the tickets. Assuming, in this illustration, that the theatre at which the performance is going on is not the same charity as the one which is attempting to raise the funds, the question that arises is whether the participation of 50% of an activity which is not a fundraising event per se can be construed to be a fundraising event on the part of the fundraising charity.

The answer appears to be quite probably that it can. If the tickets reserved by the charity are held out for sale for fundraising purposes, and particularly if there is a higher price involved, then this would appear to constitute an event for the charity. It does not, of course, constitute such an event for the theatre which is putting on the show for all 2,000 people, and it must charge VAT to the charity which is buying the fundraising event tickets (unless it is culturally exempt) as though there were no fundraising event going on. Despite this apparent positive outcome of such an "event within an event", it is the kind of scenario where clearance from HMRC in writing in advance would be a wise precaution.

As discussed, there is a different treatment for auctions of donated goods in that these are zero-rated for VAT, rather than exempt, and this can allow a potentially significant increase in recovery of VAT incurred on the costs of the event. This only applies to the sale of goods which have been donated for that purpose, and not to the sale of services (e.g. auctioning a holiday would not be included), nor to the sale of anything that has been bought in for the auction. Where the zero-rate does not apply, the sale is exempt.

Auctions also carry special Gift Aid rules. Although a purchase price cannot technically be a donation, HMRC accepts that participants often pay far in excess of an item's worth to benefit the charity. Where the item has a clear market value outside the auction, then that open-market value is deemed to be the benefit for the purposes of the donor benefit limits. If the purchase price is sufficiently "excessive", then the value ascribed to the purchase may be found to fall under the benefit limits. Where there is no widely available equivalent market value for the goods, none of the purchase price is taken to be a donation, and Gift Aid is thus unavailable. An example of an auctioned service which could arise in a cultural body is auctioning an opportunity for a walk-on part in a play. This would be exempt from VAT (not zero-rated as it is a service rather than goods). Gift Aid could not apply as the "product" being auctioned does not have a market price.

Costs of fundraising

So far in this chapter the focus has been mainly on what to do with the income streams from fundraising. But fundraising inevitably involves costs, and some of the VAT on those costs can be reclaimed (where taxable supplies are made as a consequence of the fundraising), and some cannot (such as where exempt supplies are made as a consequence of the fundraising). The question of how to apportion the VAT on your costs between these taxable uses and exempt uses is a very big subject and one which will largely be dealt with by the finance operation within the charity. Nonetheless, this issue should be discussed with the finance director in order to determine a realistic budget for any fundraising project. Obviously, any budget for fundraising should include VAT that cannot be reclaimed, including a share of VAT on overheads that cannot be reclaimed. If the fundraising budget is expressed purely in net of VAT terms, it would in many cases underestimate the cost of generating the funds. The following remarks are designed to give positive observations on things that might affect whether VAT applies to these costs, and if it does, whether the VAT could be reclaimed.

The first aim must be to reduce the amount of VAT incurred from suppliers in the first place. All charities can purchase their advertising without paying VAT. This is not true of a subsidiary company of a charity. Where, for whatever reason, the activity is placed within a subsidiary company, and that activity is advertised, VAT will be charged. One example is where a subsidiary company carries out a one-off fundraising event, and pays for the advertising. VAT has to be charged, and is not reclaimable on the grounds that the event is exempt from VAT. But the chances are that most activities are carried on through the charity itself, and any advertising should be free of VAT.

Much of the charity's printing bill will also be VAT-free. Most newsletters are subject to a zero-rate of VAT. Yearbooks, and any brochures or programmes for activities, will also usually be free of VAT. There are certain circumstances where this might not be true, such as where the brochure is entirely pictorial, with no meaningful text, or where more than 25% of the leaflet/programme consists of forms for completion by the user, to be returned to provide the organisation with information. Also, there is a possibility that if a leaflet is printed on paper which is too thick, it may be subject to VAT rather than zero-rated. These issues have to be investigated to ensure that the minimum VAT burden is placed upon purchases.

Mailing packs are a key area where the VAT cost can be controlled. For arts organisations most mailing packs advertise performances or exhibitions, rather than schemes for general fundraising, but they are also often dealt with by a fundraising department. The general rule is that a mailing pack will often be wholly zero-rated where the majority of the contents of the pack would themselves be zero-rated if charged for separately. But this will only apply where a single supplier provides the entire pack. The zero-rated components which can categorise the entire package will usually be leaflets relating to the performance or exhibition. However, by concession, charities may also enjoy a zero-rate on pre-printed letters which carry personalised address details, and on campaign envelopes with over-printed campaign messages. As long as the mailing package does not contain anything other than a printed item (avoid ball point pens), if the majority of the items would be zero-rated by a manufacturer, then the entire package will be zero-rated. Charities should check with their mailing house that the full zero-rate is applied where at all possible. VAT issues should be factored into the original design of any such campaign.

In general, the VAT on the costs of fundraising will be recoverable either by reference to the overall activities of the organisation, or to the particular VAT treatment of the benefits provided to supporters. Until fairly recently, certain assumptions were made by charities (with the encouragement of HMRC) that the cost of soliciting grants and donations was a non-VAT recoverable cost per se, because the income to which those costs directly gave rise bore no VAT. Apart from the fact that this may not have been true of certain classes of activity where benefits were concerned (see above), it was a dubious proposition in any case. This is because the donations only exist to allow the mainstream activity of the organisation to go ahead, and it is therefore sensible to "look through" the donation and see how it supports the commercial activities of the organisation. Nonetheless, many arts organisations were aware of the illogicality of HMRC's position, and succeeded in continuing to reclaim VAT based on the overall activities of the charity without having to lose VAT by reference to the stream of donation of grant income which they also generated.

This favourable approach has been confirmed in a relatively recent High Court decision in the case of the Church of England Children's Society, backed by a landmark decision in the European Court of Justice concerning the treatment of raising capital for commercial companies.

This means that an arts and cultural organisation which generates donations and grants from its fundraising activities can enjoy VAT recovery on its costs to the extent that those donations and grants are used to cross-fund taxable supplies made by the organisation. Hence, if the charity is a theatrical company that does not make supplies under cultural exemption (for whatever reason), and whose supplies therefore are entirely taxable and whose taxable supplies are effectively cross-subsidised by the donations and grants, then the VAT incurred in running the fundraising operation is wholly recoverable.

Of course, it is rare for the position to be anything like so simple, particularly as many cultural organisations carry out an educational or outreach programme which is free of charge, and specifically non-business, and this can erode levels of VAT recovery. However, a fundraising executive needs to arrive at a clear picture of the likely rate of VAT recovery on activities to determine the genuine investment in an activity and to control the level of return the investment should enjoy.

What to do if you are unsure

The time will inevitably come when a fundraiser is unsure of how to proceed. Probably the most sensible option is to seek professional advice. This is not only because a particular set of circumstances is not templated exactly in comments made in this book, but also because an organisation may have received certain assurances from HMRC in the past which materially change the way the issue should be handled. The difficulty is the potential cost, and fundraisers are naturally cautious about incurring a specific cost for an idea which may not come to fruition, or which may not prove to be particularly lucrative, and it is a judgment as to whether the fees will give good value for money to you. However, organisations should invariably inform their advisers about the scale of the activity being considered before asking them to advise. Without an idea of how much the issue is worth to the organisation, the advisor cannot possibly tailor their own actions to deliver value for money.

This leaves a second port of call, which is to approach HMRC itself, usually through telephone enquiry lines. The first health warning to give about these enquiry lines is that the answer received to a query is often incorrect. This is frequently based on a failure by the officer responding to understand quite what the fundraiser is talking about. Given the fact that everything said is a phone conversation, it is extremely difficult to prove what was said, and what was comprehended, in order to determine who is at fault should the advice prove incorrect. Despite the recent tendency to give reference numbers for queries in order to try to track file notes of these interactions, there still remains a very distinct problem around culpability in the (not infrequent) event of the advice being incorrect. The response from these helplines should therefore be seen as nothing more than one of several potential opinions, or a "steer in the right direction".

To have any certainty, the matter needs to be set out in writing. This can be done without professional assistance, but often is best done with it, since, yet again, a written submission is prone to contain ambiguities and may give rise to misunderstandings, all of which should be lessened by the involvement of professional advice. In particular, failure to disclose all of the relevant features of, say, a fundraising scheme, could invalidate the written response received from HMRC. Ensuring that everything is materially complete, without including a raft of irrelevances, is vital to ensure that the response can be relied upon. It is also important to put the case in a way which does not appear to beg a negative answer from the outset. Tax officers are like committed givers in one particular sense: once they have adopted a notion or an idea with regard to your affairs, it takes a great deal of effort to persuade them to change their point of view. The written submission should give all the relevant information, but present the most positive arguments in one go, so that it stands the best chance of receiving a fair written response.

Clearly, obtaining advice either from HMRC or from advisers does risk unfavourable comment on the arrangements. The benefit of receiving this negative input is that changes can be made to improve your chances of a tax-efficient outcome. In situations where tax efficiency is absolutely essential, the risk can be warded off almost entirely. However, there may be situations, particularly where a scheme or an arrangement is in its infancy and therefore very small, where it appears pointless to the fundraiser to obtain advice, because the potential downside in monetary terms would be limited anyway. In that case, since taxation essentially involves the taxpayer making decisions, and waiting to see if they are accepted by HMRC, it is usually appropriate for the fundraiser (or their finance director) simply to move ahead with their own interpretation of the arrangement. But, should the scheme expand in financial terms, it must be remembered that the original reasons for not obtaining written clearance or advice will have been superseded, albeit gradually, leaving a potential exposure which unwittingly has not been addressed.

The final warning in this area is not to expect too much from your auditors. There is a common perception that an auditor must spend so much time delving into the detail of every aspect of the organisation that they can pick up every single possible area of taxation risk. But as a tax treatment can differ significantly between apparently identical models, or where the differences are apparently minute, it is not reasonable to expect an auditor to pick up such differences. Whilst there may be, in certain circumstances, a case to be made against an auditor for having failed to point out the difficulty with an approach, more often than not, this would not be reasonable. In any case, an auditor will always be looking backwards to what has gone before, and will only be able to pick up liabilities that actually do exist, and cannot be rectified. The aim must be to seek to address problems before they occur. So the auditor cannot be the wicket keeper for your loose delivery. The key strategy must be to bear down on taxation risks at the beginning of a process.

Chapter Ten

Guidance for boards, senior management and development staff

W hat are the implications of all this for organisations promoting the arts and heritage, and trying to develop sustainable support from individuals?

We have learned among other things that:

● Most donors and prospects are drawn from visitors and audience members.

● In many cases, organisations have an underdeveloped asset in the box-office and similar booking systems that enables them to identify those who attend regularly, what they like and, from their address and other information, quite a lot about them.

● Some of these people may have the capacity to make regular gifts, to increase their current support, and to make significant donations in their lifetime, but have never been identified and have never been asked effectively.

● Some of those who attend regularly, or have attended regularly in the past, and might support at a relatively modest level, might not be able to make a significant donation in their lifetime. But they may be charitably disposed. They might consider leaving a legacy to other organisations they support. But they do not (with some exceptions, such as The National Trust or The Art Fund) think of the cultural organisation they love, and that has given them such pleasure, as a charity, and they have never been asked for a legacy.

● We know that people tend to give no more than they are asked for. Some potential major donors are asked for too little, too soon. If people do not have a relationship with an organisation as someone who attends regularly, they have to be introduced and cultivated and involved for some time before they are asked for a significant gift.

● Cultural organisations are very well placed to embark on a strategic programme of engagement, involving the artists, performers, curators, conservators, librarians, designers, carpenters, gardeners and scene-painters who deliver the mission.

We also understand various aspects of the general marketplace for charitable giving, particularly the attitudes of the "donor-investor".

Passion for the cause and relationships with recipients

A constant theme of this book has been that a passion for the cause is the most powerful determinant of major and sustained charitable giving. Donors report consistently and across all sectors their desire to:

- Make a difference and be a catalyst for change.
- Be appreciated and respected for their support and the expertise that is the source of their wealth.
- Be concerned with governance, effective management and accountability.
- Build relationships with key people in the recipient organisation to reinforce the commitment to the cause and make giving enjoyable and fun. These should include those who deliver the mission, ultimate beneficiaries (where appropriate) and other donors.

We also note that badly managed relationships are the main cause of many regretted donations. Interviewees added that while an introduction from someone they respect may influence an initial relatively low level contribution, serious commitment will only develop as a result of the factors above.

We have also learned (from *Why Rich People Give* and later analysis) three other key points about the characteristics of the wealthier.

Disposition of wealth

People are unlikely to leave large legacies to charities unless they have a relationship with them. The 50% of interviewees with a charitable trust are more likely to leave a charitable legacy to their trust than directly to a charity, but virtually no-one had been asked effectively for a legacy. This is reinforced by the article on legacies in Chapter Eight.

Being self-made

The majority of wealthy people derive the bulk of their wealth from their business and professional efforts rather than from inheritance. For such people to transfer the focus of their financial efforts to giving away money, in addition to or in place of accumulation, requires an explicit process of self-reflection and self-education, as well as time and a decision to focus on this. This is particularly the case for those who do not come from a philanthropic tradition. In the UK this is partly about the attitudes and values of society, as well as the expectations and responses of decision-makers and opinion-formers to wealth creation and entrepreneurs.

Adverse or cynical reports about the supposed motivations of major donors, particularly if they are also giving time as board members or volunteer in another capacity, are unhelpful.

Sensitivity to sound financial management

Whereas there is a relatively high level of trust in non-profit organisations in the UK, charities should not be complacent, and, as we discuss in Chapter Two, with reports issued by organisations such as the charity New Philanthropy Capital, increasing amounts of information will be easily available in the public domain. Organisations promoting cultural activities may not be scrutinised as closely as those engaged in social welfare, but increasing transparency and accountability will be expected across the board.

Benefits and tax relief

We also know that as well as passion for the cause, people give, and continue to give, for a mixture of motives. Among these are those benefits offered by the institutions themselves, including privileged access and various forms of recognition. We have learned (in Chapter Nine) that the area of benefits and tax is fraught with difficulty and that there are numerous pitfalls for the unwary.

Can it be left to the development office?

We have seen that passion for the cause is the most important factor in determining the likelihood of encouraging sustained support of a cultural organisation – complemented by flawless management of the relationship with the donor once they have made an initial commitment. For support at a lower level this will be managed through the development office on the basis of a systematic model. But larger donations demand a bespoke approach that must be based on an understanding of what the donor likes and expects. This in turn will be drawn from research and listening to the donor.

What is clear, however, is that while the development office can have a significant impact on the interpretation of the donor wishes, and on the development and management of links with those who support at a relatively lower level, the core mission and the quality of what can be delivered is largely driven by factors wholly or partly outside its control. The main issues are discussed below[1].

a) The most important is the nature and quality of the artistic mission of the organisation itself, and the specific aspects of the permanent collections, exhibitions, performances and education and outreach work being undertaken or promoted at any one time. The development office can only present what is on offer; that is why sponsorship in particular – by individuals or corporates – is so hard to predict and is so variable, since some painters, poets or plays are more "commercial" than others.

b) The nature of the organisation itself – art gallery, performing arts company, presenting house, garden – will determine the response of the marketplace. At the moment the visual arts are riding high, especially in terms of corporate membership and entertainment. Opera and theatre companies, orchestras and dance groups can offer involvement with actors, writers, musicians, dancers and singers. (Tate has made the point in its promotional materials that *"conversations with.... clients are not restricted to interval times, nor interrupted by the resumption of a performance"*.) Museums and galleries and libraries may be able to introduce donors to curators or conservators. Some organisations are further advanced than others in developing individual giving schemes which exploit these opportunities. Presenting houses or festivals sometimes find it difficult to offer access to performers, whether at rehearsals or private events, and can compete for individual support with the companies appearing in their venues.

c) The reputation for competence and sound financial management will also have an impact. Although the artistic quality is most important, it is more challenging to raise money, and certainly to solicit legacies, in the face of adverse media coverage about board dissension, senior management splits or financial instability.

d) Another key determinant is the extent to which those who create the mission – the painters, curators, performers, writers, conservators, craftspeople – participate in the cultivation and involvement of donors and prospects. This in turn depends on how well the development function is understood and accepted within the organisation. This will be in part a reflection of the general corporate culture and planning process, and the extent to which development is seen as a key element of a varied funding portfolio.

Participation in cultivation events should not be undertaken as a favour to the development office, but because those involved understand that it is part of their

1. *Some of this is drawn from a private benchmarking survey of the development activities of eight major London arts institutions commissioned by the Royal National Theatre in 2000, undertaken by Theresa Lloyd.*

role, and indeed job description. This features in several case studies, and is reviewed in Chapter Eight.

e) The quality and commitment of the volunteer leadership is another major factor. The participation of a dedicated and effective group of people who are themselves givers, who are passionate about the organisation, who will involve their friends and peers, who will attend events and support the staff, is crucial. These people might be trustees, a development council, an active committee of a circle of high level givers, a supporters' syndicate. The development office will have some influence on this factor, based on the quality of its servicing and support, and the strength of its own links, but the relationship will be with the whole organisation, not only the development office.

The importance of volunteer participation in cultivating donors and asking for money features in several case studies, and is explored in detail in Chapter Eight.

e) The nature and range of entertaining facilities and the catering have a major impact on what the development department can offer. Depending on how these are managed within the institution as a whole, or at a touring venue, the development office may only have limited influence on the management of events and other entertainment arrangements.

f) The ability to identify and communicate with regular visitors is very important. Most organisations recognise (and all should) that their audience or visitors offer the most potential for encouragement to join or move up a ladder of giving.

Communications with those on the marketing and development database feature in several areas in this book, and are discussed at length in Chapter Six.

g) A linked but separate factor is the quality of the research information and database systems within the development function. Some organisations already make a significant investment in prospect research, database management systems linked to their box office, wealth screening and the maintenance of up-to-date donor files.

It is not enough to have such systems if they are not used and interpreted effectively. The purpose of all this is not only to find out about donors, but also to listen to them. As with marketing generally, the starting point should be where people are and what they think about you.

Database management is discussed in Chapter Six. Research, wealth screening and data protection are covered in Chapter Eight.

Taking these two latter points together, we see that an integrated approach to marketing and development is essential.

h) The need for a team of experienced high quality development professionals cannot be emphasised too strongly. In reality, although some donors may become involved as major givers, most start at a lower level and indeed as visitors and ticket-buyers. How they are identified and encouraged at an early stage will depend on the determination and flair of the development staff.

Early relationships will be with someone on the development team, and even when volunteer leaders, artists and senior experts are involved, it is the development staff who ensure that everything works smoothly, that non-development people are fully briefed, and that the relationship is serviced flawlessly. Good communications and good manners lie at the heart of successful individual giving.

There is a shortage of effective and well-trained people, and organisations can lose staff through a combination of a reputation for not being a good training ground or not supporting the development function, and because they pay less than others. However, salary levels also vary according to the level of responsibility – for example, whether seeking capital as well as revenue funding. Key factors in staff retention include the quality of the working conditions, the investment in training and, again, the respect and perceived importance of the development function within the organisation.

Apart from factors such as salary and promotion, development office staff move in order to work with organisations whose mission they support. This not only means that they will be more committed, and more able to empathise with donors, but also that they are more likely to gain internal acceptance and credibility. The importance of this is recognised by, for example, the Royal Academy of Arts, that pays for development staff to study for the art history diploma at Birkbeck, University of London, and gives half a day a month for art training.

There is a discussion on recruitment in Chapter Eight.

i) Some organisations make a significant investment in PR and communications that is separate from the development function but whose effectiveness underpins the reputation of the organisation and its ability to attract private sector support. Investment in communications and branding varies widely. Linked to this we note that the personality and profile of the director and the chair of the organisation can have a major impact, particularly on individual donor engagement.

The importance of corporate communications is discussed in Chapter Eight.

What does this mean for the organisation?

Development – the creation and sustaining of long-term relationships for the benefit of the institution – is something which must be undertaken by, and seen as the responsibility of, the whole organisation, from chair to caretaker. Everyone should be able to take pride in a flourishing network of supportive contacts.

The role of the development office is to orchestrate the initiation and management of those relationships, liaise (often behind the scenes for higher-level support) between donor and institution, interpret their vision and concerns to each other, and ensure flawless servicing and regular communication.

None of this can be achieved without investment.

Investment

A key element in success is, as we see in a number of case studies, the level of investment. In Chapter Eight there is a detailed discussion on investment ratios. Too many boards behave as though they somehow believe that development activities can thrive without the necessary investment, or that they "can't afford it" – sometimes these include industry leaders who would be aghast at the idea of cutting back on marketing and promotion spend, especially if times are hard.

Because it takes time to build up the relationships that are at the heart of a development function, and because recruitment of donors is more expensive than retention, those who are now investing in, for example, extensive audience development, higher-level giving schemes, long-term development of major donors, or corporate membership are spending more than those who are maintaining them in a steady state.

Although this, and the different ways of reporting costs explored in Chapter Eight, make benchmarking and comparisons complex, it is clear that it is unlikely that an effective development office will operate below an investment level of about 15%, and for some, 30% or more may be necessary to achieve their goals.

What can we conclude?

So, pulling together what we have learned from donors, from our case studies and from our experts, what are the lessons?

For the board of trustees

- Oversee the delivery of an outstanding artistic mission.

- Be aware of, and participate in, the debate about the future funding of the culture sector, and the need to strengthen independent financial sustainability and organisational capacity.

- Implement the guidelines of the Charity Commission on trustee recruitment, induction and training, and be aware of the duties and responsibilities of trustees, as set out on its website and in various documents.

- Ensure that the chair gives credible messages about the importance of development to the organisation by taking a leadership role in some aspect of the development activities.

- Adopt a strategic approach to development, regarding it as an investment in long-term financial sustainability – and the creation of a network of advocates.

- Ensure that the chair is involved in thanking major and loyal supporters.

- Recognise that the participation of at least some trustees in the cultivation of prospects and nurturing relationships with donors is essential.

- Ensure that there are givers and getters on the board.

- Consider the best way to engage volunteer leadership in the development process, and establish an effective structure to support it.

- Ensure that the contribution of volunteers is understood, respected and reported.

- Ensure that everyone on the board understands the principles of tax-effective giving, and the pitfalls relating to Gift Aid and VAT.

- Ensure that at least one person on the board really understands the development process, can monitor and mentor the development team, particularly the head or director, can review its plans and budgets before they are presented to the board for approval, and can represent and champion them to their peers.

- Ensure that the organisation is a philanthropic priority for all members of the board, and everyone gives according to their means.

- Recognise that investment in development is a risk, and ensure that there are management systems in place to manage that risk.

- Encourage the development of a corporate culture of engagement, and ensure that the chief executive and senior staff participate in nurturing major relationships, and have the resources to do so.

- Invest in leadership training for the senior management team.

- When times are hard, do not insist that the development office also cuts resources if the only reason for doing so is that the leadership lacks the courage to explain why it is necessary to invest in fundraising at this time.

- Monitor the development activity and the performance of the volunteer leadership and senior management support of it on an annual basis, and implement systems to addresses any shortcomings.

- Maintain awareness of the strategic funding environment within which the organisation is operating.

For the chief executive and senior team

- Plan and deliver a first-class cultural programme.

- Ensure that the board is fully aware of the strategic funding environment, the funding mix of the organisation, and the sensitivity to variances in particular areas.

- Ensure that a proper business planning, budgeting and management accounting and reporting system is in place and is used.

- Ensure that the principles of a corporate culture of engagement with donors are understood and implemented throughout the organisation. This means that fundraising and the development of relationships with individual supporters are seen as integral to the mission of the organisation; securing long-term financial security should complement the programme activities.

- Job descriptions, work plans and person specifications at senior level, including artistic programme implementation, should take account of the need to give effective time to nurturing relationships with potential and actual major donors.

- Make the case, and make time for, investment in leadership training for the senior management team.

- Ensure that targets are set for the development office that are based on a market analysis and detailed budgeting, not the funding gap. If there is an externally set target, such as for a capital campaign, allow sufficient time and resources for it to be planned effectively.

- Ensure that budgets take account of the need for long-term investment in developing relationships, and create an understanding of concepts such as return on investment and lifetime value of donors. Monitor investment carefully and regularly using Key Performance Indicators as well as financial information.

- Ensure that marketing and fundraising activities, and the messages that underpin them, are integrated and mutually reinforcing.

- Ensure a strategic approach to corporate communications, internally and eternally, including first-class brand and reputation management.

- Use the annual report as a means of communicating to stakeholders the mission, achievements, plans and costs of running the organisation.

- Ensure that the development office is fully staffed with the highest quality professionals, supported by first-class systems.

For the development office

- For major donors, be prepared to invest in initiating and managing relationships in a way that addresses the interests and concerns of the donor, shows how they have made a difference, and is tailored to their wishes.

- Consider how to involve high-level supporters in a way that demonstrates respect for the expertise that is the source of their wealth, and addresses legitimate concerns about governance and accountability.

- Involve trustees, artists and senior staff in the cultivation of prospects and donors and in helping them to develop a real understanding of the issues facing the organisation, supported by an agreed programme of engagement, recognition and feedback.

- Ensure that within the fundraising department there is one "account manager" for each major donor, whether the donor allocates resources from their personal resources, a family trust or from corporate assets.

- Ensure that those likely to solicit support from potential major donors understand and promote tax-effective giving, and that all donors are credited for the gross amount received.

- Insist that there is a link with the system that keep details of your visitors and ticket-buyers (and members, if these are held by the marketing department), and make the case that these are assets of the organisation, to be managed in the most effective way for its long-term benefit.

- Ensure that there is a highly competent and creative approach to managing the research, analysis and wealth screening of the database of supporters, to maximise the return on investment and the lifetime value from ticket-buyers, visitors, Friends and other supporters.

- Develop and promote a legacy strategy that builds on the personal relationship between donor, charity and its senior staff, and is seen as an extension of an individual programme of engagement.

- Ensure that there is the capacity to plan and budget for the department, and manage and monitor the return from the different income streams.

- Design and implement a system for the effective management of volunteers.

- Ensure that there is technical expertise within the department, and sources of professional advice when needed in data protection and tax issues.

- Invest in continuing professional development for the development team, including looking outside the culture sector.

- Understand the possibilities of strategic alliances, such as sharing events with social welfare charities and community foundations.

- Ensure that everyone throughout the organisation understands the most important factor in individual giving – someone has to ask!

Conclusion

The aim of this guide has been to show that the development of relationships with individuals should be seen as fun, creative and rewarding in every sense.

An ethos that has its centre in partnerships between those who share a passion for the particular art form or heritage pursuit, supported by an effective professional fundraising operation, strengthens the sense of mission and purpose of the whole organisation. It also creates a network of advocates among stakeholders and opinion-formers. A wide base and range of individual committed supporters who understand and love the mission and are confident in the management team is a bastion against the vagaries of political volatility and corporate fashion. Achieving development goals enables the organisation to plan with confidence and becomes a virtuous circle of engagement and trust.

Everyone who has contributed so generously to this book has done so in the belief that it is in the interests of everyone in the cultural sector that the experience of supporting cultural organisations, of whatever size and in whatever sphere or region, should be so rewarding that people will want to do it again, and again... as more than one person observed, a rising tide lifts all the boats.

It is hoped that the guidance in this book will help arts and heritage organisations to ensure that the relationships with their donors are enjoyable, flawlessly managed and sustained so that their goals are realised and culture flourishes.

Contact details

This list provides the contact information of those who so generously helped with case studies, expert articles and general encouragement.

Case studies

Birmingham Contemporary Music Group
Stephen Newbould, artistic director
stephen@bcmg.org.uk
www.bcmg.org.uk

Chickenshed
Kate Varah, director of business
    development
katev@chickenshed.org.uk
www.chickenshed.org.uk

Community Foundation serving Tyne &
    Wear and Northumberland
George Hepburn OBE, chief executive
gh@communityfoundation.org.uk
www.communityfoundation.org.uk

English National Opera
Kirsty MacDonald, development director
kmacdonald@eno.org; www.eno.org

Foundation and Friends of the Royal
    Botanic Gardens, Kew
Lucy Blythe, chief executive
L.Blythe@kew.org; www.kew.org

Hallé Concerts Society
Fiona McLeod, director of development
development@halle.co.uk
www.halle.co.uk

Handel House Trust
Christopher Purvis, chairman
christopher@purvis.co.uk
www.handelhouse.org

National Galleries of Scotland
Peter Thierfeldt, head of fundraising
pthierfeldt@nationalgalleries.org
www.nationalgalleries.org
From October 2006, Peter is director of
external relations and fundraising, Royal
Scottish Academy of Music and Drama
www.rsamd.ac.uk

National Portrait Gallery
Pim Baxter, communications and
        development director
pbaxter@npg.org.uk; www.npg.org.uk

National Theatre
Oonagh Desire, head of individual giving
odesire@nationaltheatre.org.uk
www.nationaltheatre.org.uk
John Rodgers, director of development
jrodgers@nationaltheatre.org.uk
www.nationaltheatre.org.uk

National Trust
Justine Webb, head of major gifts
justine.webb@nationaltrust.org.uk
www.nationaltrust.org.uk

Orchestra of the Age of Enlightenment
Judy Digney, director of development
judy.digney@oae.co.uk; www.oae.co.uk

Royal Academy of Arts
Sarah Cook, head of revenue fundraising
Sarah.Cook@royalacademy.org.uk
www.royalacademy.org.uk

Royal Opera House
Ruth Jarratt, director of policy
   development
Ruth.Jarratt@roh.org.uk
www.roh.org.uk

Royal Shakespeare Company
Kirstin Irvine, head of development
   (revenue)
kirstin.irvine@rsc.org.uk
www.rsc.org.uk

South Bank Centre
Karen Whitehouse, director of
   development
kwhitehouse@sbc.org.uk
www.sbc.org.uk

Southbank Sinfonia
Michael Berman, chairman
mb@sagnet.co.uk
www.southbanksinfonia.co.uk
Paul Nicholson, general manager
paul@southbanksinfonia.co.uk
www.southbanksinfonia.co.uk

Tate Foundation
John Nickson, director
John.Nickson@tate.org.uk
www.tate.org.uk

The Place
Nigel Hinds, executive director
www.theplace.org.uk

The Sainsbury Centre for Visual Arts,
   University of East Anglia
Nichola Johnson, director
n.johnson@uea.ac.uk

The Watermill Theatre
Susan Foster, development director
susan@watermill.org.uk
www.watermill.org.uk

The Wordsworth Trust
Michael McGregor, director of
   development
m.mcgregor@wordsworth.org.uk
www.wordsworth.org.uk

Tyneside Cinema
Mark Dobson, chief executive
mark@tynecine.org
Gillian Spry, director of fundraising
gspry@tynecine.org
www.tynecine.org

Welsh National Opera
Lucy Stout, director of development
lucy.stout@wno.org.uk
www.wno.org.uk

Young Vic
Caroline Jones, development director
carolinejones@youngvic.org
www.youngvic.org

Contributors on specialist topics

Act IV
Rebecca King Lassman, executive
   director
rebecca@activ.org.uk
www.activ.org.uk

Bates, Wells and Braithwaite Solicitors
Lawrence Simanowitz, partner, charity
   development
l.simanowitz@bateswells.co.uk
www.bateswells.co.uk

Brakeley Ltd
William Conner, managing director
william.conner@brakeley.com
www.brakeley.com

Chapel and York Ltd
David Wickert, director
david.wickert@chapel-york.com
www.chapel-york.com

European Association for Planned Giving
James Myers, chief executive
jim@plannedgiving.org.uk
www.plannedgiving.org.uk

Factary
Christopher Carnie, director
chris@factary.com
Elizabeth Dixon, senior research director
lizdixon@btconnect.com
www.factary.com

Richmond Associates UK Ltd
Moyra Doyle, managing director
mdoyle@richmond-associates.com
www.richmond-associates.com

Smee and Ford
Richard Radcliffe, legacy fundraising
    consultant
rradcliffe@smeeandford.co.uk

Tara Arts
Jatinder Verma, artistic director
vaio@tara-arts.com
www.tara-arts.com

The Jerwood Foundation
Alan Grieve CBE, chairman
alan.grieve@jerwood.org
www.jerwood.org

Victoria & Albert Museum
Damien Whitmore, director of public
    affairs
d.whitmore@vam.ac.uk
www.vam.ac.uk

Contributors of complete chapters, case study development and research, and analysis support

David Dixon, director
Dixon Raines and The Phone Room
david.dixon@dixonraines.com
www.dixonraines.com
www.phoneroom.co.uk

Graham Elliott, partner
haysmacintyre
gelliott@haysmacintyre.com
www.haysmacintyre.com

Susan Mackenzie, interim director
Philanthropy UK
susan@philanthropyuk.org
www.philanthropyuk.org

Janet Reeve, strategic fundraising
    consultant
janet@janetreeve.com

Other

In addition to those listed the following
people provided significant input:

Breda Daly, former development director
of The National Theatre, who provided
the case study on the National Theatre
Development Council
breda.daly@btinternet.com

Laura McCaffrey, editor and designer
laura.mccaffrey@blueyonder.co.uk
www.everythingeditorial.co.uk

Nicky Pritchett-Brown, sponsorship and
    development director
Edinburgh International Festival
nicky.pritchett-brown@eif.co.uk
www.eif.co.uk

Phillip Spedding, senior project manager
(Maecenas Initiative and A&B World)
Arts & Business
philip.spedding@AandB.org.uk
www.AandB.org.uk

Bibliography

These resources were recommended by
our contributors:

Publications

AEA Consulting (2004) *The Maecenas
Initiative: A Review of Charitable Giving
Vehicles and Their Use in the US and
Canada* Arts & Business

Allford, Marion (1993) *Charity Appeals:
The Complete Guide to Success* London:
J M Dent & Sons

Burnett, Ken (1992) *Relationship
Fundraising* The White Lion Press

Burnett, Ken (1996) *Friends for Life:
Relationship Fundraising in Practice*
The White Lion Press

Burk, Penelope (2003) *Donor Centred
Fundraising* Chicago: Cygnus Applied
Research Inc

Grace, Kay Sprinkel (2005) *Beyond
Fundraising: New Strategies for
Nonprofit Innovation and Investment*
New Jersey: John Wiley & Sons

Grace, Kay Sprinkel (2001) *High Impact
Philanthropy: How Donors, Boards and
Nonprofit Organisations Can Transform
Communities* New York: John Wiley &
Sons, Inc.

Hart, Ted; Greenfield, James; Gignac,
Pamela; Carnie, Christopher (2006)
*Major Donors: Finding Big Gifts in your
Database and Online* Hoboken: John
Wiley and Sons

Hill, Liz and Whitehead, Brian (2004)
The Complete Membership Handbook
Directory of Social Change

Hogan, Celia (2004) *Prospect Research:
A primer for growing nonprofits*
Salisbury, Massachusetts: Jones &
Bartlett Publishers

Hudson, Mike (2003) *Managing at the
Leading Edge* Directory of Social Change

Hudson, Mike (1995) *Managing without
Profit* Penguin

Institute of Fundraising (2006) *Codes of Fundraising Practice* London: Institute of Fundraising

Lloyd, Theresa (2005) *A Guide to Giving: the essential handbook for those who would like to support charities and social causes through giving and investing tax-effectively* 2nd Edition edited by Susan Mackenzie, Philanthropy UK

Lloyd, Theresa (2004) *Why Rich People Give* Association of Charitable Foundations

Nicholls, Judith (1994) *Pinpointing Affluence* Chicago: Precept Press

Rhodes, Frank HT ed. (1997) *Successful Fund Raising for Higher Education: The Advancement of Learning* Phoenix, Arizona: The American Council on Education and The Oryx Press

Sargeant, A and Less, S. (2002) *Major Gift Philanthropy – Individual Giving to the Arts* Henley Management Centre

Walker, Catherine and Pharoah, Cathy et al. (2002) *A Lot of Give: Trends in Charitable Giving for the 21st Century* Hodder & Stoughton Educational

Wilberforce, Sebastian ed. (2001) *Legacy Fundraising: the art of seeking bequests* 2nd ed. London: Directory of Social Change

Government reports

DfES (2004) *Increasing voluntary giving to higher education: Task Force report to Government* available to download: http://www.dfes.gov.uk/hegateway

HM Treasury (2003) *Goodison Review: Saving Art for the Nation* available to download: www.hm-treasury.gov.uk/media//BE44A/goodison_review_138.pdf

National Audit Office (2004) *Income Generated by the Museums and Galleries* available to download: www.nao.org.uk/publications/nao_reports/03-04/0304235.pdf

Websites

ACEVO (Association of Chief Executives of Voluntary Organisations)
www.acevo.org.uk

Arts Marketing Association
www.a-m-a.co.uk

Arts & Business
www.aandb.org.uk

Arts Councils
Arts Council England
www.artscouncil.org.uk
Arts Council of Northern Ireland
www.artscouncil-ni.org
Arts Council of Wales
www.artswales.org.uk
Scottish Arts Council
www.scottisharts.org.uk

Association of Arts Fundraisers
www.artsfundraisers.org/about.htm

Charities Aid Foundation
www.cafonline.org

Charity Commission
www.charity-commission.gov.uk

Clore Leadership Programme
www.cloreleadership.org

Community Foundation Network
www.communityfoundations.org.uk

Directory of Social Change
www.dsc.org.uk

Department of Culture, Media & Sport
www.culture.gov.uk

EUConsult: The European Association of
Consultants to and about
Not-for-Profit Organisations
www.euconsult.org

European Association of Planned Giving
www.plannedgiving.org.uk

Fundraising UK Ltd
www.fundraising.co.uk

Google Alerts
www.google.co.uk.alerts

Inland Revenue Charity Unit
www.hmrc.gov.uk/charities/index.htm

Institute of Fundraising
www.institute-of-fundraising.org.uk

International Journal of Nonprofit and
Voluntary Sector Marketing
www.ingentaconnect.com/content/
jws/vsm

NCVO (National Council for Voluntary
 Organisations)
www.ncvo-vol.org.uk

New Philanthropy Capital
www.philanthropycapital.org
The Gas
www.fuel4arts.com

Magazines/newsletters

The Art Newspaper
www.theartnewspaper.com

Arts Professional
www.artsprofessional.co.uk

Arts Funding Watch (newsletter of the
Foundation Center in the USA)
www.foundationcenter.org/afw

Philanthropy UK newsletter
www.philanthropyuk.org

Professional Fundraising
www.professionalfundraising.co.uk

Third Sector
www.thirdsector.co.uk

Additional Information contents

Arts & Business benchmarking survey 2004/05 – Private investment

Summary of results

Business investment has increased by more than 6% between 2003/04 and 2004/05 to reach £119.2 million. Individual giving has also increased by 10% over this time, reaching £244.2 million in 2004/05. Individual giving has shown a continuing upward trend since 2001/02, increasing by more than 43%. Trust and foundation investment has decreased by 15% following high investment levels in 2003/04, reflecting the mercurial nature of this investment stream which is strongly influenced by large, one-off awards. This means that the share of the private investment cake belonging to business has remained steady from 2003/04 to 2004/05, at 26%, while individual giving has claimed the 4% lost by trust and foundation investment.

Why we collect these figures
The issues around funding for the arts remain serious. The arts have not done particularly well in recent spending reviews and the future looks uncertain. Since 1976, Arts & Business has conducted an annual survey of arts organisations across the UK, asking how much and what form of money they secure from business. Since 2000/01, we have also asked the amount received from individuals, trusts and foundations. We are the only country to produce these figures on an annual basis.

This information helps us to map trends in private sector investment in the arts in the UK and enables us to provide arts organisations, businesses and government with valuable year-on-year comparisons to inform fundraising strategies and understand the funding needs of the UK arts community.

The findings from this survey strengthen our belief that arts organisations will only survive in a mixed economy. We maintain that private sector funding should always be a supplement, never a substitute, for public funding. We need a combined effort to ensure that the structures and resources required to support arts in the UK can adapt to the political, social and economic climate.

Art matters. It matters at all levels of society. It shows people excellence, it inspires people, and it gives people hope. It must move centre stage. In the UK, the arts are more integrated with social life and business than almost anywhere else in the Western world. Let's work together to keep it this way.

Colin Tweedy, chief executive of Arts & Business writes: *"For the second time, Arts & Business is combining the figures for business investment in the arts with individual and trust and foundation giving and producing the definitive figure for private sector support of the arts. In 2004/05, this figure reached £452.1 million, more than a 3% increase from 2003/04."*

Private investment in the arts: overview

How the arts survive in a mixed economy

Private investment in the arts in the UK exceeded £400 million in 2003/04 for the first time since Arts & Business started collecting these figures. The 2004/05 level of private investment of £452.1 million compares favourably to the main public funders of Arts and heritage in the UK. For instance, Arts Council England receives on average more than £410 million in parliamentary grant-in-aid and distributes over £150 million from National Lottery Funding. DCMS funding to architecture and historic environment was over £170 million in 2004/05. This places businesses, individuals and trust and foundations as key players in the arts funding landscape, complementing the crucial role of the public sector in the arts.

Attracting private investment

Some arts organisations believe that attracting private investment is an onerous and unrewarding task. However, our survey reveals that over three-quarters (78%) of respondents received private investment between 2003 and 2005, and half received private investment in both 2003/04 and 2004/05. Of those that did not receive private investment, 68% did not seek it in either year, missing the opportunities that the private sector can offer to increase the reach and impact of their activities.

Concentration of private investment

While the figures on private investment in the arts are encouraging, there are serious issues around the concentration of this investment. In 2004/05, 77% of total private investment was shared amongst only 53 organisations (3% of respondents), most of them major organisations with turnover of more than £5 million. On the other hand, 85% of respondents received less than 9% of the share. Close to two-thirds of respondents with £100,000 or less in turnover said they lacked the time, fundraising skills or money to raise private investment. This illustrates the need to strengthen the development functions of small arts organisations.

Size matters

Major arts organisations, with budgets over £5 million, face different fundraising challenges to small and medium-sized organisations. While major organisations can target a diverse range of sources of private investment, small arts organisations with limited resources tend to rely heavily on one source of funding. For instance, arts organisations with turnover of less than £100,000 on average receive close to 54% of their private investment from businesses, with individual giving accounting for less than 19% of the share. On the other hand, major organisations receive close to 36% of total private investment from businesses, with individual giving accounting for 30%. It is for this reason that Arts & Business has focused much of its work on individual giving – the Maecenas Initiative – on supporting and developing skills amongst the small to mid-scale arts sector.

Future outlook

The growing importance of the private sector in supporting the arts in the UK is highlighted by the high levels of confidence in future private funding. Nearly 88% of respondents expect levels of private investment to increase or remain the same in 2005/06, with only 12% expecting it to decrease. In fact, we project total private investment in the arts to surpass £500 million by 2006/07.

The Olympics are an opportunity for the whole of the UK to see the arts and sport at the centre of national life. Too often, in previous Olympic Games the cultural provision has not survived the pressure from other growing budgets. We must not see this replicated in London 2012. We are committed to working with the private sector and Government to ensure that the cultural community receives the very best promised provision. The arts in the UK are bold, inventive and world-class. They are a good cause to be celebrated, recognised and cherished. Businesses are committing significant investment in advance of London 2012 – does this mean there will be less available in their budgets for the arts? Arts & Business is working to ensure that businesses balance their portfolios and invest in the arts to reflect the need for diverse involvement with the community.

Breakdown of private investment
Regional distribution
London remains the biggest player in the arts sector in terms of share of private investment. Of the 53 organisations receiving over £1 million private investment in 2004/05, 33 are in London. This accounts for 72% of total private investment in the UK in 2004/05, down from 76% in 2003/04.

Over half (51%) of responding organisations in London reported an increase in private investment from 2003/04 to 2004/05. While the strong dominance of London is partly explained by the presence of one large heritage organisation, other UK regions face serious obstacles that prevent them from fully exploiting the potential opportunities the private sector can offer.

Outside London, Scotland is the biggest recipient of private investment, receiving 6% of the UK share in 2004/05, up 1% from the previous year. However, Scottish organisations report facing increasing competition for private investment from other fundraising-wise charities and arts organisations.

All but two regions (East and London) saw an increase in their percentage share of UK private investment in 2004/05, with the West Midlands seeing the greatest rate of share growth from 2003/04 at 86.07%. These increases are in most cases due to one major investment to one arts organisation. For most regional arts organisations, issues such as low profile, lack of networking opportunities and poor advocacy remain obstacles to increasing their share of private investment. Close to two-thirds of respondents in the East Midlands, South West, South East and Yorkshire reported not having enough resources (including staff, time and money) to increase their levels of private investment.

Regional breakdown by source
Nine regions saw increases in business investment from 2003/04 to 2004/05, while three (East, North West, Yorkshire) saw decreases. The North West saw the greatest increase in individual investment (up 62%). After the West Midlands, Yorkshire saw the greatest increase in trust and foundation investment (74%). The healthy growth in private investment in the arts experienced in the West Midlands is mostly explained by increases in business investment (up 50%) and trust and foundation investment (up 149%).

Artform breakdown
The strong influence of one organisation puts heritage as the top recipient of private investment in both years. This is followed by the traditionally strong sectors of visual arts/galleries and museums, respectively taking a 13% and 11% share of the UK total in 2004/05.

Crafts saw the greatest increase in UK share of private investment from 2003/04 to 2004/05, rising by 155%. Arts services also saw a strong increase, although this is largely due to a rise in trusts and foundation investment.

Artform breakdown by source of private investment

From 2003/04 to 2004/05, business investment saw the greatest increase in crafts (85%), followed by community arts (80%), and heritage and literature/poetry (both 64%). All but three artforms (museums, libraries/archives, and other combined arts) saw an increase in business investment between the two years.

All artforms saw an increase in individual giving in the period, except dance which saw a drop of less than 1%. Crafts, festivals, film/video, libraries/archives, museums and music all saw increases of over 30%.

Methodology

In total, 3,525 arts organisations were surveyed this year and 1,333 responded (38%). Additional information was gathered from our records of business investment in the arts through New Partners and annual reports, giving a total of 1,703 organisations included in the results. Investment in awards and prizes are also added to the business figures, following research by Arts & Business into sponsored arts awards.

The purpose of the grossing procedure (applied to figures on previous page) is to obtain as good an estimate as possible of the total private investment in the arts in the UK. For organisations that replied to the last survey (2002/03) but not this year, and we know still exist, we assume that they experienced the same levels of growth as organisations that replied to both surveys. The amount is calculated based on the investment reported by this year's non-respondents in the 2002/03 survey, and adjusted by the overall percentage change reported by organisations responding to both surveys.

This year data for both 2004/05 and 2003/04 were collected, following a pause in the survey last year. This time was used to revamp the survey format and include questions on obstacles to fundraising, making it more relevant to and useable by the arts community. A full report was published in September 2006.

Further information

For any questions about this survey please see **www.aandb.org.uk** or contact the research, evaluation and information team via **research@aandb.org.uk**.

Board development and training

The Clore Leadership Programme

By Sue Hoyle, deputy director

The Clore Leadership Programme has been established to help to develop a new generation of leaders for the cultural sector in the UK; and with this objective in mind we established our Fellowship Programme in 2004. It has been born out of the knowledge that, whilst there are some outstanding leaders running our theatre and dance companies, museums, galleries, libraries and orchestras, they tend to happen by accident rather than by design. The Clore Leadership Programme, which was initiated by the Clore Duffield Foundation, aims to put some of the "design" in place, providing training, skill development and leadership experience to a range of people who have the genuine potential to take on senior positions in the next few years.

We take between 25 and 30 outstanding individuals each year with a track record of achievement, either within or outside the cultural field, and offer them an intensive modular programme (lasting a year or longer) of residential courses, tuition opportunities, workshops, secondment, research, coaching and mentoring. There is a very high demand for places on the programme and the quality of selected applicants has been very high indeed. Their average age is mid-thirties, more than half are women and they come from all areas of artistic activity and different places around the country. Some are already in senior positions in major cultural institutions, ready to take a further step up. Some are artists, wanting to make the leap into administration; others have founded their own small organisations but now want to move on to something bigger or to grow their organisation.

The Fellowship is tailor-made to each individual, but also includes some shared learning in areas such as development and fundraising which we believe are essential components in the portfolio of responsibilities required of cultural leaders in the 21st century. Other subjects covered in the tuition include financial accounting and accountability, governance, relationship management, charitable law and practice, branding, marketing, and strategic planning. Our hope is that, by investing in the skills and personal development of remarkable individuals, we will help to bring about a real improvement in cultural provision.

Our view has always been that the Fellowship Programme will only ever be applicable to a relatively small number of people: those with outstanding leadership potential, the ability in the future to take on the most senior of roles, a track record, and the commitment to devote a year or more to the programme.

Already the evidence demonstrates the success of this approach. Amongst the first two groups of Fellows, the experience of their Fellowship, and the rich variety of learning components in their programme, have had a transformational impact. Their knowledge, skills and self-confidence have grown remarkably, and already they have been courted for significant posts within the sector. A curator has been appointed director the Van Gogh Museum in Amsterdam; the general manager of a regional chamber orchestra is now director of the BBC Scottish Symphony Orchestra; and the artistic director of a studio theatre has taken up the post of chief executive of Northern Stage in Newcastle. Not only have their careers been enhanced, but they have gained the knowledge, skills, experience and networks they need to transform the quality of cultural life in the UK.

In addition, we aim to meet the development needs of those in the middle ranks of many cultural organisations, or at the top of small organisations, or currently working on a freelance basis – those who might fall under the general heading of "emerging leaders". To achieve this we are providing short, two-week intensive residential leadership courses, available at a number of different business schools and universities around the country.

The content of the two-week course includes general leadership issues, intensive personal development work, training in management skills and requirements, issues such as governance, charity law and planning, work on media and presentation skills, fundraising, marketing and lobbying, a series of case studies on change management, and intensive small-group work on a range of cases and issues.

Our first short course was held at Ashridge business school in July 2006. We aim to provide six such courses in the first year, and eight in the second, and we shall be monitoring over the coming months the impact the first courses have had on participants.

Board membership and fundraising

Chair, Contemporary Dance Trust, The Place

Role description
About The Place (www.theplace.org.uk)

The Place is the leading international centre of excellence in the development of contemporary dancers and dance-makers. It is run by Contemporary Dance Trust, a company limited by guarantee and a registered charity. Its governors are volunteers and non-executives.

The depth and breadth of The Place's activities is unique:

○ A vocational dance school providing conservatoire-level training at undergraduate and postgraduate levels: London Contemporary Dance School. All courses are validated by the University of Kent. The school is a founding affiliate of the Conservatoire for Dance and Drama.

○ A touring dance company: Richard Alston Dance Company.

○ A dance theatre: the Robin Howard Dance Theatre presenting cutting edge contemporary dance performances and Dance on Screen, an annual festival of dance for the camera.

○ Learning and access services including Shift and JDC, The Place's youth dance companies.

○ Support programmes for professional dancers and dance-makers, offering advice, support and professional development and incorporating Videoworks, with its unrivalled dance video collection and digital editing and recording facilities for dance film-makers.

Contemporary dance is impossible to imagine without The Place which established its home near King's Cross in 1969. Ever since, The Place has been at the cutting edge of the development of all aspects of contemporary dance. Its resources are recognised across the world for the high levels of professional support they provide to contemporary dance artists working to fulfil their potential.

Its building was extensively rebuilt and refurbished in 2000 and 2001, largely funded by an Arts Council England capital lottery grant.

The Place receives regular funding from Arts Council England, the Higher Education Funding Council for England (through the Conservatoire for Dance and Drama), the London Borough of Camden, trusts, foundations, businesses and individuals.

Overview of the role of chair

The chair of Contemporary Dance Trust is responsible for leading the board of governors.

The board is responsible for the overall stewardship and overview of The Place's vision, development and performance:

○ Approving policy, strategy and plans.

○ Challenging and supporting the executive team.

○ Appointing and setting pay and conditions for the executive team.

○ Maximising incoming resources.

○ Setting overall budgets.

○ Ensuring implementation of policies and plans.

○ Ensuring The Place meets its legal and financial obligations.

Governors are volunteers and non-executive:
○ Committed members of The Place's team, keeping up-to-date with its activities and plans.
○ Advocates for The Place.
○ Helping to attract resources to support The Place and its work.
○ Supporting the executive in specific areas as required.

The chair of the board is responsible for leading the board:
○ Chairing board meetings and appropriate committee meetings.
○ Ensuring that the board, its committees and governors fulfil their responsibilities.
○ Representing the board to external stakeholders, staff and other bodies.
○ Providing guidance to the executive team on behalf of the board.
○ Acting on behalf of the board as appropriate between meetings.

Four members of staff report to the board through the chair, who sets their objectives, appraises and supports them. The posts are:
   Theatre director
   Artistic director
   Executive director
   School director
Together, these posts form the executive leadership of The Place, known as the executive team.

The chair is offered particular support by the executive director, who is responsible for facilitating their work and that of the executive team and the company secretary.

The role of the chair is:
○ Voluntary, requiring a variable time commitment averaging around 24 days a year, often in periods of between one and three hours, either in the daytime or during the evenings.
○ Offered for a period of three years, following which the chair may be invited to stand for re-election for a second period of three years. The maximum term the chair may serve is therefore six years.
○ Supported by the Trust by arrangement with the chair, especially through administrative services provided by the executive.

Job specification

The principal responsibilities of the chair of the governors are:
Leadership
○ To lead the board of governors, collectively and individually.
○ To ensure that the board fulfils its leadership responsibilities for the trust.

O To enable all governors to make a full contribution to the board's affairs and work as a team.
O To advise the Trust on the development of policy and strategy.

Accountability
O To ensure that the key issues are discussed by the board in a timely manner and with the appropriate information to support decisions.
O To ensure the Board fulfils its responsibilities under:
> Company law
> Charitable law
> The Combined Corporate Code (Higgs and Smith)
> HEFCE guidelines
O This includes in particular ensuring that the board undertakes appropriate evaluation/appraisal of its performance, that of its committees and its governors, including an annual evaluation/appraisal of the chair's performance by the governors.
O To ensure the board is enabled by the executive to fulfil all its responsibilities, including for instance:
> That all governors receive a full induction and a regular updating of their knowledge about the Trust and its work.
> That governors receive all due information in a good and timely manner.
O To set objectives for, appraise and support the members of the executive team.

Advocacy
O To represent the Trust externally and to promote its interests in all appropriate fora.
O To share in fundraising for the Trust.
O To represent the board to external stakeholders.
O To represent the board to the Trust's staff.
O To represent the Trust on the board of the Conservatoire for Dance and Drama.

Any other responsibilities that may reasonably be required.

Person specification

The successful candidate will be a passionate and effective high-level advocate for The Place and its work:
O A committed champion of The Place's "big picture", delegating day-to-day concerns to the executive.
O Interested in and sensitive to dance and its needs.
O Experienced in working in complex organisations at a senior level.
O Effective in working in a voluntary, non-executive role.
O Sensitive to the professional and personal pressures that affect The Place.

The Young Vic Development Council

Terms of reference
The Development Council of the Young Vic was founded in April 2006 as a sub-committee of the Executive Board.

Membership and attendance
Membership	Up to 12 members (but not less than eight)
	Including up to two board members (but not less than one)
Quorum	Six members
Secretary	Development director to act as secretary to committee
Attendance	Development director, artistic director or executive director, and development staff by invitation
Frequency of meetings	Four full council meetings per year

Responsibilities

a) To contribute to the long-term financial stability of the company by working, with the support of the development team, to help secure maximum revenue and capital income from the private sector, including individuals, trusts and the corporate sector.

b) To review strategic issues relating to any aspects of fundraising, discuss and agree tactics and responsibilities for individual prospects, on the basis of previously reported developments for each prospect and agree action points and a timetable.

c) To ensure that the executive board receives a regular report on the sources and level of sums received, progress at an overall strategic and micro-strategic level.

d) Members of the council will be asked to take responsibility for an agreed category of donor or sponsor consistent with their own interest and experience as well as the Development Plan 2005, and in any event to use their professional expertise and contacts to advise and introduce major prospects.

e) To contribute to the development of original ideas for donor or sponsor identification, prospecting, solicitation and recognition in a manner consistent with the Young Vic's values.

f) To act as hosts at a number of company events each year. This will usually involve attending a performance and/or pre- or post-show reception or dinner and acting as sole or joint hosts for a group of existing or potential donors.

g) To act as advocates and ambassadors for the company, to propose and introduce potential supporters at the appropriate time and to contribute to the cultivation, solicitation and after-care of supporters as agreed.

h) To meet or speak with sub-groups, co-members, the development director or other development staff as appropriate for a review of progress in their agreed areas.

Member requirements

○ Attend full Development Council meetings at a minimum of two per year.
○ Attend sub-group meetings at an agreed and appropriate level.
○ Be informed of and utilise the resources and support provided by development staff.
○ Adhere to overall policies developed by the Young Vic's executive board.
○ Foster a positive working relationship with other council members and Young Vic staff.
○ Be aware of and abstain from any conflict of interest.

Qualifications/skills

○ Understand the Young Vic's artistic vision and be sufficiently familiar with the work on and off stage to be able to articulate and present it to prospective supporters.
○ Be willing and able to commit time and resources to fundraising for the Young Vic.
○ Bring Wealth, Wisdom, Work or "Wow".

Term

Founder members are co-opted by the interim chairperson and development director. Subsequent members will be nominated and co-opted by the membership.
Members serve for a one-year term.
Members may be re-elected for additional terms.
Departing members will be encouraged to recruit their own replacement.
The Council will annually review the member job descriptions and make appropriate changes.

Induction

Members will be asked to complete an induction into the Company's work at their convenience within six months of joining the Council. This is to enable all members to advocate for and support the Young Vic most effectively. It will include, but not be limited to:
a) Observing a workshop delivered as part of our Teaching, Participation and Research (TPR) programme with young people and community groups.
b) Meet members of the cast or creative team of a show to discuss the production process.
c) Meet members of the Young Vic Company in any other department to discuss their work.
d) Identify any particular areas of fundraising you would like to develop knowledge of (e.g. corporate CSR, sponsorship or events) and allow us to arrange training or other personal development session at your convenience.

In addition, we will ensure you have the opportunity to meet with members of the full and executive board as well as development staff.

Measurements of success for the Young Vic Development Council
For review after one year of operation (e.g. May 2007)

Draft for discussion May 2006

Fundraising	
1) Number of NEW prospects identified and progressed	15 each
2) Number of events co/hosted	1 each
3) Number of approaches/asks made and/or facilitated	10 each
4) Number of NEW gifts received by the Young Vic that can be linked to the above activity	5 each
5) Total amount raised over one year	TBC
Attendance	
1) Attendance at full council meetings	3 each
2) Attendance at subgroup meetings	TBC
3) Availability for one-to-one meetings	TBC
Giving	
1) Personal gifts made at agreed minimum level or frequency	TBC

Capital campaigns and feasibility studies

The table opposite demonstrates an approach to categorising prospects in a way which takes into account the probability that they will support a specific appeal.

Gift range up to	Potential donor	Voluntary lead conduit	Staff lead contact	Current probability	Estimated value	Comments	Action	Next steps
Individuals								
£1,000,000	A	AB	MN	15%	£150,000	No further progress since the last meeting. We should pursue this with AB.	MN	
£150,000	B	BC	MN	80%	£120,000	B has indicated that they are willing to help us put on a major fundraising event at [place]. They also indicated that they may be able to increase their existing pledge.	BC	
£1,000,000	C	CD & DE	OP	10%	£100,000	Opportunity to meet at [place] missed as C out of the country April-May.	OP	
£500,000	D	AB	QR	15%	£75,000	D has been asked to support the purchase of the [collection], as a stepping stone to more substantial support. However, he has not yet responded.	AB	
£250,000	E	AB	QR	30%	£75,000	QR attended the New Year's Eve Party at E House.	QR	
£100,000	H	AB	ST	20%	£20,000	H was unable to attend the event at [place]. He was asked to speak at the [event] in January, but was unable to attend.	AB	
£50,000	IJ family	FG	ST	40%	£20,000	FG visited the Trust on 7 March. She has offered to speak to her brother, IJ, on our behalf.	FG	
Sub-total	**£410,000**							
Foundations								
£500,000	KL Foundation	AB	MN	10%	£50,000	Following a meeting with AB and MN, the chair has put forward an application to the [foundation] to endow the [foundation] to endow the post of curator.	MN	
£500,000	M Trust	BC	MN	5%	£25,000	No further update since last meeting.	MN	
£100,000	N Foundation	AB	MN & OP	20%	£20,000	An application to the [foundation] has been put on hold while the [foundation] reviews its funding priorities.	MN	
£50,000	O Charitable Trust	AB	QR	30%	£15,000	No further update since last meeting.	QR	
£50,000	P Fund	BC	QR	20%	£10,000	BC had lunch with the director on 23 February. He indicated that he is a good friend of IJ.	QR	
£50,000	R Foundation	CD	ST	10%	£5,000	ST has been in contact with R regarding a loan of material to the anniversary exhibition.	ST	
£10,000	S Trust	CD & DE	ST	10%	£1,000	ST has written to ask S to participate in the 2007 symposium.	ST	
£100,000	Lady T	BC	ST	0%	£0	Lady T was instrumental in us securing a £13,500 grant for the [collection] from the [charitable trust]. The trust has indicated that we will not receive further grants for the foreseeable future.	ST	
Grand total	**£561,000**							

Endowments

Lifetime legacies

"Lifetime legacies" are a form of planned giving which encourages donors to make an irrevocable pledge of an amount that they might leave as a legacy, but are deterred from giving now because they wish to retain the income from the capital against future uncertainties. They provide the donor with tax relief and regular income in their lifetime while guaranteeing the recipient institution capital on the death of the donor.

Such schemes have been prevalent in the US for some time (under the name Charity Remainder Trusts). They are thought to account for over $100 billion of charitable assets and 40% of endowments. A broad-based coalition of charities, individuals and umbrella organisations is advocating their introduction into the UK. For that to happen there would have to be a change in the tax regime, so that the donors benefit at the time of the pledge from the kind of tax reliefs their estate would receive with a traditional legacy.

Current tax relief rules prevent donors from deriving an income from gifts of assets to charities. What is proposed is that when the donor makes a commitment of a capital sum it would be placed in a trust for the future benefit of a designated charity. The present value of the future receipt by the charity would be calculated on the basis of factors such as the donor's age. This value would form the basis of a deduction against the donor's taxable income. Ideally, this tax credit could be carried forward over future years.

The trust would pay income to the donor during their lifetime. This income would be liable to income tax. Like a legacy, gifts into the trust should qualify for capital gains tax relief. When the donor dies, the capital sum goes to the recipient charity. To minimise the risk of abuse, and the cost of administration, only standardised forms would be used, approved by the Inland Revenue and Charity Commission.

Informal research (which is being supplemented by research being undertaken by the Institute of Fundraising) suggests that lifetime legacies would appeal to the type of major donors that charities are keen to attract but with whom they have had limited success so far. The targets would be not so much the super-rich who could give out of capital anyway, but the mass-affluent – those who are wary about reducing their asset base for fear that they might need to use it to supplement income at a future date.

Advantages to such a scheme include:

○ The charity receives a clear and irrevocable commitment from the donor. This offers greater security than legacies, which do not always materialise.

○ The charity can rely on eventual receipt of a lump sum; this would have critical impacts on fundraising for capital projects or endowments. Even for a building project, a charity could undertake capital expenditure commitments at current costs knowing that committed funds would be forthcoming in due course.

○ The commitment of the lifetime legacy to a cause about which the donor cares passionately means that the donor enjoys the rewards of involvement and appreciation by the charity during their lifetime.

○ Lifetime legacies address the issue of potential donors' fears about financial insecurities in old age and their desire to safeguard their future income needs. This was a major finding of the research for *Why Rich People Give*.

Charities enjoy exemption from most forms of taxation because they serve a public good. Donations to charities benefit from additional tax incentives. Legacies enjoy both capital gains tax and inheritance tax exemption. The lack of tax incentive for lifetime legacies seems inconsistent with this general philosophy.

As with any fundraising mechanism, charities would have to learn how to present the idea and explain the benefits. The involvement of the financial services sector would be crucial; they would need to understand and incorporate this type of planned giving into their client services.

As we consider a new Charities Bill, the Government should also consider how to strengthen the financial security of the institutions which underpin civil society. The lifetime legacy should be a central plank of that strategy. With widespread ownership of assets among the post-war generation coming up to retirement, and an historically low number of children to whom they might leave this wealth, the time is right to develop these ideas in the UK.

Seven steps for donor development

Step	Terminology	Characteristic of each step NB: each step should be where we are now in the solicitation process not where we have come from	Tools
1	Identify	Identify a prospect, ie. have reason to believe that they may be able and inclined to give to [ABC]. It is a good discipline to rank at this stage with an estimate of: • The level of a possible gift. • How likely they are to give at present.	Using: • Desk research. • Volunteer information. • Database.

Step	Terminology	Characteristic of each step NB: each step should be where we are now in the solicitation process not where we have come from	Tools
2	Research	Research everything we need to know to guide steps 3-7 towards a successful conclusion! Research their 'propensity' to give (eg why should they give to *[ABC]*?) Asking the following questions: • What are their resources? • What is their connection to *[ABC]*? • What are their interests? • What is their goal in life? • Who is the key influencer? NB:Learning and adding to research profile will not stop; whenever we review strategy we should be informed by an updated profile.	Using: • Volunteers. • Detailed profiles. • Initial meetings with prospect ("getting to know them" and listening to them).
3	Plan	Plan the next stage of action and discuss what will happen with each subsequent step in the solicitation process. Remember: • The plan should aim to deal with all possible concerns that the prospect may have. • Take into account all aspects of prospect's relationship with us and all research, meetings, volunteer discussion etc. • Plan how we will involve/cultivate, ask, close and reciprocate. Finally: • Agree a prospect check with all concerned (volunteers and staff).	
4	Involve/ cultivate	• Remember to involve both partners. • Implement decisions planned at Step 3. • Involvement will also help gather more information on the prospect's needs which may alter our research decisions and plans (but hopefully not radically if Steps 1-3 done properly). • Listen for concerns/clues that you may have missed. • Actively try to uncover and deal with all objections/concerns. • Warmth.	Invitations. Research profiles. Volunteer.
5	Ask	• Delay the ask until you and they are ready. • Have your lines ready (tailored). • Ask for a lot. • Be open minded and ready for surprises (have three projects in mind). • Sell idea before talking about money. • Answer objections and queries. • Summarise the meeting. • Write immediately and suggest the next stage.	Briefing notes. Double-teaming.

Step	Terminology	Characteristic of each step NB: each step should be where we are now in the solicitation process not where we have come from	Tools
6	Close	Aim for: • Agreement to the sum. • Agreement to a particular project. At: • The right time. With: • Knowledge of payment schedules, etc.	Briefing notes.
7	Reciprocate	• To make sure that people are not forgotten and that they will give again in due course. • How should each person be looked after/kept involved. • Thank, Thank, Thank.	Prospect care systems.

Recruitment

By Moyra Doyle, managing director, Richmond Associates UK

Recruiting a fundraiser for a critical position

Key points in the recruitment process
The brief
As in any project the quality of the brief will have a strong bearing on the success of the recruitment process and the quality of the appointment made.
Key points
- ○ Decide who will be on the recruitment committee and ensure that those involved have a shared commitment and understanding of the fundraising goals.
- ○ Be realistic about recruitment timescales and check that those involved will be available as required.
- ○ Gain full agreement on a realist budget required for fundraising.
- ○ Create an organisation chart that reflects the importance placed on fundraising.
- ○ Offer an opportunity that has flexibility in terms of remuneration, additional benefits, working conditions and hours worked.
- ○ Be able to describe the organisation's values and culture.
- ○ Be clear on who will lead the recruitment effort and what resources are available.
- ○ Prepare full information for candidates containing background information about the organisation, the job description, organisation structure, the role, critical success factors of the role, key responsibilities, and person specification. This information pack should also contain clear guidelines on how to apply, the closing date and selection process.

With a clear brief those responsible for the recruitment effort will be in a better position to present and differentiate the opportunity through the most appropriate media to attract and source applicants of the right calibre and quality during the recruitment stage.

Key points
- Try to differentiate the opportunity by emphasising the organisation's artistic vision and values. For many prospective candidates this will be inspirational.
- Advertisements should give an honest and realistic description of the job as this is proven to improve retention.
- If you are working with a recruitment consultancy, make sure the personnel are interested in your sector and understand your values as they will be the representative face of your organisation.
- Make sure your advertisement and information for candidates adhere to employment and data protection legislation.
- Be accessible to potential candidates and provide them with realistic deadlines.
- Advertise the opportunity though appropriate media; expensive broadsheet advertising may not always be the most effective.
- Make sure that all potential candidates receive the information about the opportunity in good time to make their application.

Selection
It is important to retain an objective attitude when deciding which candidates to interview. Refer to the person specification and rate the candidates against the essential criteria. If your organisation uses psychometric assessments, decide when in the process you want to apply them and make sure the candidates are aware of this. Unsuccessful candidates must be informed in good time and thanked for their interest in the opportunity and the organisation.

Interview
When inviting candidates to interview it is important to offer a few options as good candidates are usually busy people. A first informal interview is much appreciated by candidates – especially for senior level appointments. The best interviews are a two-way process of giving and getting information. If your final stage of interview is a formal panel including trustees and senior management, make sure that everyone is in agreement about what you are assessing and the role each panel member will play. Candidates are making their own assessments of the organisation and the opportunity at every stage of the interview process – being open and managing the process efficiently is important for success.

At the final stage it is often the most suitable candidate who will be selected rather than the most eligible. Ideally, the preferred candidate will be both eligible and suitable.

Offer stage

This can be one of the most delicate stages in any recruitment process. Be clear about who is handing the negotiations and what the parameters are. Candidates are in high demand and may be in receipt of several offers – so yours needs to be handled carefully and remain a top priority. If you have listened carefully to what the candidate has said they are looking for in their next career move, then this negotiation should be reasonably straightforward. Flexibility is often worth more than salary to candidates at certain stages of their career.

Once you have concluded the negotiations, follow up promptly with an offer letter and employment contract. Make sure that these are "subject to satisfactory references" and that these are followed up – preferably by phone.

Conclusion

In essence, approach the recruitment of a fundraiser as you would any other critical, important project for your organisation. Think it through carefully, make sure you know what you are looking for, and remember it's a two-way process. If you choose the right person they can make a huge difference to the future of the organisation. A final word of warning – "appoint in haste – regret at leisure" – take time to get it right.

Research

Sample in-depth profile by Factary

PROSPECT NAME	Doe: Sir Joe (John) Doe, OBE
HOME ADDRESS	100 Fortnum Row
	London SW1 1MM
BUSINESS ADDRESS	Doe Investments plc
	100 Mayfair Place
	London W1 1XX
TELEPHONE	020 000 0000
DATE OF BIRTH	1 January 1950
KEY DIRECTORSHIPS	Doe Investments plc – founder and chairman
	JD plc – non-executive director
	Previously:
	Multinational Bank plc – founder, chairman and president
	Innovus Ltd – non-executive director
KEY TRUSTEESHIPS	The John Doe Foundation – settlor and trustee
	Disabled Children's Sports Foundation – vice president
WEALTH ESTIMATE	The wealth of John Doe and his family is estimated in the press at £400 million based on the value of his company, Doe Investments and sale of Multinational Bank plc.

LIVERY & CLUB MEMBERSHIPS	Liveryman, The Musicians' Livery Company Wilde Hampstead Golf Club
LEISURE INTERESTS	Theatre, opera, golf, horse racing, horse breeding
BRIEF BIOGRAPHY	John Doe was educated at Hampstead Park School, London. He read economics at Old Hall College Oxford, where he was a prominent member of the Spotlight Theatre Company. After college he trained as a chartered accountant before working in banking in Canada for five years.He returned to the UK to found Multinational Bank Ltd, which he built up over 10 years. It was floated on the Stock Exchange in 1995 and four years later he stepped down as chairman. With funds from the company's subsequent sale he focused his energies on establishing The John Doe Foundation, a charitable trust giving mainly to the performing arts. During this time he took on non-executive directorships with leading investment companies, to which he brought his well-documented keen financial eye and charisma, his time at Innovus being the most influential.

By 2003 Doe had brought many of his closest colleagues from Multinational on to the board of his new company Doe Investments. The company continues to expand under Doe's leadership with JD plc as its subsidiary buying out smaller operations.

Described in the press as a *"loss to the stage when he chose the City"* Doe has never lost his love of the performing arts, and is perhaps as well known for his interest and support of British theatre as for his business success. He also finds time to have an active role in his stud farm on the Somerset levels. In 1999 Doe divorced Patricia Howle, a Canadian heiress, with whom he has two sons, Peter and Alex. Alex trained as an actor and was very successful until a car accident in 1995 left him unable to walk. He helped his father to found the John Doe Foundation, through which he campaigns for disabled actors. Doe married BAFTA-winning actress Polly Grieves at his villa in Southern Tuscany in June 2003.

PHILANTHROPIC INTERESTS	The Theatre Council – chairman Mayfair Festival of Performing Arts – joint chairman Disabled Children's Sports Foundation – vice president The John Doe Foundation – settlor and trustee The majority of funds in the John Doe Foundation are earmarked for the Mayfair Festival and performing arts

projects, especially those which involve disabled performers in the UK and overseas, especially Canada. However, some funds are directed to charities concerned with horses and sports.

Doe owns a ranch in Canada where he has plans to set up a theatre summer school for both disabled and non-disabled young people.

Peter Doe has recently set up his own foundation. Grants from these foundations have mainly been made to theatre and architecture in the UK and Canada.

KNOWN MAJOR

He is reported to have donated between £1 and £2 million to the Bromwich Festival of Performing Arts through his foundation.

£100,000 to the Horse Health Trust from his foundation in 1999/2000

£25,000 to the New Greenwich Theatre in 2005

£20,000 each to Opera Future and Perform South in 2006

BUSINESS NETWORKS

Doe Investments plc

Corporate finance and management

Terence Smith, chief executive

Non-executive director of Revolution plc, Redfield plc and BioInvestments plc, he is former chief executive of GP plc.

Adam Scott, finance director

Non-executive director and shareholder at GP plc and non-executive director of Scott Holdings plc.

Tom Fernandes, head of corporate finance

Non-executive director of Fox Venture Capital plc, former chairman of Aristotle.com and a director of the London Institute of Music and Performing Arts

Tony Maloney, non-executive director

Chairman and shareholder of Dynamo Finance plc, non-executive director and shareholder of Sharestock plc and chairman and shareholder at Big News Ltd

JD plc

Independent corporate management and subsidiary of Doe Investments plc

Ann Bankwell, chair

Former finance director of Innovus Ltd

Julia Nation, finance director

Non-executive director of Strand Theatre Company

William Just, non-executive director

Lawyer and trustee of The Art Fund

Innovus Ltd
Venture capital and fund management
Billy Fortune, director
Trustee of the Mayfair Festival of Performing Arts
Sal Ling, fund manager
Non-executive director of Polestar plc
Norman Foreman, non-executive director
Former chairman of 2 Capital Ltd
Wilson Grace, non-executive director
Chartered accountant and former director of Ark plc
Multinational Bank Ltd
Investment banking
Terence Smith, non-executive chairman, as above
Adam Scott, finance director, as above
Tom Fernandes, former fund manager, as above
Tony Maloney, former non-executive director, as above
John Givver, former director, as above
Mary Stokes, fund manager
Trustee of The Animal Charity

PHILANTHROPIC
NETWORKS

John Doe Foundation
Peter Doe – chair of trustees
Alex Doe - trustee
The Hon Chris Fotherly Highwood – trustee and treasurer
Caroline Shaw, JP – trustee and correspondent
Mayfair Festival of Performing Arts
Claire Rome – joint chairman, former director of World
Theatre Company and founder of Royal Pinter Theatre
Company
Professor Michael Flare – trustee, playwright and journalist
Dr James Sherbourne – trustee, director of The College of
Opera
Deborah Likh – trustee, major shareholder in Rillard plc and
founder of the Performing Arts Museum
Disabled Children's Sports Foundation
Princess Charlotte – patron
Lady Erica Price – chairman
Olympic goldmedalist
Peter Mills – trustee
former chairman of Commonwealth Games Board
Dr Richard Lees – trustee
author, physiotherapist and trustee of St Peter's Foundation
Elizabeth Montford – trustee

former director of the Heidleburg Institute

Charles Pine – trustee, director SPT Rugby plc

OTHER
NOTEWORTHY
RELATIONSHIPS

Prince Robert – Doe and Prince Robert met at Oxford and have been close friends ever since, the Prince is often involved in Doe's charity work. They also share ownership of Doe's stud farm in Somerset.

RECENT NEWS

May 2006; Doe was involved with US private equity group, Capital Venture Plc in a rescue package for the troubled computer software company Softouch.

Sir John received his knighthood in 2004 for his services to charity.

August 2006; Among the guests at John and Polly Doe's Tuscany home were Prince Robert and his children, sportswear tycoon, Ollie Slalom and theatre designer, Dan du Champs.

ANALYSIS

WEALTH

Sir John's wealth is principally held in the shares of Doe Investments plc, in which he has a 45% stake. The company's investment portfolio has been performing well this year, and City analysts are predicting further growth. Sir John's dividends from the company were £34.4 million last year and should be higher this year.

MOTIVATION

Sir John has shown a high degree of motivation for organisations like ours, supporting a range of arts and similar causes. It will be important to emphasise the arts elements of our organisation.

CONNECTION

We have a direct connection with Sir John via Prince Robert, our trustee. The two are known to get on well, and our analysis is that this relationship is the key to a substantial gift from Sir John.

GIFT CAPACITY

Based on his income and the high level of motivation he has shown for causes like ours, we estimate his gift capacity for our organisation at £4 to £5 million.

SOURCES

We used the following sources to compile this profile;

SOURCE WARNINGS

Research was carried out without contact with the prospect, so relies on secondary sources.

RESEARCHER

Dirk Douglas

DATE

September 2006

Briefing note – Factary

CONFIDENTIAL
CONTACT NAME:
CONTACT ADDRESS:
CONTACT TEL. NO:
TIME/DATE/VENUE OF MEETING:
STAFF ATTENDING MEETING:

Overview and cultivation strategy
This area to be used for summing up in bullet points key information about the
prospect, including wealth and target gift and recommendations for cultivating the
prospect.

Relationship with our organisation
This area to provide a chronological list of all past meetings and involvement with
the prospect.

Family and education
To include information about parents and siblings; early, middle and higher education;
and early influences.

Career and professional achievements
To include details of past and present career, together with professional
achievements. This area should also include in-depth information about the
companies with which the prospect is currently involved.

Philanthropic interests
To include past and present trusteeships and other not-for-profit roles. Also include
known past gifts and affiliations to charities in this area.

Networks and connections
Incorporate a "map" of the circles in which your prospect moves.

Recent news
Use this section to include any important developments surrounding your prospect's
personal, business or philanthropic life to include company news.

Tax and VAT

By Graham Elliott

Gift Aid donor benefit limits
Relevant value test

Amount of donation	Value of benefits
£0 – 100	25% of donation
£101 – 1,000	£25
£1,001 +	2.5% of donation

Aggregate value test:
The value of the benefits received in consequence of making the donation.
Plus the value of any benefits received in consequence of any Gift Aid donations by the same donor to the same charity earlier in the same tax year.
Must not exceed £250.

Rules concerning gift aid on admissions to heritage property (April 2006)
Admission will not be regarded as a "benefit" (and accordingly Gift Aid will be claimable) as long as:
Either: The visitor makes a donation that is at least 10% more than the admission charge for the equivalent right of admission.
Or: The donation secures admission to the property for a 12-month period, for example, through a season ticket or a membership scheme. Access should in general be unlimited whenever the property is open to the public during that 12-month period, but charities may exclude from the right of admission up to five days in each 12-month period when the property is otherwise open to the public and still qualify.

Transactions with substantial donors (April 2006)
This legislation is lengthy and complex. Readers should refer to S.506A ICTA for full details. The following is a brief summary:
○ Charities may be required to pay tax by reference to non-qualifying charitable expenditure if they supply benefits in a variety of ways to "substantial donors".
○ Substantial donors are those who gift at least £25,000 in 12 months or £100,000 in six years. The gifts referred to above are "relievable gifts" (i.e. they attract a tax relief by reference to charitable giving).
○ The tax liability will arise on a payment from the charity to the donor. It also applies where a charity enters into any form of transaction with, or investment in, the donor at what HMRC deems as other than "arm's length" terms.

Telephone fundraising

By David Dixon

Suggested script

Introduction

Good afternoon/evening _____, my name is _____ and I'm calling on behalf of *[Organisation]*. Could I speak with _____ please?

Is this a convenient time for me to call?

❏   Arrange call back.
➤   Thanks…

I'm following up a letter from _____, about our urgent appeal to secure the refurbishment of the organisation through which we hope to raise around half a million pounds from our audience. Could I just ask out of interest?

Engagement question

(Keep some of these questions back for subsequent negotiation)
○   What was the last performance/exhibition you saw here?
○   How long have you been visiting *[Organisation]*?
○   Do you know anyone who has attended one of our workshops?
○   What do you enjoy about *[Organisation]*?
(Get chatting and describe the importance of the organisation to town and the region.)
Thanks for telling me that! We always appreciate the chance to talk to our audience. Just to return to _____'s letter…

Case for support

Did you get chance to look at the information which was sent with the letter?

If Yes: Well, then you'll have a good idea of the scale of the work we need to do and the exciting new organisation which will emerge when we've finished.
If No: Not to worry, do have a look when you get chance.
○   We urgently need to make improvements to and update our facilities. These improvements are necessary as we strive to secure the future of *[Organisation]* for generations to come.
(Don't pause – go straight to first feature ask, clearly stating the amount you are asking for.)

➤   First regular gift ask

Many of our audience have chosen to support *[Organisation]*'s transformation with a

small regular gift of £10 per month. As I mentioned, *[Organisation]* cannot secure its future without your help – please could you help us to undertake these works with a gift of £10 per month?

❑ Gift confirmation
➤ Go to second regular gift ask

Case for support two
In order to reach our target, every gift is appreciated. I hope you share my enthusiasm about *[Organisation]*, I realise £10 per month might sound a bit much. If just 100 of our audience members could give just £5 once each month we would raise around £6,000 towards this work. I cannot stress enough how essential it is that we carry out this refurbishment. Please would you help us with £5 per month?

❑ Gift confirmation
➤ Go to single gift ask

➤ **Single gift ask**
A regular gift isn't appropriate for everyone. Many people I have spoken to have chosen to make a one-off gift instead. Just today I have received gifts of £50, £100, £150 and more. The average is around £75. Could you help with a gift of that amount? If 1,000 of our audience made gifts of this amount we would raise £75,000 towards our appeal target. Could you help with £75? (And negotiate from here where possible.)
❑ Single gift confirmation

➤ **Regular gift confirmation**
Thank you so much!
Just to confirm _____, I've put you down for a donation of £XX every <<freq>> (Confirm amount and check address details) which will be made by direct debit. We will put a form in the post to you shortly. All you need to do is just to fill it in and return it in the freepost envelope supplied.
❑ Gift Aid ask where applicable

➤ **Single gift confirmation**
Thank you so much! The easiest way to make a gift is over the phone as we can take all the details here and now. Shall I wait while you get your credit card?

❑ Credit card donation (They take Visa, MasterCard, Switch / Maestro & Delta)
➤ Offer to send forms
Just to confirm _____, I've put you down for £XX.. (Confirm amount and check address details). We will put a form in the post to you shortly. All you need to do is

just to fill it in and return it in the freepost envelope supplied
- ❑   Gift Aid ask

➤   **Gift Aid ask**

Incidentally, if you are taxpayer in the United Kingdom, *[Organisation]* can claim tax back on your gift, increasing its value by almost 30% at no extra cost to yourself. Would we be able to do that?
- ❑   Gift close

Gift close

Thank you so much for your donation _____ and for taking the time to talk with me today. Goodbye.

"Maybe" close

Well if you agree, I'll send you a form for your consideration. It's great to get feedback from our audience and I am sure you will agree with me on the importance these works have for the future of *[Organisation]*. Thank you for taking the time to talk to me today. Goodbye.

Refusal close

It's great to get feedback from our audience and even if you can't support us on this occasion, I am sure you will agree with me on the importance these works have for the future of *[Organisation]*. Thanks for taking the time to talk to me today. Goodbye.

Sample telephone fundraising financial and statistical report

Client:		Calling date:			
Start date:		Group: all groups			

		TODAY		CUMULATIVE	
PLEDGES	**Gift type**	**Number**	**% of contacts**	**Number**	**% of contacts**
DEFINITE					
	Direct debit	18	13.95%	107	10.63%
	Credit card	2	1.55%	25	2.48%
	Single gift	13	10.08%	76	7.55%
	Gift Aid	0	0.00%	2	0.20%
Totals		33	25.58%	210	20.85%
MAYBE					
	Regular gift	6	4.65%	89	8.84%
	Single gift	5	3.88%	104	10.33%
	Unknown	9	6.98%	90	8.94%
Totals		20	15.50%	283	28.10%
REFUSALS					
	Soft no	30	23.26%	114	11.32%
	Hard no	20	15.50%	181	17.97%
	Financial	23	17.83%	189	18.77%
	Already given	3	2.33%	27	2.68%
Totals		76	58.91%	511	50.74%
TOTAL CONTACTS		129	100.00%	1007	100.00%
DONATIONS		Year 1	4 years	Year 1	4 years
Calculated from definite pledges	Direct debit	£1,103	£4,412	£7,424	£29,696
	Gift Aid on direct debits	£329	£1,318	£2,218	£8,870
	Credit card	£100	£100	£760	£760
	Cheques	£375	£375	£2,070	£2,070
	Gift Aid on single gifts	£0	£0	£500	£500
Totals		£1,907	£6,205	£12,972	£41,896
AVERAGES		Year 1	4 years	Year 1	4 years
Calculated from definite pledges	Direct debit inc tax	£79.58	£318.33	£90.11	£360.43
	Single gift/C.C. inc tax	£31.67	£31.67	£28.02	£28.02
Average per definite pledge (inc tax)		£57.80	£188.03	£62.61	£201.45
Average per contact (inc tax)		£14.79	£48.10	£13.24	£42.61
Retires (incorrect data, deceased, moved)		21		79	

The original Medici

The complex approach to recognition of donors is not of course new. Indeed, it is interesting to consider this in the context of 15th century Florence – a period dominated by the munificence of a family whose name has become a byword for patronage of culture – the Medici. As bankers and self-made entrepreneurs, they and their networks offer many parallels with the "new philanthropists" of today. They created new ways of doing business, akin to the venture capitalists and hedge fund managers of the 21st century. In the early generations they did not often hold power directly, although they were of crucial political significance; they exercised influence through favours and strategic investment.

Cosimo il Vecchio (1389 – 1464) was extremely generous to a wide range of charities and religious foundations, and a knowledgeable and major supporter of what were then the contemporary arts, crafts, architects and thinkers. Contemporaries seemed to have regarded him as motivated by genuine piety, as well as a love of beauty, and no doubt an eye on the prestige of the family. But then, as now, there were cynics: one is recorded as observing that his generosity was spurred by the fact the "he knew that his money had not been over-well acquired".

So with him, and his son Lorenzo il Magnifico (1449 – 1492) we see, as in *Why Rich People Give*, the same complex mix of passion, wanting to make a difference, feeling good, desire for a reputational legacy, guilt, civic pride and pleasure in the company of like-minded donors and the artists and thinkers themselves.

While we may think that the idea of free access to libraries is relatively new, or at least initiated by Carnegie, we see in the Dominican monastery of San Marco the legacy of Cosimo's most lavish patronage. He not only financed major extensions of the buildings, but established a huge library. This was furnished with wonderful manuscripts and books sourced from Europe and the near East; all the religious items were given to the monastery, on condition that they should be accessible to all. Was this Europe's first public library?

Apparently, the monks suggested that perhaps he need not support them on so grandiose a scale, to which he is reported to have replied *"never shall I be able to give God enough to set him down as my debtor"*. (It should be added that in this case at least money didn't buy influence; later in the century San Marco became the centre of resistance to the Medici!)

But it was not only the Medici themselves who created the great buildings and art of Florence. Other families made their contributions with their own mix of motives. In the mid-fifteenth century Brunelleschi was commissioned to build Santo Spiritu in Florence[1], later described by Bernini as *"the most beautiful church in the world"*. The church was funded by local families, mainly through the sponsorship of side chapels. A member of the Frescobaldi family gave 1000 florins, a considerable sum at that time, on condition that *"no coat of arms other than that of the Frescobaldi were placed in…his chapel"*. As with so many other projects, major donations were complemented by more modest contributions. In this case monks from the nearby monastery sacrificed a meal a day as a money-raising example to others.

And it wasn't only aristocrats and bankers who patronised the arts. When Florentines queued to view one of the most important and influential paintings of the Renaissance, the 1427 fresco of the Trinity by Masaccio in the church of Santa Maria Novella, they saw not only a stunning apparently three-dimensional representation of the Trinity, but representation of the donors as a crucial element in the overall design. Judge Lorenzo Lenzi and his wife are immortalised for ever through their patronage of a 26-year-old painter who was breaking all the rules – presumably as risky a venture then as it would be now.

As well as personal pride, the patronage of the time showed considerable civic pride, and certainly by the end of the 15th century we see recognition that the beauty of Florence was an appropriate complement to and reflection of its strong governance, political stability and successful economy. For example, Lorenzo's uncle, Giovanni Tornabuoni (another banker) commissioned Domenico Ghirlandaio's wonderful frescoes in his eponymous chapel in the church of Santa Maria Novello. Apart from the depiction of family members in the frescoes (for example, among the ladies present at the births of John the Baptist is the donor's sister, Lorenzo's mother) the whole chapel is a celebration of Florence; we see a prominent inscription on an arch in one of the frescoes which reads: *"The year 1490, when the most beautiful city, renowned for abundance, victories, arts and noble buildings profoundly enjoyed salubrity and peace"*.

A crucial factor in the achievement of this state of abundance and peace was that patronage of the arts wasn't something that happened after a great city and stable society was created; it was an integral part of the creation of such a society.

---

1. *I am most grateful to The Rough Guide to Tuscany and Umbria for drawing attention to some of the Florentine examples quoted.*

Cultural Giving

The Chickenshed 100 Club

Essentially, this is a scheme through which members purchase a form of raffle ticket which is entered into a draw at regular intervals. The first ticket drawn wins a cash prize, and usually there are three of four such prizes. Prize money is paid from the ticket proceeds, and the net income benefits the organisation. The basis of the Chickenshed scheme is as follows:

- The 100 Club started in about 1990.
- Members must be 16 years old or over and must commit to one year's membership. Each club has up to 100 members. As soon as this figure is reached, membership is closed and a new club is set up. There is no limit to the number of memberships anyone can hold, either within a club or across clubs.
- Members pay £60 for a year's membership or arrange a standing order for £5 per month for each number held.
- The total gross income for each club for one year is £6,000.
- For each full 100 Club the prizes are: 1st £500, 2nd £250, 3rd £125 and 4th £125 for each draw, making £1,000.
- The draws take place three times a year, so the total prize money is £3,000.
- From each full 100 Club, Chickenshed receives £3,000 per annum.
- At present there are 135 members who have 170 numbers between them.
- Several members buy two, three or four numbers.

A Chickenshed member of staff is present when the draw is made by a person who is neither related to nor a member of the Club. Once a year, the entire 100 Club membership is notified of the winners. The Company has not had a gambling licence in the past, but it is continually reviewing legislation.

Because of the potential winnings, the 100 Club membership contribution cannot be Gift Aided. However, on average about a third of winners donate part or all of their winnings back to Chickenshed, and that donation can then be Gift Aided. The revenue from the 100 Club is about 20% of the voluntary giving from individuals (excluding galas, appeals and events). Furthermore, a significant percentage of the 100 Clubbers also donate regularly to Chickenshed through other schemes or through appeals. About £30 a member (a little less allowing for promotion and administration) compares well with the net revenue from some Friends schemes.

The involvement of employees from across the company is an interesting additional and positive facet.

As Kate Varah, director of business development, says: *"Chickenshed gets great value out of our 100 Club – it provides a steady income stream and the members (including some of our staff!) really enjoy participating."*

Transnational giving in Europe: facilitating cross-border philanthropy

By Ludwig Forrest, project manager, King Baudouin Foundation, Brussels

Legal and fiscal barriers
The potential of cross-border giving is growing. The European population is increasingly mobile, and as a consequence there is an increasing dispersal of assets across several European countries and more and more donors wanting to support foundations and charities abroad. But huge fiscal and legal barriers still impede transnational generosity. Most European countries do not grant income tax deductibility to donors wanting to support a foreign beneficiary in another member state, and even tax (with gift or inheritance taxes) such gifts, donations or legacies at the highest applicable rate. This unequal treatment of national and cross-border philanthropy infringes the fundamental freedoms guaranteed by the European Community treaty.

Two steps to enable cross-border giving
The Walloon case[2], pending before the European Court of Justice, could therefore be very helpful in at least tackling one of these two problems, as other member states could be required to modify their legislation to ensure, as a minimum, equal tax rates on gifts and inheritances, regardless of whether the beneficiaries are domestic or reside in another member state. To obtain a completely free European cross-border philanthropy, equalisation of gift and inheritance taxes is only the first step. Non-discriminatory tax deductibility for donors would be the second. But adapting national income tax deductibility rules and providing tax deductibility to resident donors supporting foreign beneficiaries could be more difficult to implement and less acceptable to member states. It is therefore quite realistic to think that in the near future an important improvement is more likely to happen with regard to gift and inheritance tax rates rather than to income tax deductibility rules.

Overcoming barriers: how TGE works
The Transnational Giving Europe network is therefore an important private initiative that provides an efficient solution and a serious alternative to the problem of non-discriminatory tax deductability. At European level, TGE is the only practical and secure solution for tax-effective cross-border cash donations. The TGE network – a partnership between the Charities Aid Foundation, the King Baudouin Foundation, the Fondation de France, the Oranje Fonds, Maecenata International and, since

2. The question is whether the Walloon region of Belgium is infringing hte treaty of Rome by imposing strict conditions on granting tax relief on gifts to charities located in another member state.

early 2006, the Foundation for Poland – enables donors, both corporations and individuals, resident in one of the participating countries, to financially support non-profit organisations in other member states, while benefiting directly from the tax advantages provided for in the legislation of their country of residence. A donor resident in one of the participating countries and wishing to make a gift to a public interest organisation in one of the other member states can contact the foundation in the country of his/her residence. The home foundation establishes contact with the foundation in the recipient country for an assessment of the beneficiary (which is another non-profit organisation). If the evaluation is positive, the donor makes the gift to his home-country foundation which then provides the donor with a tax receipt and transfers the gift to the recipient country foundation in favour of the beneficiary organisation.

By providing such a secure and tax-effective cross-border giving framework, TGE is of course particularly interesting for national organisations with prospective donors abroad. Receiving tax-free contributions from foreign donors, appealing to expatriates, approaching global partners such as multinational corporations, benefiting from borderless interest in a specific cause, or capitalising on global exposure offered by the internet is within arm's reach. The TGE network enables organisations to extend fundraising to foreign countries, without having to set up branches or sister organisations for that sole purpose and without having to master different national laws. Two concrete examples of beneficiaries using TGE are museums having donors abroad and high schools or universities relying on donations from individuals and companies and having a significant number of alumni in other countries.

Steady growth, great potential
Figures for the TGE network are showing a steady increase. The transnational gifts settled through the network amounted to 315,843 euros in 2002, 515,329 euros in 2003 and 601,658 euros in 2004. Last year, 1,395,217 euros was transferred with the help of TGE. These rising figures could be considered satisfactory but, still, they could be better. First, a lot of beneficiaries and donors across Europe are not yet aware of the TGE option and this must be improved by effective promotion. Second, TGE will only show its full potential when extended to most of the EU member states. TGE is currently operational for donations from and to Belgium, the UK, France, the Netherlands, Germany and Poland. But extension to new EU countries is on its way. Foundations and associations interested in the goals of the Transnational Giving Europe network and keen to allow both national beneficiaries and national donors to receive or give tax-effectively across borders are more than welcome to contact the network. After five years of facilitation of cross-border gifts between five countries, the network is now mature enough to extend the scope of its activities to other European countries.

Index

A number of topics recur throughout the book. This index focuses on signifcant references.

Index